Praise for *The Empty Envelope*

"Richly conveying a multigenerational detective story of loss, grief, broken family connections, and sudden revelations, Weinstein and Weinstein draw in the reader to different continents—and truths that were unspeakable for far too long. Worlds within worlds open as the mystery unravels. The hard-fought-for peace that accompanies knowledge (instead of silence) and understanding (instead of shame and stigma) is on full display. Poignant, at times breathtaking, *The Empty Envelope* is profound, moving, and deeply relatable in today's world."

—Stephen P. Hinshaw, Distinguished Professor of Psychology, UC Berkeley, author of the award-winning *Another Kind of Madness: A Journey Through the Stigma and Hope of Mental Illness*

"I was so moved by what the authors unearthed and synthesized into an extraordinary work of mystery, love, connection, and return. The family and historical narratives and the inclusion of psychological theory are woven together seamlessly. Only when we are able to reconstruct the past, can we more fully live in the present."

—Stacy Friedman, Senior Rabbi, Congregation Rodef Sholom, creator of the REAL Mental Health Initiative

"Powerful, powerful piece of writing. This volume can be read as a profound reminder that adversity, albeit ever looming, can be overcome, even if it takes several generations to realize positive outcomes. This is a book about hope and possibility as much as a tome fraught by despair, tragedy, and misfortune."

—Ross D. Parke, Distinguished Professor of Psychology Emeritus, UC Irvine, co-editor of *Children in a Changing World: Sociocultural and Temporal Perspectives*

"With keen psychological observations, the book traces how a family tragedy reverberated intergenerationally and across continents, layered with experiences of expulsion, displacement and immigration due to Nazism and war. Family archeology at its best—sensitive, self-reflexive, and very well written."

—Diane L. Wolf, Professor of Sociology Emerita, UC Davis, author of *Beyond Anne Frank: Hidden Children and Postwar Families in Holland*

"A compellingly-crafted book. *The Empty Envelope* begins with a conflicted mother-daughter relationship. Through careful historical detective work, the two perceptive authors produce an intriguing, richly textured, and gripping story."

—Kogila Moodley, Professor of Sociology Emerita and first holder of the David Lam Chair of Multicultural Studies, University of British Columbia, author of *Race, Culture, and Politics in Education: A Global Journey from South Africa*

"This book turns a personal family story into a gripping and universal tale."

—Muffie Meyer, documentary filmmaker, co-director of the award-winning films *Grey Gardens* and *Benjamin Franklin*

"Totally engrossing! There are three stories, wrapping in and out of each other—a grandfather, the inquiries themselves, and the emotional saga through the generations. It is a remarkable piece of writing for the success with which the authors are able to tell these three stories at the same time."

—David Hollinger, The Preston Hotchkis Professor of History Emeritus, UC Berkeley, author of *When This Mask of Flesh is Broken: The Story of an American Protestant Family*

"A lovely story of self-discovery through family reconstruction. The letters and material found make this not only a compelling family tale but also an important historical one."

—Paula S. Fass, The Margaret S. Byrne Professor of History Emerita, UC Berkeley, author, *Inheriting the Holocaust: A Second-Generation Memoir*

"This book is a wonderful example of 'filling in the gaps' and the empty envelope becomes the metaphor for our need and desire to do so."

—Christina Marsden Gillis, Founding Associate Director of the Townsend Center for the Humanities, UC Berkeley, author of *Where Edges Don't Hold: A Small Island Miscellany,*

THE EMPTY ENVELOPE

The Empty Envelope
Family Secrets and a Grandfather's Legacy

Additional copies may be ordered from the publisher for educational, business, promotional or premium use.
For information, contact ALIVE Book Publishing at:
alivebookpublishing.com

Cover Photograph of Taborstrasse, Alamy
Family photo of suicide note envelope

Book Design By Alex P. Johnson

ISBN 13
978-1-63132-277-8 Paperback
978-1-63132-278-5 Hardback

Library of Congress Control Number: 2026904168

Library of Congress Cataloging-in-Publication Data
is available upon request.

First Edition

Published in the United States of America by ALIVE Book Publishing and ALIVE Publishing Group, imprints of Advanced Publishing LLC
3200 A Danville Blvd., Suite 204, Alamo, California 94507
alivebookpublishing.com

PRINTED IN THE UNITED STATES OF AMERICA

10 9 8 7 6 5 4 3 2 1

THE EMPTY ENVELOPE

FAMILY SECRETS AND A GRANDFATHER'S LEGACY

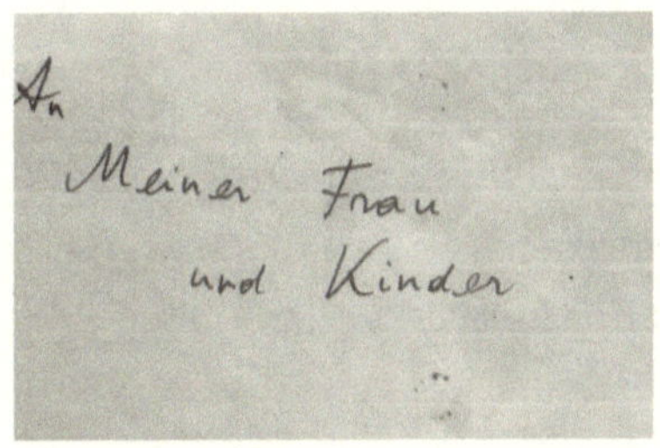

RHONA S. WEINSTEIN
AND
HARVEY M. WEINSTEIN

History, like a vast river, propels logs, vegetation, rafts, and debris; it is full of live and dead things, some destined for resurrection; it mingles many waters and holds in solution invisible substances stolen from distant soils. Anything may become part of it; that is why it can be an image of the continuity of mankind.

—Jacques Barzun, 1974

In order to create something universal, you must pay very great attention to the specific.

—Lorraine Hansberry, 1959

To Max, Lotte, and Hedy, of blessed memory

To Hannah Barenbaum and Dan Picker,
of blessed memory

Contents

Prologue

Turets, Belarussia—1872

They came to the synagogue from miles around. Word had spread rapidly, "Have you heard him sing? A voice like an angel." And when they saw the small boy, five years old, almost lost in his prayer shawl as he hunched over the lectern, surrounded by the elderly bearded men of the village, they could hardly believe their ears. "So melodious, so sweet a sound that brings tears to my eyes." They sat in rapt silence as the high notes filled the sanctuary.

A shtetl in Belarussia in the late 19th century, several hundred villagers gathered for Saturday prayers, enthralled by the voice of one little boy. He was known as a child prodigy, an unusual child who embraced the word of God and the Torah, whose wisdom was beyond his years—an old soul in a young body. His parents were so proud, to have such a son was a gift beyond all imaginings. They doted on him and basked in his fame. Heeding the advice of the village scholars, they sent him off when he was five years old to a leading Jewish academy, a yeshiva, in a town about thirty miles away, and ultimately, to another one in the city of Minsk. Without family and surrounded by other boys, he spent his days in a cold and drafty room, seated at a long table where he studied the scriptures. Partnered with another boy, he and his fellow student would debate the meaning of the words, argue about the truth of various commentaries, and search for connection to the Almighty. But he was lonely—he missed the warmth of his mother, his younger siblings, and all that was familiar.

Eight years later, the boy was approaching puberty and he returned to his village. Another Saturday morning, the same sanctuary, an attentive audience. But this time, not only would he chant the prayers, but he would impart his knowledge and challenge his people to live a moral life. For four hours, this thirteen-year-old boy, for he was still a boy, lectured his elders, holding them accountable to God and each other. It was a sermon that none present would ever forget, its impact spread near and far. As the villagers left, they marveled at his wisdom and congratulated themselves on having such a holy one in their midst. "He will do great things," they said, "He will bring fame to the village and will long be remembered."

But he was restless. The protective cocoon of the shtetl ensnared him like a trap, suffocating his eager mind with its conformity and traditions. He could not stay still. He roamed the countryside, he sang, he preached, but he could not find peace within himself. He felt alone, set apart from his peers. He began to chafe at the strictures of his religion and longed for richer intellectual soil.

And so he fled his homeland, traveled westward, and was exposed to different cultures. He immersed himself in the literature, art, and music of the wider, secular world of Western Europe but happiness eluded him. In Vienna, he married, fathered three children, and pursued a career as a writer and musician. Achieving some success, he became well known in the intellectual world of Vienna. But never did he reach the heights that had been predicted in his childhood. The great expectations held for him and by him were irretrievably dashed. Everything became too much, his failures overwhelmed him. In the last act of his life, he put his head in a gas oven and it was done.

What causes a child prodigy to crash and burn? How does a suicide shape a family and the generations that follow? Surely every life leaves a legacy of memories, at least for the survivors. Yet, his very existence was blotted out, his life buried along with him. He became a family secret, never to be discussed again.

Could there be traces of his sojourn on this earth and its aftermath—left behind and waiting to be found?

Part I

REVELATION

Chapter One

Cincinnati—1969

Everything is illuminated in the light of the past.
—Jonathan Safran Foer, 2002

In 1969, Rhona's mother Lotte revealed a family secret, opening the door to what had been hidden. Rhona was twenty-three at the time, already out of the household and married for two years. But instead of telling her daughter, her only child, she confided in her son-in-law, Harvey, in the most unlikely of settings.

* * *

Harvey—

We were in Cincinnati, in an elegant 19th century home overlooking the Ohio River, to celebrate the rabbinic ordination of Michael, Rhona's future cousin. This was a happy occasion with most of Rhona's immediate family in attendance—her mother Lotte and her father Alec, and Lotte's sister Hedy, her husband Benno, and their daughter Hannah, soon to be married to Michael. Lotte's brother Max and his wife Cecile were unable to travel for the occasion. The mood was light, the atmosphere festive. The salon spoke of grandeur, and the music and food of another era. Lotte was in her element, in an environment of grace and style that likely awakened memories of her youth in early 20th century Vienna. With Strauss melodies in the air, Lotte asked me to dance with her.

As we stepped onto the dance floor, she took control. "Lead," she said to me, but as much as I tried, her grip was iron-tight. As in so much of her life, she needed to steer those around her. And yet, there was a girlish quality to her smile and even a flirtatious air in how she moved her head and body.

As we danced, Lotte hummed along to the music and spoke of her past. She described the culture and civility of Austria. Perhaps the memories were idealized but clearly Vienna had been the center of her universe, and perhaps, still was. But when the music stopped, she suddenly looked very serious, "I have something to tell you," she said. I could not imagine what had changed her mood.

"I'm listening," I responded.

She pulled me to the side of the dance floor, "I don't think I told you that my father killed himself."

I was stunned, "Does Rhona know?"

"No," she replied.

"But why not?" I pressed her to go further.

She looked embarrassed, perhaps, even ashamed: "I couldn't. But you're studying psychiatry so I thought that you would understand."

"When did this happen?" I asked.

She went on: "In 1921, in Vienna, when I was sixteen. He was with my brother Max in our flat. My mother, Hedy, and I were in Bad Ischl, in the country. He had taken us there to a hotel and returned to the city with Max. Max awoke in the middle of the night and smelled gas. He found my father with his head in the oven. Papa was gone. Max never got over finding him."

I took a deep breath, "Was this a surprise to your mother or to the rest of the family?"

She looked sad. "I never really knew my father," she said: "He was an enigma. Never home, often in his head when he was. I don't think my parents got along very well. And he and I had many quarrels as he did not want me to express any opinions."

She turned away. I never had seen her so vulnerable. In fact, she ruled the family, telling Alec and Rhona what to eat, wear, even what to think. I knew that for Rhona, it had been a difficult childhood. What was I to make of this?

"I think it is important that you tell Rhona," I said. She straightened up, pushed her shoulders back, and led the way to where Rhona was talking with others.

* * *

Rhona—

I can still see my mother walking towards me that night, her lips pursed, her stride determined. She grabbed my arm, pulling me away from the others. In the midst of this celebratory occasion, she repeated what she had told Harvey. I struggled to take in her words— suicide, Vienna, her father—all jumbled together.

One line reverberated: "I never really knew my father." I could have said the same about her.

That night, there was no room to explore this revelation as we were jostled by the crowd, gathering to toast the guest of honor. What was true before, remained so afterwards. She rarely talked of her past nor shared much about her inner life.

How well can children come to know their parents as people, to learn about the pain they carry? And yet children are keen observers of their parents' mood and behavior. When deprived of explanation, they draw their own interpretations. As we grow older and reflect on our familial heritage, it becomes even more vital to understand who our parents were and what shaped them, if only to put to rest misunderstandings and old hurts. I only knew what I saw, what I heard, but I was ignorant about so much.

My attempts to learn more proved largely futile. Only Max, called home to be with his father at the time, was able to add a few more details about that traumatic night. Haltingly, he described waking up in the middle of that night, choking on the terrible smell of gas and running down the long hall into the kitchen. There he found his papa, with his head in the oven. He turned off the gas, pushed out the window, and pulled him from the oven. But, as Max said, "He was already dead and there was nothing I could do to save him."

Beyond repeating the bare bones story of their father's suicide, its details seemingly frozen in time, the three siblings, Max, Lotte, and Hedy, had little more to say. "We didn't really know him," they all echoed.

Here it was—the truth about my grandfather's premature death. A tragedy for him and for my family. So many questions were stirred up that evening. Who was he, what kind of life did he live, and why did he choose death? Why did he put his son, the eldest of his three children, in harm's way? Why was his tragic act hidden from me and my younger cousin Hannah, his only grandchildren, until our adulthood? What effect did his suicide have on the family—especially for my mother and her mothering of me? And could this man, Eisig Lubetzky, and the long-held family secret explain the darkness of my childhood home?

Chapter Two

The Montreal Family—1946-1968

Dead and living mixed together.
—Anna Margolin, 1929

Rhona—

In every flat my parents rented, two framed and faded photographs, in the formal style of the early 20th century in Vienna, were placed on the honey-colored bureau in their bedroom. The images were oriented so that they faced each other. On the right, there was my grandfather, Eisig Lubetzky. Sporting a mustache, thin with balding hairline, he wore a three-piece suit. Seated on a chair with his legs extended, cigarette in his right hand, he appeared solemn and lost in thought. On the left, was my grandmother, Musa Brainin, a beautiful woman, yet with a matronly and serious air. Her long hair was twisted in a chignon and a string of pearls graced her neck.

Musa was the only grandparent I knew. She lived with us, unhappily so, until I was twelve. But as I passed by these photographs each day, I wondered about Eisig and his life. When I asked, I was told only that he had died young.

An undated family portrait of Eisig, Musa, and their three children—Max, the eldest, Lotte, the middle child, and Hedy, the youngest—also hung on my parents' wall. That Lotte had emigrated to Montreal in 1925 at the age of twenty, well before the rise of Hitler, had critical implications for the fate of our immediate family. It was her steadfast efforts that saved the lives of her mother, sister, and brother from death at the hands of the Nazis. But she was unable to rescue Eisig's brother, her cherished Uncle

Gabriel. These facts I knew, but in the silence about the past, I did not appreciate their emotional impact.

An only child, I struggled alone to make sense of this small family of mine. To interpret the silence. To decode the whispered German, usually reserved for secrets and displays of emotion. To decipher their Viennese sensibility of style, manners, and culture, never abandoned despite living in the markedly different world of Montreal. And to understand my mother and our relationship.

I remember happy family dinners, always with much loved Viennese food. These would include wiener schnitzel with lemon slices, fried potatoes, gherkin salat (cucumber salad), sweet and sour red cabbage, and end with a Nusstorte mit Schlag (nut cake with whipped cream)—prepared exactly the same way by Lotte or Hedy. German filled the room as Lotte, Hedy and her husband, Benno, also from Vienna, and Max chattered away, while my quiet father, unable to speak the language, sat deep in his own thoughts. Hedy's daughter Hannah, fifteen months younger than I and also an only child, was like a sister. We, the next generation, would listen as Uncle Max played the piano, composing silly songs about us that evoked peals of laughter. His many made-up stories were thrilling and fueled my imagination.

But while the rich intellectual and cultural traditions made family events warm and loving, there was always an undercurrent of despair—apparent in the photographs displayed or hidden away, in the stories that were told or went untold. Tension filled the air, revolving around my grandmother who was part of the household for twenty-two years, from the time of her arrival in Montreal in 1936 to her passing in 1958. The early death of Eisig had apparently left behind an emotionally frail Musa and a close but ambivalent relationship between the three siblings, with reverberations for their new life in Montreal far away from Vienna.

This sadness and these family tensions were a mystery—the roots of which I could not grasp but could clearly feel.

I remember a photograph of the young Lotte, attractive and dramatic, dressed in a knee length black taffeta dress, silk stockings and high heels, sitting at a mirrored dressing table, a cigarette in hand. She is looking confidently at the camera. This was Lotte in her twenties, newly arrived in Montreal, fun-loving, always with a boyfriend in tow, so full of life. My father Alec, ten years older and a Romanian immigrant, was tall and handsome, quiet in nature and pensive, deeply committed to his profession of medicine. He had emigrated with his family in 1904 at the age of nine, to escape the poverty and antisemitism that plagued his homeland. As a young man, he took his first job in a tailor shop as a clothes presser to support the family and continue his education. Against great odds, he became a physician, one of the earliest Jewish graduates in medicine at McGill University, at a time when Jews were subject to strict admission quotas. While the photos at the time of their courtship and marriage in 1933 show happy faces, these early pictures did not match the parents I knew.

To the world, my mother was vivacious, fiercely intelligent, and a caring friend to so many, offering food and comfort. Alway active in the parent-teacher council, she worked hard to create the best of educational opportunities for me. Widely-read, she would forcefully share her views on every subject, beginning with this refrain, so familiar to our family, "Now let me tell you!" At home, she showed a different side—a self filled with sadness and fear, a self consumed by obligation and the need to control, a self with a critical tongue, and a self that felt bony-hard to the touch.

Anticipated loss lingered in the air of our household. That both parents were older (forty-one and fifty-one, when I was born in 1946) exacerbated their fears about not living long enough to raise a child to adulthood. "We may not always be here for you, so be strong," they would say. My mother also harbored worries that my life was in constant danger—when a dog approached, crossing the street, riding a bike, and later, driving a car. Even when I went on a date, she would sit by the window, fearfully awaiting my return. Home had to be protected too, its beige curtains drawn, locks on the windows and doors checked multiple times a day.

When a parent breathes rapidly and grasps a child's hand ever so tightly, a child inhales the perceived threat. This I must have revealed, when at the age of four, in a class at the Montreal Museum of Fine Arts with the famed Canadian artist Arthur Lismer, I painted every canvas with bold strokes of black. I still remember the feeling of exuberance and freedom. According to family lore, Lismer told my mother that I harbored dark feelings inside, needing to find expression.

Lotte's prophecies about the lurking dangers were often confirmed, eroding my confidence in a secure world. She had multiple miscarriages before my birth, and when she was in her fifties, she lost four very close friends within a few years—to a car accident, suicide, and cancer. It was then, when I was in middle childhood, that she cautioned me to never love anyone. "Loss is inevitable," she said, "and love hardly worth the effort." Her conclusion, held lifelong, tore at my heart at a time when I was looking for reassurance and hope.

My grandmother's presence in the home was an undeniable burden. While there are photographs of Musa holding me as a baby and gathering for tea with her Viennese lady friends, this was not the Bubbe I knew. There were her demands—relentless and all-encompassing—and the fact that she could not be left alone in the house. This, along with my birth, had turned my mother into a full-time homemaker. Sick and bedridden, Musa cried from pain most days, missing Vienna and unable to cope. After school, I would venture into her room. The curtains were drawn, the darkness enveloped her, her head barely visible in the bedclothes. As I entered, I could smell a faint sickly odor—musty, sweet and at the same time, pungent—the scent of a failing body. Musa did not "go gently into the night" and the years of her illness weighed heavily on the family, most of all on my mother, whose care of her was heavy with duty and rage.

As I stood by her bed, Musa would whisper in broken English that Lotte was poisoning her with injections. "Sei vorsichtig, be careful" she warned me, "Your mother may hurt you too." I was left to wonder whether I could even trust my mother. But perhaps it was Musa who misunderstood that the injections, three times a day, were necessary to control her diabetes. I felt as if both my grandmother and mother were "poisoning" my mind.

And yet there were those who offered comfort. My gentle father, Alec, provided some protection and he enlarged my world. When I was disappointed that we could not afford the toy kitchen set I coveted, he created a play version in my bedroom closet, with shelves, an overhead light, a stool, and toy dishes. I found peace there behind two closed doors—closet and bedroom—sheltered from the screaming fights between Lotte and Musa. He would take me for walks in the Snowdon district, visits to museums, even a weekend trip to Quebec City. I would accompany him on his hospital rounds and to his downtown St. Catherine Street office, reading in waiting rooms until he would reappear. In the evenings, he introduced me to what he called the Encyclopedia Britannica game, our exploration of the long line of heavy volumes that graced the bottom shelves of our bookcases, his proudest acquisition. I could open any volume, pick an entry, and together we would read it aloud. This shared pastime clearly fueled my desire to become a scholar. My happiest times were with my father.

There was much I wanted to run away from in my childhood home. I suspected my father felt similarly. Left to his own devices, he turned even more inward. When he was not working, he sat in his wingback chair in the living room, reading philosophy and writing poetry, which he scribbled on scraps of paper and stuffed in drawers, escaping from what, for him, must have been an intolerable situation. His disaffection for Musa mounted and led to arguments between my parents. He no longer wanted my grandmother to live with us. The tension mounted between my father and my mother who never left Musa's side. Conflict rose in the extended family between Lotte, Hedy, and Max over who would take care of Musa. My father wanted my aunt and her husband to take her to live with them but they were intransigent, they would not have her.

The stress reached a crisis point when I was ten years old. I can picture the front hall of our flat, its door partially open, and I can see the stairs down to the outside door, to the street and freedom.

" I can't stand it anymore," my father pleaded. "Put her in an institution or I will leave."

My mother sobbed, "I can't, I have to care for her."

I cried out to my father to take me with him, "Don't leave me here with Mama and Bubbe."

But he left me behind.

My parents never really recovered from this confrontation. Weeks later he returned, staying until that fateful day, decades on, when he, afflicted with Alzheimers' disease, was placed in a geriatric hospital. While they were cordial with each other, I never saw overt affection. I never saw them hug or kiss. Still, there must have been a tie that bound them together. He was always kind to her and for years she devoted herself to caring for him before he entered the hospital. Even after his placement, she visited him daily until his death.

My Aunt Hedy, too, was a loving presence in my life. A slight woman, with a beautifully sculpted face and short brown hair carefully coiffed—Vienna lived in her as well. She had a radiant smile, her warmth would embrace me like a comfortable blanket. Although she worked full time in the manufacturing of men's socks, a business that she and her husband Benno had started, her home was sunnier and filled with laughter not conflict, as Benno had a wonderful sense of humor. It became a refuge, sleepovers were cherished, and I loved having my cousin Hannah as a sister-in-life, so close in age. Yet, there was another side of Hedy, quiet and somewhat depressed, but buoyed up by the extroverted nature of her spouse.

Uncle Max also brought laughter to my heart, through his story-telling and music. A small man, thin with a beaked nose. What he lacked in stature, he more than made up in personality. Max was full of energy and always moving—he talked rapidly, joked constantly, and was an outrageous flirt, even after he married his third wife, Cecile. Without steady employment, he frequented neighborhood restaurants, like Murray's and the Snowden Delicatessen, kibbitzing with the waitresses and charming those around him, while nursing a single cup of coffee. He had been a pianist of enormous talent in Austria and later in the Jewish hotels of the Catskills in New York state, before arriving in Montreal. He even became my piano teacher, but in that role, he would transform from the happy go-lucky, funny uncle into a demanding tyrant, accusing me of not doing my best and letting him down. There were days where he so criticized my playing that I quit piano lessons entirely, unable to salvage my interest and self-esteem. There were periods of time when Max disappeared, and when I walked to his nearby apartment, he refused to answer the door, telling me to go away. It was only as an adult that I learned of his alcoholism.

While the Lubetzky side was small, it was Musa's large extended family, the Brainins, who both animated and dominated our life. It included her eight siblings, spread across the world—some living in Montreal close by and others in New York, London, Berne, and even as returnees to Vienna—with an age difference of twenty-six years between the eldest and youngest. The youngest was Liesl, who with her husband Sam Ortenberg, arranged for Lotte to emigrate to Canada. Its patriarch, the eldest, was Reuben Brainin, a Yiddish and Hebrew writer of international renown, greatly revered by his relatives. It was a creative and accomplished family—producing musicians, writers, artists, and cosmopolitans. There also was a mystique about them, a glimpse of a larger world beyond what I knew. Over the years, as we met many members of the extensive and multigenerational Brainin family, there was no mention of my grandfather Eisig, who had married Musa. It was as though Lubetzky had never existed for them. While visible every day on my parents' bureau, memories of him had no place in our lives.

In 1958, my grandmother died. Her passing did not alleviate the family tensions. In fact, the world became darker as my mother's full attention turned toward me, just as I was approaching my teenage years and yearning for greater autonomy. Caretaking became control—over my dress, my eating, my behavior, my choices, and even my opinions. The rules were iron-clad and any transgressions were harshly criticized. Even the refrigerator was off-limits for me. Although I inherited my mother's Viennese sense of fashion and appropriate fit, I bristled at her need to clothe me well. Trips to specialty salons were followed by lunches out and then visits to the Viennese dressmaker. Two sisters, Lotte and Hedy, shopping for beautiful outfits for their daughters. But what my mother wanted for me—never my choice—often came at a steep price. As I fingered the expensive fabrics, I awaited the inevitable recriminations over the cost and the accompanying sigh from my mother that "Now, there is nothing left for me." Shopping became a guilt-ridden ritual that I despised.

In truth, every potentially positive interaction turned negative in the face of her sharp tongue, undercutting what could have been moments of pleasure. I spoke out many times—not politely nor kindly—as I asserted my independence from her tight control. The more I rebelled, the colder she became. I yearned for a mother who was not afraid of the world and exuded a positive spirit. A mother whose energy was focused outward, not on me.

It was hard to find a place for my emerging self in the family and in the largely segregated Jewish Montreal of the 1950s and 1960s. There was much I shared with those around me, many coming from immigrant families and silent about the past. The majority of mothers I knew were full-time homemakers. At that time, the expectations for girls were limited. If they included a university education, it was to be obtained while still living at home and would lead to early marriage. But our family was also different. We were secular Jews and did not belong to a synagogue. We were not part of the upwardly mobile Jewish community, renting rather than owning a home and never members of a country club. Despite its implications for the family income, my father devoted himself to providing medical care to the underserved and poor Chinese immigrant community, well before the advent of Medicare. He was paid in Chinese food, with Chinatown restaurants open to us for evening meals. He also befriended others who, like him, had faced discrimination, bringing a Black professor and a Chinese physician and their families into our circle of friends. Having interracial friendships was not typical at that time for most in the Jewish community. I came to model myself on my father and I longed to find a larger world, one free of judgment.

It was at sleep-away camp each summer, beginning at the age of ten, that I found the freedom and sense of exhilaration missing in my constrained life at home. This was a unique camp in the Laurentian Mountains, north of Montreal—a place of close relationships, deep discussions, and passion for nature, Judaism, literature, music, and the arts. All children, whatever their differences and needs, could thrive. Fictionalized by Leonard Cohen in his book "The Favorite Game," Pripstein's Camp was legendary for the number of psychologists, psychiatrists, and social workers it produced. There, I had my first taste of the kind of adult I hoped to become and the career I would pursue. This second home cemented my interest in psychology, fueling my curiosity about the different qualities of the worlds in which children develop.

McGill University and its undergraduate honors program in psychology opened the door to the excitement of research and its applications. I became passionate about this field of study and had big dreams for a woman at that time—to earn a Ph.D. and to become a professor. This goal clashed with the future that my mother had envisioned for me. It became clear that her tight control over my life and its inherent obligations would interfere with my capacity to become an independent adult and a scholar.

When I began a doctoral program at McGill, I was still living at home, paralyzed by inaction. I wanted to flee but did not know how. It was Harvey who threw me a lifeline and would ultimately help me escape.

* * *

Harvey—

Rhona was twenty-years-old, a university junior when we met, and I was in my third year of medical school. We had dated probably three or four times when I was invited to dinner with her parents. The family flat in Snowdon, a solidly middle class area in Montreal's west end, had a European and intellectual air about it. China dishes, original paintings, comfortable furniture, and books everywhere. Peaceful at first glance.

Rhona and her mother greeted me, her mother elbowing Rhona to the side. This was a hint of what I would see in the years to come. Lotte ushered me into the dining room, where the table was formally set and out came traditional Viennese fare. With her lilting accent, Lotte was the European grande dame, the elegant hostess. What struck me most was her dominance of the conversation, with an opinion on every subject but what was surprising was her deep grasp of multiple topics—politics (Canadian and global), literature (German, English, Jewish), philosophy, history, and more. I could see at once where Rhona's intellectual curiosity came from. Initially, I was bowled over by Lotte's charm and engaging ways. She and I would sit at the kitchen table and talk in an easy banter—a naturalness, sadly, that Rhona had never experienced with her mother. My interactions with her were fun and she even would tease me about dating her daughter.

At first, I was a little cowed by Alec. As a medical student, I was in awe of older physicians, especially surgeons. He was tall and stocky, and talked sparingly, but as I got to know him, I was struck by his patience, gentleness, and his ability to make space for the needs of his wife. Where Lotte was practical, impatient, and focused on fighting (with words) the vicissitudes of the world, Alec turned to books, nature, and in his quiet way, to social action.

While attracted to so many aspects of Rhona's family, I also noticed the absence of color, light, laughter, and affection in the household. Often, the mood was silent, even dark. Beige and grey everywhere, curtains drawn, and so quiet you could hear a pin drop. When I saw Rhona's room—decorated by her mother entirely in beige—I realized how little opportunity she had for her own self-expression. I learned very quickly that Lotte controlled much of what Rhona did and where she went. She was allowed to drive only to the university and to her cousin Hannah's house, with the clock ticking until she reported in, informing Lotte that she had safely arrived. It appeared that Rhona spent much of her time figuring out how to escape the control she felt at home.

I began to see that Lotte was intrusive, demanding, and that she dominated every aspect of family life. And Rhona's father was above all this—disappearing into his reading or his work life. I knew that if I did not support her escape, we would have no future together.

In the fall of 1967, I helped Rhona to separate from her parents. I found her a roommate, one of the nurses in the hospital where I was an intern, and together, we told her parents that she was moving out. In Lotte's mind, leaving the family home before marriage brought shame on all of them. The departure was deeply painful—through the same door where Rhona's father had once left the family behind. I can see Lotte at the top of the stairs, her face suffused with rage, calling Rhona names and throwing her clothes down the stairway that led to the street. But if Rhona and I were ever to build a life as a couple, we had no other choice. The deed was done. Our marriage followed three months later.

* * *

We left Montreal for Yale University in New Haven, Connecticut in 1968: Rhona, to continue graduate school in psychology and Harvey, to do a residency in psychiatry. Ultimately, we emigrated to the United States—moving to the San Francisco Bay Area and a life even further away in California. Despite the distance, Rhona remained the ever-dutiful daughter, flying back to Montreal multiple times a year, calling often, and fully involving her parents in our lives. While intensely ambivalent, she was also deeply tied to them, at great cost to herself. She was, after all, the only child and a daughter. Despite the separation, both physically and emotionally, Rhona's mother became a constant third presence in our marriage, standing between us, dominating our lives. Harvey became the protector, guarding against her intrusiveness.

Lotte's revelation that night in Cincinnati, so early in our marriage, marked just the beginning of a long journey. Her father—this shadow figure immortalized in a photograph on her bureau—became the subject of our shared quest to reconstruct the long-buried story of Eisig Lubetzky and understand his legacy. And perhaps to shed light on the forces that shaped Lotte's life and led to the fraught relationship between mother and daughter. The disclosure of Eisig's suicide opened a door to Lotte's past, just a crack, but it failed to unlock more memories. The silence continued.

This mystery that colored Rhona's childhood became Harvey's inheritance as well. Not surprisingly, we bring the past, be it painful or happy, into the marriage we build. And Lotte's demands also brought that past into our present. That she chose her son-in-law as the recipient of the longheld family secret about her father's suicide, evoked in him as it did with Rhona, the need to learn more. Thus, the drive to unravel this puzzle became an enduring aspect of our relationship as a couple, now more than fifty years in the making.

As Rhona was to learn, her adolescent struggles to have an independent voice mirrored those of her mother. Each of their lives was marked by ambivalence. Both fled their homes yet remained attached, in dutiful obligation to their mothers. Both carried the scars of a suicide—a tragedy enacted on a dark night, in a second floor flat, on a tree-lined street in Vienna—the living legacy of a life lost to despair.

Chapter Three

Leave and Return—1968-1998

You are the bows from which your children
as living arrows are sent forth.
—Kahlil Gibran, 1966

We would learn little more about Eisig Lubetzky for almost thirty years. Surprising perhaps, given the backdrop of a growing interest in genealogy worldwide, with many swept up in searching for their ancestral history. But preoccupied by so much, we did not think to utilize the emerging archival resources and in fact, we did not even know where to begin. Our own busy lives took hold—professional training, dual careers, twin sons, life cycle events, illnesses, and deaths. We were also caught up in the weighty demands emanating from our families of origin—from Rhona's mother and Harvey's father. Daily living was all encompassing and the opportunity to ask questions, to delve further into Rhona's grandfather's life, passed.

But just after Lotte's revelation, we took our first trip to Vienna in 1969. We invited Rhona's parents to join us at our expense but Lotte adamantly refused, determined never again to set foot in the city of her birth.

We wanted to experience the culture of Vienna, and see where Lotte and her family had lived and where her father ended his life. Soon after arriving in the city, we took a taxi to the upscale 18th district, to a beautiful tree-lined street and the address on Messerschmidtgasse that Lotte had given us. Standing in front of a dignified stone building of three stories, we studied the second floor windows on the right side, belonging to the flat that once had been theirs. On this first visit, we carried a letter of introduction from Rhona's mother, written in German, which asked if we might see the family's former home. After ringing the bell beside the tall wooden doors, we were buzzed into the entrance hall, graced by a wide circular stairway. A burnished wood railing, high ceilings, an Austro-Hungarian architectural treasure.

A woman about Lotte's age slowly descended the stairs and asked what we wanted. Upon reading the letter, her face whitened in shock. From the little German that Rhona understood, it appeared that this woman remembered Lotte and her family. She had apparently taken over their apartment and belongings, when on short notice, Hedy and their mother Musa fled Vienna for Montreal more than three decades ago. She screamed "Mein! Mein!" Shaking her fist at us, she forcefully ushered us out of the building, slamming the door shut. We later learned that Rhona's family had the right to reclaim their former home and its contents as restitution, but taking legal action was beyond what the family wanted to pursue. Its current occupant was afraid that we had come to repossess the flat.

During this first trip, we also made a long pilgrimage on the electric tram, from Schwartzenbergplatz to the city outskirts, to visit the Wiener Zentralfriedhof, the Vienna Central Cemetery. There we entered the oldest of the two Jewish sections, virtually destroyed by the Nazis during Kristallnacht (Crystal Night) in 1938, but with 60,000 graves still intact. The name reflects the broken glass of the Jewish-owned stores, buildings, and synagogues that were desecrated on that night. After searching rows of overgrown brush and crumbling tombstones, many no longer upright but instead hugging the ground, we found Eisig's final resting place. Standing askew above his grave, a small and square stone was held by a gold metal frame, its lettering faded and barely legible. We could scarcely make out the name: Eisig Lubetzky, 1872-1921. Following Jewish custom, we placed small rocks on the top of this monument, honoring his memory and leaving evidence that we, his granddaughter and her husband, had visited. The state of decay in a forgotten section of the cemetery saddened us. That his name was almost lost underscored that the memory of his life had been erased. It was as if he had never existed.

This first of many trips to Vienna evoked a great attachment to the city. With no Lubetzkys left there, we established relationships with the Brainin family members who had returned after World War II. We explored the romantic restaurants and cafés, attended the opera and concerts, and admired the couture of the Viennese women, elegant and expensive. It was a taste of the Vienna that Rhona's Lubetzky family had carried in their hearts to Montreal, the nostalgia that most immigrants feel as they long for their homeland. But the remnants or remembrances of the Holocaust were not visible to us during that first visit, hidden from view, except for one acknowledgment. At that time, our Brainin relatives were careful not to identify themselves as Jews. As one cousin whispered to us, if he had done so, it would have inhibited his professional advancement.

* * *

In 1972, we moved to Northern California and a number of years later, we were followed by Hedy's daughter Hannah and her husband Michael. Now the two cousins lived near each other and were able to raise their families together, just as their mothers had done—a deeply meaningful gift of connection. But with this relocation, our lives were 3000 miles away from parents in Montreal. While more common in the U.S., this was unusual for the time and the traditions of Jewish Montreal. Hedy, Benno, and even Alec accepted our move westward and to a different country with grace but Lotte was inconsolable. And, as difficult as it was for Lotte when Rhona first left home and then moved to New Haven, this decision to settle in California was perceived as a permanent abandonment.

Despite the distance, now with two sons, we made the trek back to Montreal many times each year, brought Rhona's parents on our vacations and for visits to California, and were in touch regularly by telephone. The frequency of visits and telephone calls increased with Alec's illness and more so, after he passed away in 1985. There was a familiar rhythm to our interactions. With Lotte, each contact began with a countdown—how many days and how many minutes were left for this visit or this telephone call—the clock ticking fast toward the inevitable separation. Whatever we did to include Rhona's parents in our lives was, for Lotte, never enough. At various points, we considered bringing Rhona's parents, and then, Lotte, to California to live but the difficulties of obtaining health insurance and its prohibitive cost made that impossible. Lotte even asked Rhona to leave her marriage and career behind, to return to Montreal and give her the life that other mothers had. A life with weekly Friday dinners and Sunday teas, shared birthday celebrations, and daughter-accompanied visits to doctors.

Parents can give their children wings to pursue their individual dreams or create tight bonds to keep them close to their elders and extended families. For both of us, the constraints of our pasts had made us dreamers, needing to be free to build meaningful lives for ourselves and with each other.

Lotte's anger toward Rhona for leaving her could not be assuaged and their interactions became a nightmare of recriminations, guilt, and tears—an ever-present shadow on our household. Finally, Lotte told Rhona that she was not the daughter she had wanted. In truth, neither was Lotte the mother Rhona had desired.

* * *

Also, during these years, the 1980's and early 1990's, Harvey's own family mystery came into full view. He grew up in a Montreal family whose life had been destroyed—business and home lost—when his father was hospitalized in a psychiatric institution after several panic attacks. The year was 1954; Harvey was twelve-years-old and his father was forty-eight. When his father returned six weeks later, the man he knew was gone. In his place was a man who could barely talk, could not arise from bed, did not know who Harvey was, had strange mannerisms, and hummed constantly. During the next six years and through multiple long hospitalizations, his condition worsened. While he recovered some of his faculties, even enjoying family life, the brain damage he suffered rendered him unable to work ever again.

Harvey's choice of psychiatry as a career was driven by the need to understand what had happened to his father, but this was not understood until 1979, when the truth was revealed in a book by John Marks titled *The Search for the Manchurian Candidate*. His father had become an unwitting victim of mind control experimentation—carried out by the eminent psychiatrist Ewen Cameron at McGill University in Montreal, and funded by the CIA in the United States and by the government of Canada. The experimentation at this site, among many others, was part of the notorious CIA MKULTRA brainwashing program that lasted some twenty-five years. Harvey then spent most of the next decade, commuting from California to Washington, DC, to uncover what had been done under the guise of psychiatry. His research supported a lawsuit against the CIA, assisting the attorneys representing a group of victimized Canadians, one of whom was his father. This research became the basis of his book *Psychiatry and the CIA: Victims of Mind Control* published in 1990.

Each of us had brought a family mystery into our marriage. Perhaps that was what first drew us together, led us to choose psychology and psychiatry as our professions, shaped our desire to flee Montreal, but also kept us deeply tied to the fate of our families of origin. Buffeted on all sides, we were clearly a sandwiched generation.

* * *

In 1995, when Rhona's mother was ninety-years-old, we were forced to move her to a chronic care hospital, a move laden with conflict. This decision was the culmination of a long downward trajectory. "If you ever move me into an institution, I will never speak to you again," Lotte said. As the years passed, these words became a repeated refrain, a threat that hung over us.

Lotte had been living alone since the death of Rhona's father ten years earlier. As her cognitive faculties declined, due to repeated small strokes and vascular dementia, she was no longer capable of living on her own, even though her sister's apartment was in the same building, just four floors below. Firing every caregiver we hired, she sat by the front door of her apartment all day, phoning Hedy repeatedly and waiting for her to arrive with each meal. She could not be trusted to use the stove, as she left the gas burners on, endangering the occupants of the building. Hedy could no longer survive under this barrage of telephone calls, carrying full responsibility for her sister. We were warned by the staff of Lotte's day program that the situation was desperate and we needed to act immediately.

We visited three geriatric care settings with Lotte and asked her to make a choice. Bitterly, she chose the one where she had placed Rhona's father and where he died. The day before her "removal" as she called it, we took her out for a special lunch followed by a shopping spree in an exclusive dress store. Now the tables were turned, as we clothed her. She chose two classically tailored suits, made with the finest wool weave, to wear in her new home. While clearly inappropriate for life in an institution, her selections reflected the impeccable Viennese taste to which she clung and which we fully supported, given what lay ahead.

The morning we arrived to take her to the geriatric hospital was deeply traumatic. Elegantly dressed, Rhona's mother refused to look at us. She marched out of her beloved apartment—lined with precious books, paintings, and photographs—head held high without so much as a backward glance. Once in her private room at the geriatric hospital, she sat glued to the bed, unmoving, as we brought in her bedroom bureau, two of her favorite chairs, paintings from home, and her clothes. We placed family photographs all around, trying to make the space look familiar.

True to her promise, she never spoke to her daughter again. When Rhona visited from California every two months, Lotte would turn her head away, seething with anger and refusing to engage. Perhaps it was her dementia speaking but the words were hurtful: "I love Amina (pseudonym for her caretaker) more than I ever loved my daughter," she would say. Over that first year, her words trailed away and she became largely silent.

Sometimes in the midst of her confusion, Lotte would cry out for longingly for her mother, inconsolable to any touch. Desperate to soothe her, Rhona once held up the photographs of each of Lotte's parents. But at the sight of Eisig, Lotte screamed, terror in her eyes, "No, Papa! No, Papa! No." She was unable to say more. What was frightening her? Was she thinking about his suicide or had he threatened her in other ways? Who was her father—this dark, brooding, and bearded man who lay at the heart of their family secret?

It was a long three years—multiple bouts of pneumonia, increased paranoia, and even physical aggression towards staff. We saw a gradual and then a rapid physical deterioration. In the face of her decline, we tried to live our lives.

The countdown to Lotte's end began with an urgent telephone call to Rhona from her doctor: "Your mother has pneumonia, the third time since January. You need to decide whether or not to treat her, as each time she is greatly weakened. When someone is ninety-three and their quality of life is so diminished, pneumonia can often be their best friend. My recommendation is to let her go, peacefully, of course. You must come to Montreal immediately to sign papers about next steps."

Harvey was about to leave on a month-long research trip to the Balkans, a location where communication would be extremely difficult. It was a trip too complicated to cancel, given multiple collaborators, translators, and scheduled meetings. With Rhona's blessing, he accompanied her to Montreal to help make the difficult decision and to say his goodbyes before he set off for the Balkans.

Thus, began the pilgrimage to Montreal, this time to witness Lotte's death. Our long plane ride offered much time for reverie. Flying over the city as we were landing, we watched for the familiar landmarks—the downtown skyline, the St Lawrence River, the flanks of Mount Royal, and the glorious dome of St. Joseph's Oratory. We immediately drove to the geriatric hospital, pulling up into its familiar circular driveway, racing upstairs to Lotte's floor, and rounding the corner to her room. Painfully thin, Lotte was non-responsive, awkwardly placed in a wheelchair, with her head hanging down on her chest and her mouth wide open. She did not react to touch, to her name, or to our voices. The doctor reiterated that antibiotics would do little to help her. She had stopped eating, her bodily functions were failing, and death could come in three days, at most a week. We needed to make the decision for her. Together with Hedy, we decided to follow the doctor's recommendation.

Three days turned into an agonizing three weeks, without food or liquid and marked by alternating periods of quiet and agitation. Lotte was dying, her daughter by her side, the daughter whom she felt had abandoned her. The scene was a microcosm of the relationship, both unable to give, both unable to love. Aunt Hedy, frail at ninety-years-old, would come by taxi each day for a brief visit. Late at night, back at Hedy's apartment, Rhona and her aunt would reminisce and cry together.

* * *

Rhona—

On the twenty-first day at my mother's bedside, my work life in shambles, I decided to make a brief trip back to California to settle my academic obligations and return for the longer haul. The hospital social worker advised, "Tell your mother that you are leaving and when you will return. Although she appears comatose, she can still hear you." I did so and within hours, I saw a change in my mother's condition, her skin tone darkening and a bluish tinge appearing in her extremities.

That night, a favorite nurse, Angel, called Hedy's apartment and said to me, "Come quick, love. Your mother is on her way." And so, we returned to the hospital. My mother's breathing had become rasping and irregular, although after each cessation, she drew another deep, sighing breath. Hedy and I stood on either side of her, each holding a hand, but words did not come.

Just before one o'clock on the morning of July 8, 1998, I picked up a bound book of my late father Alec's poems, gathered many years before, and read aloud the lines of "Requiem," an offering for the soul: "When I die, as all must die, do not sigh, do not cry. Silently let me rust. Remembrances do not bury, just bury me."

And with the last lines of his poem, "Till I'm set free, again to feel moments of eternity . . . . passing glimpses of serenity," my mother took her final breath.

It was a raw and unfinished ending, not a time for reconciliation between mother and daughter nor for love professed on either side. An ambivalent loss, filled with unresolved feelings, leaving enormous pain in its wake and no path for resolution.

There was no time to mourn. The hospital room had to be cleared for its next occupant by eight o'clock in the morning. Despite my grief, I set about the task at hand. While emptying my mother's bureau, I found a large manila envelope, which I immediately tore open. Inside lay three spiral-bound notebooks, and a small, faded, and beige-colored envelope. A telephone directory reflected my mother's long and richly-peopled life, with many of the names crossed out, indicating their deaths. Another notebook listed the tasks that she had completed each day: "Monday, dusted the living room tables; Tuesday, vacuumed the living room rug and the couch." So it read—all the cleaning accomplished in her small apartment, over the weeks, months, and years. The final notebook contained a compilation of events in her life—appointments, money paid for coffee or the hairdresser, and a sentence, repeated many times over: "I love Tamara (pseudonym for a beloved nurse at the day program)." Did this record-keeping reflect her way of coping with cognitive decline or did it represent a compulsive listing that she had routinely maintained?

And in this last book, there was even one mention of me—the date of my birthday graced the first page. Seeing my name there, I then remembered what else I had found, upon cleaning out my mother's apartment. A large box, within it, in piles tied with ribbons, lay all of my school records, my letters from camp, trips, and California, and pictures galore of me and the family. Despite the harshness of Lotte's words and ultimate silence, there lay evidence of a mother's love for her daughter. And still one more pile, a thick one, contained obituary notices for lost friends. Love and loss, side by side.

I turned to the small and discolored envelope. On its front, written in German, in flowing black cursive: "An Meiner Frau und Kinder." To my wife and children. And on the back flap of the envelope, my mother had written, "I think this is the envelope that contained the suicide note my father wrote to my mother."

The flap was open, the envelope empty.

Where was the letter? Who had read it? What did it say and why was it kept secret?

* * *

For seventy-seven years, Lotte held on to this empty envelope, addressed to her mother and also to the children. She never showed it to Rhona.

The envelope and the questions it raised now became ours. We would never have more than this from her—no words about the past, no writings about her life experiences. But she did leave us a legacy, the truth about how her father died and an empty envelope to fill.

Chapter Four

A Serendipitous Discovery—1998

The seeds of great discoveries are constantly floating around us, but they only take root in minds well-prepared to receive them.
—Joseph Henry, 1877

A photograph, a surprising revelation, an empty envelope. If we were to make sense of the mystery that surrounded Rhona's grandfather, how could we move forward? How could we develop an understanding of the antecedents and consequences of an event that happened almost a century before—in another country, another language, another world? We remained haunted by Lotte's terror at seeing her father's photograph but we were stymied by her silence, which her death now made final.

Within six weeks of Lotte's passing, as Rhona grieved, an act of serendipity occurred—our first breakthough.

In Montreal, Abrasha Bogen, a scholar of Jewish history, was rummaging through the recycle bins of the Jewish Public Library, examining the titles of discarded books. Lying in one bin were volumes of the *German Encyclopedia Judaica,* published in Berlin in 1934. Bogen came upon a volume beginning with the letter "L," which he, as only a scholar would, read cover to cover. In it, he found a brief, bibliographic entry: Lubetzki, Isaak, Eisik (1872-1921).

Curious, he searched other sources and discovered that Lubetzky had married a younger sister of Reuben Brainin—Musa, Rhona's grandmother. Ten years older than Lubetzky, Brainin (1862-1939) was internationally-known as a

Yiddish and Hebrew writer. Emigrating from Lyady in Belarus to Vienna and later to Berlin, he was recruited to come to Montreal and was instrumental in the founding of what became known as the Yidishe-folks-biblyotek, the forerunner of today's Jewish Public Library. This unique resource contains "the largest circulating Judaica collection" in North America and emerged from the efforts of a Canadian immigrant from New York, Harry Hirshman, to bring Jewish literature to Montreal at the turn of the 20th century. Brainin also became editor of *Der Kanader Adler* (The Canadian Eagle), a daily Yiddish newspaper.

For a Jewish historian, the Lubetzky-Brainin connection was an exciting find. He knew Brainin's granddaughter Judy, who lived in Montreal but he knew nothing about Lubetzky. He called Judy and with her help, this detective scholar found his way to Rhona's Aunt Hedy. He arranged to see her, bringing a translated English version of the German bibliographic entry and a newspaper article about a Lubetzky family from Mexico.

As soon as he left, Hedy called Rhona in California, speaking so rapidly that Rhona could barely understand her: "Rhonale, the most amazing thing just happened. My papa was a famous man." Hedy was tearful, her enthusiasm infectious. She had reached out to her niece because Rhona was the one with the unanswered questions, the keeper of the family history. Her voice trembling, Hedy read the scholar's translation over the telephone, describing the life of her late father:

> Writer, cantor, and dirigent [in German, a choirmaster or director], born in Turetz [Gouv. Minsk], attended the conversatorium in Milan, was a short time professor in

> the conversatorium in Budapest, after until 1914 in the biggest synagogue in Vienna, after started as a business man. He started writing with an open letter to Max Nordau. He wrote about social and mainly Zionistic problems in Hebrew, Yiddish, and German periodicals. In *Ha-Schiloach,* appeared a few Hebrew fictions of psychological and realistic nature, also a fiction "Be-Re-schet Ha-Chet" [The Sin, 1910]. Also to mention is a very popular Yiddish brochure "What is Zionism" and critical essays about Mendele and Zangwill in *Ha-Schiloach*. Lubetzki committed suicide in 1921.

Individual lives are remembered as long as those who survive recall them or as long as they leave traces behind. This brief biography was our first written trace of the arc of Eisig's life. With Lotte's death, it felt as though a curtain had been drawn over the family's history, but this entry opened the floodgates.

It contained vital clues to his birthplace in Turets, Belarus, his multiple careers as a writer, choir director, and businessman, and even the names of some published articles, fiction and non-fiction, written in three languages. This first glimpse of Eisig depicted an unusual man of many talents who, while he remained an enigma to his family, was well known among the Viennese intellectual comunity, the Zionists, and Hebrew writers of the early 20th century in Europe.

***

Thus began what we called "The Lubetzky Project," a

shared commitment that would send us on a more than twenty-year journey of discovery across the world—from key informants to multiple archives and a rich literature, from villages in Belarus once inhabited by Jews to the streets of Vienna and Jerusalem, and to the sites where the Lubetzky relatives perished in the Holocaust. We became historical detectives, propelled on a mission backwards in time, to pursue these written traces. To capture what the cultural historian Jacques Barzun has called the "continuity of mankind," where the seeds of life shape each successive generation, for good or ill. What began as a biography of one man ultimately became a multigenerational story of many.

Without knowledge of the languages (German, Hebrew, and Yiddish), we were dependent on others to search for materials and translate these writings into English. We applied for grant funds and hired a cadre of graduate students in Jewish Studies at UC Berkeley, as well as professional translators, who had expertise in these languages, the historical eras, and the published literature. To this project, we brought a deep well of curiosity, our research skills, and a psychological lens—critical to the understanding of suicide, human development, and lives through time. Our careers, born out of traumatic experience, now gave us the capacity to study and analyse the life and legacy of a complex man.

We were forced to wait, sometimes a long time, while others scoured the literature and decoded it. It was as if an intermediary stood there between the original writings and us, a limitation we were forced to accept. Our understanding accumulated in haphazard and often surprising ways, requiring interpretation and temporal integration. In pursuing this research, these pivotal figures came alive and entered into the room with us. Over twenty years, the first file folder of findings turned into multiple boxes of archival material, ultimately allowing us to piece together the family story.

* * *

Serendipity would continue to grace our search. We began with the new information that had turned up on our doorstep, looking first for possible Lubetzky relatives, especially those who had come from Turets or elsewhere in Belarus. We reached out to the Lubetzky family from Mexico, mentioned in the newspaper article that Bogen had shared with Hedy. Our conversation with this family failed to uncover a common ancestor but it led us to Mme. Marianne Urbah of Paris, who also had also written to them about possible connections. Her branch of the Lubetzky family was originally from Turets, descendants of the esteemed Rabbi Yehudah Lubetsky (but with a different spelling). We hit pay dirt, we thought.

We wrote to Mme. Urbah, who was thrilled to hear from another Lubetzky with ancestry from Turets. Family trees were exchanged. Marianne's extensive tree reached back to 1810, tracing the descendants from Reb Leisur Lubetsky. But nowhere on that tree could we find the names of Rhona's family members, even going back to the father of Eisig. Our records had noted his name as David Eli Lubecki (likely the Polish spelling) and he may have been born some time in the 1840s-1850s. So our connection at the start lay only in a shared birthplace, the same shtetl in Belarus.

Rhona followed up with a phone call to Paris. Marianne answered and burst out with excitement, "I know of your grandfather, Eisig."

But "how?" Rhona asked.

"I've read two chapters about him in a Yizkor book titled *Tooretz-Yeremitz*," she said. We were surprised to learn that Eisig's life had been remembered in the story of the Belarussian village of his birth.

She went on to explain that these Yizkor books, more than 700 of them, are a treasure trove of our Jewish heritage. "Yizkor," she said, "means may God remember, from the root Hebrew word zachor." Often published privately, these books were written by Holocaust survivors in Israel and the diaspora, to memorialize the thousands of Jewish settlements and the millions of lives that were destroyed by the Nazis and their allies. A gift from the survivors, they ensured that this Jewish world would not vanish. Holding the collective memory of those who came from the villages of Eastern Europe, the Pale of Settlement, from Galicia, Bessarabia, and old Poland. Telling the stories of the unique characters who inhabited these shtetls, until their world was destroyed. They provide a record of who we were and who we are. Mme Urbah had led us to an important source of information. Sadly, she passed away in 2023 at the age of ninety-two.

Harvey immediately rushed to the library at Stanford University, where he worked as a physician. In its dark stacks, he found the *Tooretz-Yeremitz* volume, published in 1977 in Israel, and he brought it to our home, just a few miles from the campus. Given digital advances, these precious Yizkor books can now be accessed online through the New York Public Library.

Much of the description of Turets, Eisig's birthplace, was written by Yehudah Gesik, whose name appeared on Marianne Urbah's family tree. As we later discovered, Gesik reported the death of Eisig's family members in an affidavit filed at Yad Vashem, the Holocaust Memorial Center in Jerusalem. He identified himself as a relative, a nephew of David Eli, Eisig's father, which suggested that our family and the Paris family were related, the connection perhaps evident in earlier generations.

Two chapters, written by Moshe Ungerfeld, were indeed devoted to Rhona's grandfather: "Yitzhak Isaac Lubetzky" in English and "Yitzhak Aisik Lubetzki" in Hebrew. These were based on an article published by Ungerfeld in 1972, titled "The Man Who Escaped Himself." He described Lubetzky as a gifted child who became an itinerant cantor and preacher but was not satisfied with his life: "In a community replete with scholars, Yitzhak Isaac Lubetsky was a child prodigy, a Talmudist at the age of five, blessed with a phenomenal memory and rare musical talent. At the same time he was restless, always in a state of running away from people—and one might add, from himself."

How did Ungerfeld come to write about Eisig in the 1970s, some fifty years after his death? Born in Poland, Ungerfeld (1898-1983) studied at the University of Vienna, worked as an educator, and published regularly in Hebrew newspapers. A well-known writer and critic, he also served as the director of the Beit Bialik (Bialik House) in Tel Aviv, Israel—a museum, archive, and cultural center in the home of Israel's national poet, Chaim Nahman Bialik. There, he built an extensive public library of journalism and writings in Hebrew. He clearly knew of Lubetzky's work and may even have met him in Vienna, as he was age twenty-three when Lubetzky died in 1921.

Ungerfeld was actually Lubetzky's second biographer and his analysis was built on the earlier work by another scholar. Through a rabbinical classmate of Hannah's husband Michael, we soon discovered the writings of Nissan Touroff, Lubetzky's first biographer. Rabbi William Cutter, a scholar of Hebrew literature and now emeritus professor at the Los Angeles Hebrew Union College, was intrigued to learn about our family's Lubetzky heritage and he immediately put his students on the hunt for materials.

In short order, a large over-stuffed envelope arrived at our home. Inside, we found a chapter on Eisig Lubetzky's life and suicide in a 1953 book by Touroff titled *The Problem of Suicide: A Socio-Psychological Study*. This book grew out of a series of articles, "Essays on the Suicides of Famous Personas," published in the journal *Ha-doar* in 1945. Here was an analysis of Eisig Lubetzky's suicide alongside analyses of the suicides of Vincent van Gogh, Stefan Zweig, and a failed attempt made by Robert Schumann—noted artists, writers, and musicians of the late 19th and early 20th century Europe. In the preface to his book, Touroff wrote that from his earliest days, he was fascinated with suicide, which he perceived as an unnatural act and sought to explain. He noted that his book was the first attempt in the Hebrew literature to explore the circumstances under which individuals choose death by their own hand—a topic around which there had been utter silence. Silence about suicide, except in fiction, has a very long history. Only in recent times, has there been a movement among scholars and family members to lift the stigma and shame, share the stories, and build an understanding of predictors and consequences, prevention and treatment.

In this envelope, Cutter also included copies of two of Lubetzky's original writings. This was our first view of Eisig's work: an article titled, "Zionism and its Opponents:

An Open Letter to Max Nordeau" (1898) and a serialized novella titled *The Sin* (1910), both published in *Hashiloach*, a major Hebrew periodical of the time, and edited by the well-known scholar, Ahad Ha'am. All of these writings were, of course, written in Hebrew.

How did Rhona's grandfather appear in such distinguished company? What fueled Nissan Touroff's interest in Lubetzky and how did he learn so much about him, including the details about his suicide? Touroff (1877-1953) was born in Nesvizh (Niswitz), a town not far from Lubetzky's birthplace in Turets. He was a teacher and psychologist, a Hebrew language translator, editor-in-chief of the Israeli newspaper *News of the Land*, and former director of the Hebrew educational system in Palestine. He emigrated to the United States in 1919 and was the founding dean of the first Hebrew Teacher's College (now Hebrew College) in Boston, and later a professor at the Jewish Institute of Religion in New York.

Touroff explained his fascination with Lubetzky: "I saw him once, and the memory of this meeting has remained with me to this very day . . . grateful for this unexpected opportunity to see the prodigy whose talents I marveled at as a young boy."

Touroff also puzzled over the forces that shaped Lubetzky's life, pointing to the age-old controversy of nature versus nurture in the development of personality. He mused about the possible life trajectories for children who are ordinary and those who are extraordinary. Who lives up to their earliest potential, who exceeds it, and who fails at achieving all that was presaged? And why?

Ungerfled had written of Lubetzky's restlessnesss and Touroff, too, described Lubetzky as "one of those people who tend not to choose the paved paths, but rather prefer the dangerous leaps and shortcuts. One of these leaps once raised him to the top of the world, as it were; another led him to the bottom of the earth, from a life of kings to the act of suicide." He continued, "When it comes to Hebrew writers, this case is quite unique."

Touroff's chapter on Lubetzky was titled "From Igra Rama" (From the Top), thus proclaiming a prophecy about his impending fall. Cutter, in his book *Midrash and Medicine: Healing Body and Soul in the Jewish Interpretive Tradition* (2010), provided a source for this term in S. Ansky's play "The Dybbuk." Translated it reads: "Why, oh why, does the soul plummet from on high, down to the deepest pit? Here is the descent that enables the arising."

This image of the soul rapidly descending, to rise once again, would capture the essence of Lubetzky's life and careers. In fact, both Ungerfeld and Touroff alluded to character flaws in Lubetzky that led to periods of great darkness but both of these biographers also noted that out of the darkness emerged great creativity.

The ups and downs of his life course raised suspicions in us that there was more to explain than character flaws in Lubetzky's personality. We were also struck by the theme of prophecy in Rhona's grandfather's life—the highest of expectations held, but yet unfulfilled. How unexpected to find this ghost hidden in her family closet, when her own research as a psychologist has explored the underlying dynamics of self-fulfilling prophecies, how the expectations we hold for ourselves and others can have consequences. Her curiosity led her to study the *under*estimation of ability and here was an example of expectations *for genius*.

Touroff (1945) concluded, "Lubetzki's contribution to

Hebrew literature remains much smaller than it otherwise would have been; and still it should be remembered in the history of this literature for its own sake, and also—and especially—for the sake of the amazing personality of the contributor." Ungerfeld (1972) also pressed for a compilation of Lubetzky's work: "As of today, Lubetzky's writings have not been gathered into one volume. But now, a hundred years after the author's birth and fifty years after his death, it is indeed time to collect his writings."

Both Touroff and Ungerfeld underscored that Lubetzky's writings were important contributions to the Hebrew literature of the day. We became curious about the scope of these works, why had they not been previously collected, and what place did they have, if any, in the field of Hebrew literature. Reading this, we even imagined ourselves heeding the call and playing a role in bringing to light Lubetzky's contributions to the worlds of music, art, and literature. But we also needed to understand the forces that had stamped out and disconfirmed the prophecy of his genius.

While Lubetzky left behind published writings, did he also leave any private papers? Perhaps these could be found in Vienna where he had died, but we failed to find traces there. On a lark, we visited the Jewish Public Library in Montreal, where Bogen had uncovered the first clue.

Had Musa sent her husband's papers, upon his death, to her brother Reuben for safekeeping or had she instead brought these papers with her when she fled Vienna in 1936, perhaps donating them to the library when Brainin died in 1939? The library's holdings, however, made no mention of Eisig Lubetzky but clearly visible was the archive for Reuben Brainin, Rhona's family deity. After hours of pouring through the Brainin material, we came upon two boxes labeled "Yitzhak Isaac Lubetzky." This was a surprise even to the director of the archives, as these materials were not catalogued and were hidden from public view. A poignant reminder that the elder Brainin's contributions were privileged above those of Lubetzky, a reality that likely plagued Rhona's grandfather during his entire literary career.

Upon emptying the contents of the two boxes, we unearthed a forgotten treasure, largely in Yiddish: numerous personal letters to and from Lubetzky, published articles about him, bills, and drafts of unpublished work. The latter included essays, stories, book-length manuscripts, and a play. We solicited the help of a Yiddish-speaking Montrealer to compile a complete listing of the materials and we copied what we could to take back with us to our home in California for translation.

Among the contents, our Yiddish-speaking guide discovered a large blue notebook, dated 1907 and divided into two parts. Book 1 "opened with an impassioned account of an overwhelming need to leave home as a youngster." Book 2 bore the title "In Odessa." Barely legible scrawl filled these unpublished manuscripts. The writing mixed German, Yiddish and Hebrew, and often was so tiny that it could barely be deciphered. Words were written in every available space— the sides, top and bottom. The whole looked as though it was produced in a rush, as though there had been an eruption of verbiage. This work would prove to be exceptionally difficult to translate.

Our guide suggested that the content of this blue notebook, written in the first person, read like an autobiography. When Book 1 was translated, we saw that its details closely mirrored those of Eisig's early life in Gorodeja.

There was, however, a puzzling dedication on its opening

page: "To my dear and beloved children, my only daughter Shifrah and my only son Yaakov. This book is given to them as a present from their devoted father."

"But these are not the names of his children!" Rhona exclaimed.

We suspected, instead, that this work was a veiled autobiography. In the story, Lubetzky gave his protagonist the name Shuelik. If he hid the identity of the writer, he might have given his children pseudonyms as well. This hypothesis gained further support by our failure to find traces of a Shifrah or Yaakov Lubetzky in the archives of Vienna or Belarus. Also, the dedication to a single daughter was consistent with the birth order in Lubetzky's own family, as his second daughter, Hedy, was born after 1907, when this material was written.

Shortly thereafter, we received an email from one of our graduate student translators, who wrote us about an amazing story penned by Lubetzky, titled "A Lonely Stalk of Grain (1902)" and published in the Hebrew literary journal *Ha-Eshkol*. "You must read this piece about Gorodeja," she urged us. Gorodeja was the town that Eisig's family had moved to when he was still a boy. It was a story about Shalom, a young Yeshiva student, who breaks the rules of the Torah in his zeal for engagement in a larger world.

We now had in hand two stories, both penned by Lubetzky, about young men struggling to leave Gorodeja behind to continue their studies not only in the Talmud but also to pursue a secular education. These writings, the fruits of his literary imagination, contain autobiographic elements that might illuminate his inner world in the years of his youth and bring him to life. The list of translation tasks became longer—Yiddish, Hebrew, and German to English. And patiently, we waited.

* * *

In this early part of our search, with so many exciting discoveries, the idea emerged for a unique gift, a commemorative family volume about Eisig Lubetzky, to be given in honor of Hedy's 90th birthday. Rhona embraced this goal with fervor and the book's creation became the primary means of mourning for her mother's death.

Given Hedy's age, we worried that time might be running out. As the last surviving child of Eisig, only she could offer a first-hand account of her father and the family. With cassette recorder in hand, before the advent of the iPhone, Rhona spent many hours talking with Hedy about the family life in Vienna and Montreal. These precious interviews, taped and transcribed, reinforce the importance of learning from family members before they pass away.

"I have no memories," Hedy haltingly began the conversation.

Yet after decades of silence, with Lotte gone and new information emerging about her father, she became surprisingly open. There was much she did not know and much she had forgotten. But what she did remember revealed an intimate portrait of her parents and siblings, their difficult lives, and of the suicide and its aftermath—a perspective that we share in the coming pages. We will never know whether Lotte and Max would have told the same stories.

As the deadline for Hedy's birthday gift approached, we quickly gathered some of the original material we had collected thus far, including the translations where available and the correspondence from our search. The book begins with letters to Hedy from Hannah and Rhona, the family tree, and photographs of the Lubetzky family and of our respective families. Also included are letters documenting the family's search for the whereabouts of Eisig's younger brother, Gabriel. This handmade book, which we titled *Legacy of Isaak Eisik Lubetzky*, was bound in beautiful leather by a very skilled Russian bookbinder. Copies were also made for family members and for those who had helped in this journey.

Together, we, along with Hannah and Michael, presented our gift to Hedy in an intimate dinner at the elegant Ritz Carlton Hotel in San Francisco, in celebration of her long life. Overwhelmed by the book, she was awed by her father's accomplishments and rendered speechless that details of his suicide were discussed in a publication. Painful to her was that neither she nor her siblings had ever seen his writings or been aware of his reputation.

"Ja," Hedy said, with surprise, as she took the book. She slowly opened the cover and took a deep breath, "This is my father?"

As she turned the pages, this usually taciturn woman exclaimed over every new revelation. Her voice was tremulous and tears appeared at the corners of her eyes. For the first time, Hedy saw one of her father's political critiques about Israel, the first chapter of his novel, a commentary on his life and his death—more information about her father than she had seen in her ninety years. Her memories of him, as she had recently told us, were of a distant and cold man, a man who thought that the birthday of a little girl was of no consequence. Yet, in front of her was a novel of passion and photos of a lost time. Her hands were shaking as she put the book down and looked at us, "If only Lotte, Max, and I had known and understood." On that splendid evening, we were in tears as well.

To our surprise, this family book had a life of its own—one copy was to travel to Israel. It would be ten years before we were to learn the outcome of this unexpected journey.

These early findings provided a foundation, enabling us to follow Eisig's story and travel to the places where his history unfolded over time. And so we set out for Belarus and the village of Turets, the birthplace of Eisig Lubetzky.

Part II

EISIG LUBETZKY
(1872-1921)
TURETS TO VIENNA

Chapter Five

A Child Prodigy Escapes the Shtetl

When we were young, we thought Tooretz was too confined.
We dreamt about the big, wide world.
—Yerahmiel Markowitz, 1977

Eisig Lubetzky was remembered by his biographers as the talk of the village. Named for his grandfather Aizik (also known as Aizikov), he was born in 1872 to David Eli Lubetzky, a grocery merchant, and Khana Feiga, his wife, in the shtetl of Turets—then, part of Poland, now in Belarus. His birthplace reflected a world in which national borders were fiercely contested and frequently rearranged. Ask anyone whose parents or grandparents came from that part of the world what country their ancestors had lived in, their answer, with a shrug, would be: "Who knows? It depended on who won the war." One day, Polish, another day, Lithuanian, and yet another day, Russian.

As his father was in the business of trade, the family moved when Eisig was a child, from Turets to a neighboring commercial town, Gorodeja, sixteen miles away. This town was on the main railway line to Minsk and therefore securing and selling goods proved easier. Exposure to this railroad was likely pivotal in evoking in young Eisig a longing to engage in the wider world.

The Lubetzkys had four sons (Eisig, Motel, Feitel, and Gabriel) and one daughter, Peschke. Eisig was the eldest child and Gabriel, ten years younger. Hedy had sparse knowledge of her father's family and his homeland. She had been told of a family visit to Gorodeja in 1910, when she was two (Lotte, five, and Max, six), but given her young age, it was a trip which evoked no memories. Rhona's mother had left her the few photographs she possessed of her father's family. Captured in these photos were Eisig's parents, Eisig and his four siblings, as well as the next generation—Peschke's daughter Mirele and Motel's daughter Idele. While Gabriel was to follow Eisig to Vienna, the rest of the family remained behind in Gorodeja and Turets until 1941, when the Nazis invaded. They all perished, only the faded photographs remain.

By the end of the 19th century, almost one million Jews lived throughout Belarussia and they constituted 14% of the total population. The 1897 census records on the Jewish Geneology website show that Jews in Turets numbered 737 (46% of a total population of 1,616). In the Gorodeja of 1900, the proportion of the Jewish population was larger, at 91% (that is, 688 out of a total population of 754). The Jews were surrounded by Christian farmers and peasants with whom they traded. But in these villages, daily life and boundaries were closely circumscribed by the prescriptions of the Orthodox Chassidic community. As the historian Samuel Kassow has noted, "No shtetl stood alone." Rather, they were interconnected through a regional economy and numerous religious educational institutions that linked together neighboring villages. At that time, there were occasional anti-Jewish attacks in the area but for the most part, Christians and Jews co-existed.

The depiction of shtetl life in Sholem Aleichem's beloved *Tevye* story and its representation in film and plays conveys the intensity of these towns—the closeness of the families and the richness of their communal lives—fueling great attachment. Certainly not wealthy in riches, these shopkeepers and peddlers, blacksmiths and scholars, devoted themselves to the study of the scriptures, reading the holy word in the Torah and arguing about the meaning of each line. Tradition really bound Jewish families to the norms of the village and while each community had its mentally ill, its beggar, its alcoholic, its prostitute, no one was ever left to starve.

"My mind overflows with recollections of my home town and my heart is filled with longing—perhaps Tooretz, to me, is the story of my youth," wrote Yehudah Gesik in the 1977 Yizkor book, poignantly describing his ancestral home:

> A small town with touches of splendor, shunting aside the less attractive aspects, the poverty and inertia, the fights over who was to get maftir [last person called to read the Torah on Shabbat]. What I remember is the grove of old chestnut trees near the old churchman's home, the jasmine, the sunflower plants in the garden patches, the fruit orchards, the wildflowers, grazing land and the songs of the shepherds at dusk. I also recall the hard winters, the blizzards, the warmth inside the home, with every crack and crevice stuffed with rags to keep the warmth inside.

There was also a warmth outside their homes that defined these small communities and the wide range of community institutions that supported Jewish life. Yerahmiel Markowitz described Turets in these ways: "The Jewish community was one big family, sharing joys and sorrows, everyone turning out for a wedding or a birth, visiting the sick, and escorting the departed to their final resting place." And, not surprisingly, he went on to say: "Like in a family, there were quarrels and disputes, usually about how the community would be run best. There was no such thing as indifference."

He recounted how the Jews of Turets organized a bank, a night vigil of the sick to let the families rest, a circulating library of books in Hebrew and Yiddish, and entertainments such as plays. Audiences gathered to listen to speakers on Zionist, Jewish, and worldly matters. They gave readily to charity when they had little to give. Markowitz' descriptions of the Sabbath with its candles, the gathering for prayers in the synagogue, and the festive meal capture the joy and devotion that brought families together. Life was structured around the words of the Torah and the traditional commandments. The boys and men studied together, learning from their rabbis and texts.

Yet the joys of such religious traditions were also constrained by strict rituals and prohibitions. In a world of rigid gender-role expectations, boys were educated as religious scholars and girls were trained in the womanly arts of domestic life, as balabustas (a Yiddish word for good homemakers) and as fiscal managers, especially to support their learned husbands. Markowitz also underscored the suffocating nature of this tightly-knit community. And there were some in the younger generations who questioned and even rejected the path their elders had set out for them.

Eisig was sent away from his home early, between the ages of five and seven, to live and study with the rabbis in Minsk and at the famous Volozhin yeshiva, the first modern academic institution of its kind. When he was thirteen, he returned and amazed the townspeople with his cantorial skill and his moralistic preaching. As noted earlier, Nissan Touroff was well acquainted with Lubetzky's reputation, writing that he had "impressed the community with his sweet voice during synagogue services and his chastising sermon which lasted several hours." This was a sermon on moral conduct, instruction, and discipline, based on a section from the Book of Proverbs. Clearly, Touroff was taken with Eisig's story.

A thirteen-year-old boy, his forelocks flapping as he vigorously nodded his head emphasizing one point after another, mesmerizing the audience with the sweet sound of his music and the wisdom of his understanding of the scriptures. Eisig followed his father's wishes, as his father and the rabbis were the center of all authority. The eldest child, he was very much aware of how his behavior would influence his siblings and so, he studied, he sang, and he respected his parents. For the next three years he wandered about as an itinerant cantor and preacher spreading God's word. But this peripatetic life was soon to end as community expectations caught up with him.

Eisig's scholarly and musical gifts made him a very attractive candidate for marriage. Marriages occurred early and were arranged, and the contracts tied to dowries prescribed the obligations of these interconnected families. Boys as young as eleven or twelve were betrothed and expected to fulfill the marital role. The in-laws were expected to support the young couple, allowing the boy to study. It is not surprising then that Eisig was married by the age of sixteen to an older woman of the community. Very soon, his wife became pregnant and bore him a son. But this was not a happy marriage. Eisig began to chafe under the strictures of the town and the traditions that he had reverently followed. While many of his contemporaries lovingly remembered the dirt streets, the winter mud, the wooden houses with sacks of potatoes in the storerooms, the hydrangeas and geraniums outside the windows, Eisig became increasingly disaffected. Perhaps fueled by the characteristics of the newer market town of Gorodeja, where more modern ways increasingly encroached on the strict mores of Chassidic Judaism, he began to think about what lay beyond the confines of shtetl communities. His filial obedience to his father and his commitment to a wife began to fray.

That Eisig became a writer and drew upon his own life experiences offers us a glimpse into his soul. From his writings, we can discern the forces that may have provoked Eisig's restlessness and the depths of his despair, here described in a story titled "A Lonely Stalk of Grain." It was published in 1902 when he was thirty-years of age. He writes of a man's sense of being eaten alive, of his sinking into torpor and passivity in reaction to the isolation he experiences in the village of Gorodeja. He feels the need to escape, to flee to a new life, as he imagines a different world. But as we read the story of the protagonist Shalom, we realized that the details closely mirrored Eisig's own life. And indeed, at that time, autobiographical fiction had become a popular genre of story-telling.

In this work, Eisig describes the town of Gorodeja, where its railroad and the accompanying growth of the town sharply distinguished it from older villages. Reflecting keen observation, the story illustrates a shtetl confronting the forces of modernity:

> Gorodey, the hometown of our protagonist Shalom, was a small town. In its spirit, however, it was different

> from all the other small towns. The wind of the wide world was already blowing among its houses, ushering in an atmosphere of materialism and practicality. It was one of those special towns that multiplied under the great reign of the steam trains; one of those railway towns that were born overnight at the feet of the new trade sources opening up in the village, by the new railway station.
>
> The older towns were able to withstand the strong winds of time, alongside their orderly lives and ancient traditions, as well as the social bonds that deprive the individual of his freedom. Such towns are preserved with all the fine details they inherit from previous generations, for every single person protects the other and is accountable for the other's life and actions. But this is not the case in new towns that simply spring up, all of a sudden. These towns have no tradition, and so even the slightest rush of wind leaves a great mark upon them.

Eisig suggests that in older towns, perhaps like Turets, the social and familial bonds served a protective and yet constraining function, but in this new town, there was more freedom to be different from one's neighbors. In Gorodey, he writes: "[The villagers] were not bound together by friendship or familial ties. They were strangers to one another, and so they felt no shame before each other. They did whatever they deemed right, without considering what their neighbor might think."

In this story, he describes how even traditional tight-knit communities were not immune to change and these winds of change drove a wedge between young and old. As has been written, the wars and shifting state boundaries, pogroms against Jews, emigration overseas to America, South Africa, and elsewhere, especially following the 1903 Kishniev massacre, and the relentless progression of modernity were bound to promote resistance to tradition and the desire for a different life, particularly among the young. Eisig writes that for the older townsfolk, the pull towards the past was strong, and trade and making money diverted them, but the young were more interested in the new ideas. Because Gorodeja was a town opening to the wider world, the protagonist of his tale is caught between past and future.

One of the new movements that swept the shtetls at this time was the Western-influenced set of non-traditional principles termed the Haskalah. The young man, Shalom, anxious to shed the past, desires to adopt the philosophy of the Haskalah—to become a Maskil. The "Maskilim (in Hebrew, the educated ones)" were its leaders. The Haskalah movement of the late 18th and early 19th centuries advocated enlightenment values and secular education. It was one of the most important social movements to effect change in the shtetl communities as it challenged the power of the orthodox establishment and its adherents, the Chassidim, to frame the education and roles of men and women in society. Most importantly, it revived the use of Hebrew as a spoken language and in literature, de-emphasizing the study of Talmud. In a *Jewish Virtual Library* article, Shira Shoenberg has described how the Haskalah movement encouraged Jews to learn both European and Hebrew Languages, and to enter such fields as agriculture, crafts, the arts and sciences. It was, in a sense, an assimilationist movement.

Eisig's description of his character's desire to shatter the traditional customs of his Jewish faith may well have reflected his own drive for change:

> In one of the final years of the nineteenth century, Shalom became a "Maskil." And when I say "Maskil," I believe the word itself will suffice to describe to the reader the very essence of Shalom. . . . He became a Maskil, namely, a dreamer of dreams more exalted and beautiful than the dreams that amused the hearts and minds of the elderly Maskilim.
>
> And just like a youth who just emerged from the swamp to gaze upon the wide world and whose ambition to become enlightened marks the beginning of his blooming, Shalom dedicated himself entirely to the dreams of the Haskalah. He relentlessly voiced the great call of the Haskalah in the ears of the deaf with enthusiastic devotion; with this call, he wished to pry open the eyes of these bats [the townspeople], so that they might witness their surroundings and feel the warm glow of the light.

These words describe the transformation that Eisig must have undergone, a sixteen-year-old, married with a child on the way and obligated to follow a pathway that tradition demanded. These winds of change, the Jewish Enlightenment movement, captured his imagination, as an adolescent open to new ideas and chafing at the strictures of shtetl life. Eager to convert others to his dreams but unable to do so, evoking the image of his fellow townspeople as deaf and as bats, Eisig became increasingly restless and felt an urgent need to leave that life behind.

The theme of escape is repeated in Eisig's veiled autobiography, the unpublished manuscript written five years later in 1907 and found in the Montreal Jewish Public Library. We read about another young man, Shuelik, not unlike the Shalom character of his "Lonely Stalk of Grain," who also is determined to escape the shackles of the past, obsessed with leaving home to expand his knowledge and transform himself. Here, Eisig writes in the first person.

The protagonist Shuelik appears torn between his love for the traditional study of the Torah and also, for newer ideas and a secular education. He is angry at his parents who have held him back, ambivalent about his marriage, and rages against himself, a despair that pushes him to flee. In these painful paragraphs, we read:

> Why am I to blame when my unfortunate parents have sinned against me, intentionally or unintentionally, and have hidden from me the bright rays of the Haskalah? . . . Enough with suffering. Enough with tormenting myself! . . . My soul thirsts for Torah! [But] (1) In me there is glowing a burning fire for the Holy Haskalah! (2) Every bone in my being is crying out in one voice: "Bildung [Edification]!" (3) "Civilization!" Travel, I must travel . . . !

These yearnings for the dreams of Haskalah have deeply divided these two young men from family, marriage, and community—an isolation that Lubetzky describes in both these stories.

For Shalom in "The Lonely Stalk of Grain," the prospect

of marriage is described as burdensome and without love. The distance that he feels from his wife-to-be is enough to delay the marriage. Eisig writes:

> He feels as though there is a difference between them. She is not as near to his heart as he believed her to be. Something is missing, and she remains a stranger to him. His emotions and words do not rise to the surface. He is lonely, forsaken, and he has nothing in this world.
>
> . . . His mother and father-in-law beseech him to set the date for the chuppah [the canopy under which traditional Jewish weddings are performed], but he does not even wish to think about that. How can he enter the chuppah without ending his studies? How could he live in this current state, in this deep darkness and stifling, polluted air? He no longer resists, he lacks the will. And yet, his weakness protects him, as whenever the date of the wedding approaches, it is rescheduled once again.

For the already-married Shuelik, in the veiled autobiography, we read about his inner rage towards his wife, who is similarly perceived with distance and disgust:

> And then only now, suddenly, I notice my wife who is, as usual, sitting next to me by the table. I myself don't know why but her two imbecilic-looking eyes, which always look a bit fearful, have a strong effect on me. Yes, truly, I am always sensing her staring at me. . . . I wanted to bellow: "Vacuous bovine! Why

> aren't you eating? Calf! Why are you gawking at me like this with your silly onions? Eat, little fool, and drink and be a good person!"

But another side of Shuelik is also revealed—an awareness of his incapacity to love and a recognition that his wife does not deserve such disdain:

> So, I would want to know what she's thinking right now . . . Then suddenly I'm getting a ringing in my ears, the things she says when she turns to me oftentimes: "Shuelik, tell me the truth, do you at least like me a little bit? A little bit, a drop?"
>
> Love, what does love mean? I know, I feel that I have great pity for her. Every time I take a look at that aggrieved face, my heart starts to flutter. My legs start to shake and my eyes become like windows, and at that point I can't control myself. I have such great compassion for her! Woe, she is not to blame for anything . . . I'm scratching my forehead. I want to drive out the silly fantasies [of fleeing].

Intensely personal, both the short story and the veiled autobiography reveal the depths to which Eisig, himself, descended in trying to come to terms with his fate—a future decreed by his father and the community at large. Could he remain in a dark room, davening (praying) for hours on end, debating the meaning of obscure words in the Torah, questioning the wisdom of the prophets and sages? Was this to be his life? And bound to a woman he did not love and to her parents who supported them. In the face of these demands, his characters (and likely he) retreated to an inner world, rich with ideas and desires but remote from those around him.

This divide from family and wife, felt by Eisig's characters, also occurred with peers. The protagonist Shalom, in "The Lonely Stalk of Grain," hoping for solace in the familiar and melodic prayers, instead experiences an "impenetrable wall" between himself and his school friends:

> His Haskalah has distanced him from his friends at the school for Torah studies, despite their common upbringing and education. At times, when he is feeling sorrowful, he decides to return to the school, hoping that he might assuage his pain by listening to the melodies of the prayers, or by speaking with old friends. But whenever he sets foot at his former school, he sees that an impenetrable wall separates him from his old friends, and his present life from his past life.

Eisig concludes, "He has grown distant from them and he can never return again." The angst of his character, Shalom, is beautifully captured by the stark image of one lonely stalk of grain—born late, too close to the approaching winter, left in the field and destined to die alone:

> Oh, poor and lonely one! You weep in vain, there is no cure for you. Fortune has led to your belated birth and you must drink your cup of poison. Lonely stalk of grain! And this loneliness is the source of its poverty and torments. . . . Could it be that human beings are not unlike the stalks of grain? Could it be that

> if fortune has led to a man's belated birth, then, from the very womb, he is destined to doom and decay?

Yet, just as the hopelessness sets in, torn between madness and a vision of freedom, Shalom realizes that he must act, must leave all behind:

> At the field, among the waves of grain and whispering trees, his uneasiness would grow even more burdensome, and he would feel the burning tears of madness climbing up his throat. What should he do? He cannot remain here, in his town . . . The most important thing is to run away from this home of filth and rot unto the vast world, the dwelling place of light and sunshine. He must leave everything. But how?

And then, we read of Shalom's resolve to grasp his freedom. We learn about his final departure westward from the Gorodeja railroad station:

> Shalom, too, began to dream his old dreams again. He was free to leave his little swamp, Gorodey, and head towards the blessed land, towards other countries in which heaven is open to him . . .
>
> A few days later, Shalom was seen at the railway station, standing in line to buy a ticket. He had to wait fifteen minutes for the journey to begin, and in the meantime the younger and older residents of Gorodey surrounded him with questions, while he told them of the purpose of his trip . . . that he was leaving Gorodey for good, heading to another country

in order to study and achieve a goal in life . . . to study and become a man.

These two manuscripts, eerily similar in their stories, reveal much about Eisig's preoccupations. We cannot help but see young Eisig in Shalom and Shuelik, the fictional protagonists. These two stories follow the Hebrew literary tradition of autobiographical writing, intensely personal, almost confessional stories in which the narrator is also the subject. During this era of great change for the Jews of Eastern Europe, young men described their painful journeys as they cast off tradition and searched for new meaning. Commitment to truth, to openness about one's feelings, was the hallmark of the genre and Eisig faithfully recorded his travails, as difficult as they were.

In 1888, at the age of sixteen, Eisig Lubetzky fled from Gorodeja, taking the train to Milan to study voice at the Conservatory of Music. He graduated at age eighteen with a Gold Medal—a tribute to his talent. What did he feel as the train approached, as he got on, and as he saw Gorodeja recede into the distance? Leaving the town, his family of origin and his pregnant wife, was a significant step that broke his tie to the past but also opened rich opportunities for him to fulfill his intellectual and creative strivings.

Would Eisig thrive or, like Shuelik, come to regret the choice he felt compelled to make? The story of Shuelik, who also leaves his village behind for the city of Odessa, suggests, not surprisingly, that the journey away from the shtetl would be fraught with tremendous challenges. A second unpublished manuscript follows Shuelik on his voyage, where he struggles. His success is far from guaranteed. When he reflects back on his departure, he bemoans the choice that he felt compelled to make: "How tragic my life is! The whole world is against me. . . . Wasn't I wrestling enough with myself? Wasn't I suffering enough then? What else could I have done?"

Eisig's own words reveal his inner world as well as the world around him. While one must be cautious in interpreting all that we read as corresponding exactly to the events of his life, they track very closely.

* * *

In 2010, more than a century after Eisig's departure from the railroad station in Gorodaja, we plunged into the past and retraced his steps in Belarus. To see with our own eyes the shtetl he left behind, to view the geography of that place, and to experience this storehouse of memories. We were accompanied by Franklin Swartz and an interpreter from Voluntas (the East European Jewish Heritage Project). Voluntas, founded by Frank, an American, and his Belarussian wife, Galina, was, at that time, engaged in supporting what little is left of Jewish life in Belarus and Lithuania—providing glasses and medications, and preserving the old Jewish cemeteries.

The city of Minsk served as the base for our travels. We stayed in the heart of the city, surrounded by the grand facades of the postwar buildings, including the imposing edifice of the Belarus KGB. In our minds, the portentous size of these buildings emphasized the power of the State over the lesser importance of its people. But the mood of the people was unmistakable as it was a time of unrest and protest just before an election, where anger and despair could be seen on the faces of those on the streets. In the following years, the totalitarian nature of the State and its autocratic President would become even more readily apparent, as elections became a charade of democracy.

With Frank and our translator Alex, we drove from Minsk to Turets and Gorodeja. The beauty and poignancy of the long drive persists in our memory because of the groves of stark, white birch trees that line the roads. The same forests that hid the partisans and the Jews who were able to survive during World War ll.

Soon, we found ourselves in Turets, in the village where Eisig was born. We brought relics of the past with us—a faded photograph of Eisig's father, his siblings and their families, and a crude hand-drawn map of Turets before World War II, copied from the Yizkor book. Making our way to the town hall, we met the mayor of Turets and showed her the map. She was visibly stunned by its accuracy, as the town was little changed from that time. She was surprised as well by the text written in Hebrew, a language foreign to her. We asked whether there might be someone who remembered life before the war and she graciously agreed to lead us through the town to meet some of its oldest inhabitants.

As we walked down the dirt streets, lined with wooden houses, some brightly painted, others faded and poorly kept, it was not difficult to imagine the old days, they were now. Showing our photograph and with the help of our interpreter, we talked with elderly townsfolk as we walked. Everyone stared at the strangers in their midst. An aged local historian remembered well the Jews who lived as neighbors until the Germans came.

The mayor then took us to the home of one of the village

elders, a striking woman in her eighties, with piercing blue eyes and an intense stare, her skin tanned and leathery. An orange and black scarf wound around her head revealed wisps of white hair. With work-worn hands, she examined the photo and recalled playing with the "Lubetzky girls." Whether these girls were part of our Lubetzky family, we did not know. Exhausting our interpreter, she spoke rapidly for over an hour, clearly emotional as she described the Nazis coming into the village and her mother trying to help by hiding some Jewish neighbors. Tearfully, she told of the Jews attempting to escape, fleeing into the birch forest. Was this factual or a reimagined past, we wondered? Was this an attempt at redemption?

Inside her home, it was dark. The kitchen where we sat was small, with no refrigeration. A bushel of apples stood in the screened entry, which served as a cold storage room for provisions. Old wooden houses, the bare fruit trees of autumn, and dirt roads, it appeared that little had changed since the turn toward the 20th century. And yet, the Jews who peopled this village were gone.

Finally, we stood at the edge of a grassy field, the town cemetery. Mounds that covered mass graves lay before us—403 Jews, labeled only as Soviet citizens, were listed on a plaque. They had been slaughtered, silent sentinels guarding the memories of a lost people and a lost community. This was Turets in 2010, the village of Eisig's birth.

We drove on to Gorodeja. Eisig's vivid images of this market town were with us as we stood on a street that paralleled the railroad tracks. The blue-roofed train station, anchoring the tracks, that would figure importantly in his life as a symbol of a larger world and of freedom, looked just as he had described. We could picture him as a young man, sixteen-years-old, boarding the train and leaving his home behind.

The town of Gorodeja, however, had changed more dramatically. Most of the surrounding buildings were new. A furniture store with contemporary but ornate Eastern European sofas and tables. A simple supermarket featuring canned goods, plastic-wrapped meats, and a bakery. In fact, aside from the railroad, there appeared little there that evoked the past, the late 19th century.

Yet, surprising to us, our visit to the office of the mayor provided unexpected opportunites. Upon hearing Eisig's story through our interpreter, the mayor warmly welcomed Rhona as a citizen of Belarus, giving her a gift of two photo books about the country. Turning toward her bookcase, she pulled out a large volume that recorded the names of those who died in this town during World War ll. We found the listing of many with the name of Lubetzky but none with the first names of Rhona's family members.

"Does anyone know where the old synagogue was?" we asked, "Does it still exist?" We pressed further, "With no Jews left in Gorodeja, is there someone who might remember?"

After making a number of telephone calls, the mayor located the very building and told us that she would take us there. We followed her by car to one of the oldest structures in the town—a single-story, white ediface that was now a bakery. Earlier, it had served as the synagogue during Rhona's grandfather's time. We were overcome with emotion to find this very spot, more than a century later.

Standing in a cavernous room, we saw women, bakers in white coats around us, flour and dough-stirring machines, fresh loaves of bread and rolls. The smell was intoxicating and Rhona, in tears, was assailed by images of a young boy with a sweet voice and a fiery message. It was here where young Eisig had given the famous three-hour sermon when he was thirteen, where the Lubetzky men had prayed, and where his protagonist, Shalom, had sought refuge in the familiar melodies and rituals.

The women welcomed us openly and talked with us about a past they did not recognize. They seemed excited that this Canadian-American couple, relatives of Jews who had lived in their town long ago, had come to visit and they claimed Rhona as one of their own. They gave us bags of delicious cookies to commemorate the return of a citizen of Gorodeja and we celebrated the moment with a photograph. Amid this warm embrace, we struggled with ambivalent feelings. No Jews were left in Gorodeja—only memories from the Yizkor book, only graves, and the cold wind of a Belarus autumn. It was bittersweet to honor the memory of Eisig and also to mourn the loss of an entire Jewish community.

Finally, stopping on the long, winding road out of the town, we left our car to climb a steep hill, where large rocks, placed one by one, line the path up to the top. These rocks represent the Jews who were herded from this town to the mount, where they were shot in the back, falling downwards into a deep hole, intermingled and buried by the dirt heaped upon them. At the top, a stark but powerful metal sculpture of empty, broken window frames, signifying destroyed homes, stands in memory of the 1147 Jews who were killed there in 1941. But, as in Turets, they are not remembered as Jews. The tribute is to "Soviet citizens" who were murdered. It was difficult to reconcile the friendly welcome to Rhona as a fellow citizen with this poignant site of human evil.

Was this the place where Eisig's siblings, their children, and their father— Rhona's family— had perished? Or did it happen in the cemetery of Turets? Or at the memorial site in Minsk, where life-size statues of the lost people—heads bowed, faces etched with sorrow—now line the way down toward a deep pit. We will never know exactly where their lives ended and at whose hands. At this graveyard in Gorodeja, high on a hill, Rhona stood holding a copy of the last Lubetzky family photograph and together we said the Jewish memorial prayer for the dead, the Kaddish. The wind whistled and the chilling cold seemed appropriate to the memory of those who lay beneath us. The Jews have largely disappeared from Belarus, the geography is the same, and we are the legacy.

Long after we departed from Belarus, we held on to the image of the Gorodeja train station. Taking a train westward, like many others, Eisig left this world behind. But unlike the majority of his family, he escaped the slaughter that was to come. Instead, the slaughter came by his own hand, far earlier by twenty years than the fate of his kin.

In the eyes of his biographers, Eisig Lubetzky was a most unusual and gifted child—a child prodigy. Aspects of his early life suggested that he was destined for greatness, yet he ultimately killed himself. What, we continued to wonder, led to that kitchen, the oven, and an untimely death?

Chapter Six

Let My Words Speak For Me

To this day Lubetzky's writings are scattered in various periodicals and have not been collected in one published work. It is time that this is done.
—Moshe Ungerfeld, 1977

And so, Eisig fled Gorodeja for Milan, Italy, leaving his family behind in order to follow his dreams. Driven by his thirst for a new life, he abandoned all that was expected of him. His wife and new-born son, casualties of that drive.

Upon graduation from the Milan Conservatory of Music, he headed eastward to Vilnius, Lithuania. There, following his talent in music, he entered the Vilnius Teachers' Academy to train as an educator. This was the brief but fateful period in which the paths of Lubetzky and Touroff would cross. Awed by this personal encounter, Touroff wrote of its enduring impact on him.

Touroff and a friend had queried Lubetzky about his recent activities, to which he replied that he was "studying singing." What Touroff found most surprising was the discrepancy between Lubetzky's appearance as a young Yeshiva boy—broad brimmed black hat, forelocks, a long black coat, and fringes of a ritual shawl peaking from under the jacket—and his choice of a secular vocation as a musician and singer. His friend produced a sheet of paper on which was written a melody and asked Lubetzky to sight-read the music. In Touroff's words: "Lubetzki penetrated the page with his eyes and the sweet melody spread in the small room through a secure, strong, and clear voice—the voice of an artist-singer that needs to be heard in a large hall in front of a large audience."

Touroff was impressed with the dual talents of this young man, which he later described as "the artistic line, manifested here in his singing, and the spiritual, intellectual line, manifested in his proclivity towards (social and literary) criticism." This meeting was so profound an experience for Touroff that he followed Lubetzky's career and life over the years, ultimately including him in his 1953 book about the suicides of creative individuals in Europe.

Eisig's stay in Vilnius was cut short in 1891, when at age nineteen, he was conscripted into the Tsar's Army. Once there, he would be forced to spend the rest of his life in the military, a tenuous existence for a Jew. Fearing a dismal future, he fled Eastern Europe, yet again.

* * *

Seeking first-hand experience of his life during these years, we traced the steps of the young Eisig in Vilnius, that city known as "the Jerusalem of Lithuania," a center of religious life. With the help of a history book and a translator, we were able to find a photograph of what was then called the Jewish Teachers' College and we visited the site where the long-ago demolished school once stood, now occupied by a contemporary building.

We walked through the streets of the old Jewish Quarter, where Eisig had lived, and saw the narrow alleys lined with modest and decaying houses, laundry hanging outside, signs in Hebrew and Yiddish, and finally, the beautiful synagogue. There was a marked contrast between the picturesque squares of the old city of Vilnius and these faded Jewish quarters. We imagined what it might have been like for Eisig walking these streets in 1891, in a city then vibrant with Jewish life. Peddlers, the same washday hangings as now, horses in the street, children running—a cacophony of sight and sound. As music was so much a part of his life, we attended a concert by a chamber orchestra of young Baltic musicians, the Kremerata Baltica, in Vilnius's beautiful concert hall. It was conducted by Gidon Kremer, a Latvian violinist and son of a Holocaust survivor. For us, it was a truly magical evening of music in the city from which Eisig, the singer, had been forced to flee.

Over the next twelve years, Eisig lived in multiple countries across Europe—among them, France, Poland, Switzerland, Hungary, and Austria. During this time period, he was deeply engaged in writing and also pursuing vocal performance and teaching. Why he kept moving his residence remains unclear, although his roving ways would broaden his emerging world and cultural view and enable his learning of multiple languages.

Eisig's musical talent was recognized when in 1902, at the age of thirty, he was invited to join the Crown Conservatory of Music in Budapest as a professor of voice. Within six months, Eisig was forced to resign because he was Jewish. The invitation to Budapest had been a godsend, a recognition that his voice was the ticket to a successful career but it was short-lived. Antisemitism was endemic in Europe and even though Jews had many options in theatre, art, music, and business, their careers often were constrained by the anti-Jewish discriminatory practices that thwarted success. Eisig then moved to Galicia where, for a short period, he served as secretary of the society Ahavat Tzion (the Love of Zion), a faction of the pre-Zionist movement that argued for a Jewish nation.

* * *

In 1903, at the age of thirty-one, Eisig finally settled in the city where he would live out his days. Vienna, the center of music and culture for Eastern Europeans at that time, called to him. Vienna was a magnet for someone with his interests but the glories of its fame covered over the challenges. He became choir director at the Stadttempel, the main synagogue of Vienna, a post he held from 1903-1914 and he served in a similar post at the Kluckygasse Synagogue close to his apartment in the 20th District. He also headed a studio for voice training. As well, Eisig became active in literary and artistic circles, as a writer, political and cultural commentator, and critic, thus melding his musical and literary interests.

What a feast it must have been for Eisig to live in Vienna at the dawn of the 20th century. Despite comparisons to Paris or Berlin, casting Vienna as a pale shadow of these cosmopolitan centers, the city, in the first decades of the era, was aglow with life and ideas. Even for Jews, opportunities were abundant in many fields.

By 1910, Jews constituted about 9% of the total population of the city and in many ways their influence far surpassed their numbers. Steven Beller suggests that "Jews were the people who dominated the cultural life of Vienna" and were the principal consumers of this life. He describes the contributions of the community in many fields—psychology (Freud), philosophy (the Vienna Circle, the founders of Logical Positivism), political thought and socialism, social thought, economics, legal theory, literature (Zweig, Schnitzler), theatre and operetta, and music (especially Mahler and Schoenberg). In two fields, in art with the birth of the secessionist movement and in architecture, Jews were the critical supporters, indeed, patrons in their development.

Stefan Zweig, in his memoir, *The World of Yesterday*, gives powerful expression to the richness of the Viennese world at the time. He calls it "The Golden Age of Security" and describes a "fanaticism for art and for the art of theater in particular . . . [that] touched all classes." He further notes that there was "an uncommon respect for every artistic presentation . . . a connoisseurship . . . and thanks to that . . . a predominant high level in all cultural fields." While Jews were excluded from governance and most aspects of civic life, Zweig claims "that nine-tenths of what the world celebrated as Viennese culture in the nineteenth century was promoted, nourished, or even created by Viennese Jewry." This claim is supported in the writings of other authors.

There were two centers of cultural and intellectual ferment—the private salons, usually hosted in peoples' homes, and the coffee houses—where men exchanged ideas and aspirations. It was at a salon held at the home of Reuben Brainin that Eisig Lubetzky first met Reuben's younger sister Marie or Musa, as she was called, his future wife. A young woman, dressed in a white nightgown, long and flowing hair, her face radiant with pleasure, as she followed the youngsters in her care throughout the apartment. Musa had come from Lyady, a shtetl in eastern Belarus, to Vienna to work as a nanny for her brother's children. Eisig was entranced. Marriage and children soon followed.

However, the enchantment with Musa and family life would be short-lived.

It was in the coffee houses that Eisig could be found. We can picture Eisig leaving the family apartment and walking through the Augarten towards the Karmelitermarkt, the lively market at the center of the Jewish Quarter, named for the lovely Carmelite church that anchors the area. He spies some members of the synagogue where he is the choir director and wishes them a good morning. He is off to the Café Reklame, across the street from the apartment of Theodor Herzl (the father of modern political Zionism), where he will spend some hours drinking coffee with whipped cream ("mit schlag"), enjoying a pastry and most of all, engaging in spirited discussion with other patrons. He will take notes and for some periods of time, he will sit alone and write, occasionally looking up to take in the large windows overlooking the street, the crystal chandeliers, the arched high ceilings, and the waiters in formal garb. Cigarette smoke wafts through the room. A man stops at his table, an author, and barrages him with complaints about his recent review of his article on contemporary music. Another compliments him on his article on Zionism and its discontents. His life is in the cafés where he is most at home, his wife and children are far away. This is where the men of the intelligentsia meet. In this respect, Eisig was not so different from many of the upward striving Eastern European Jews who have come to Vienna. This is where he belonged.

* * *

While we had in hand copies of several of Eisig's writings, we remained curious about the entire body of his literary work—what it revealed about his inner life but also about its special qualities and how it had been judged. This seemed curious, as the call by his biographers, Touroff (1953) and Ungerfeld (1977), for the collection of his publications, went unheeded. Curious also, because his writings were his legacy, traces of him that remained.

Rhona contacted a contemporary scholar of the Hebrew literature of that era. Identifying herself as a granddaughter, she asked about Eisig Lubetzky's contributions to the literary canon, which the scholar dismissed with these words: "Lubetzky was an insignificant figure in Jewish literary history—a person of no consequence in the field." A more nuanced assessment is offered in the *YIVO Encyclopedia of Jews in Eastern Europe* where in the bibliographic article on the history of Hebrew literary criticism, Lubetzky is described as one of three "outstanding critics" of that time. It is true, however, that in the entry on Hebrew literature, Lubetzky's name appears only in the appendix, in a list of "Hebrew writers who are not the subject of an independent biographical entry," in contrast to the acknowledgment accorded his brother-in-law, Reuben Brainin.

Given what we knew of Eisig's prodigious talent and early renown, was there more to this story? As we puzzled over how we could gain a deeper understanding of his literary work and its contributions, serendipity, yet again, brought us an unexpected gift.

In 2008, a decade after we created the family book about Lubetzky to honor Aunt Hedy's 90th birthday, we learned of its impact. With our inquiry about Eisig's life as the nudge, a linked set of events across different continents became the impetus for a new scholarly investigation into the literary contributions of Rhona's grandfather. An Israeli graduate student, Shoshana Sperber, completed a master's thesis, written in Hebrew and titled *Isaac Lubetzky: Writer and Critic*.

Rabbi Cutter, who helped us early in the search, had passed on a copy of our family book to Professor Avner Holtzman, a noted scholar of early 20th century Hebrew literature at Tel Aviv University. Holtzman then suggested to Sperber that a study of Eisig Lubetzky would be a good topic for a thesis. It was Holtzman who had written the two YIVO entries about Lubetzky mentioned above. In Sperber's recounting, Holtzman told her that Shmuel Werses, a Professor Emeritus at the Hebrew University in Jerusalem and a recipient of the Israel Prize for Literature, had been saying for a long time that someone should research Lubetzky. Familiar with Lubetzky's work, Werses was also aware of a fascinating correspondence (1898-1901) between Lubetzky and the esteemed editor Ahad Ha'am, archived in the National Library of Israel. Ahad Ha'am was a central literary figure of the Zionist movement and the founder of the leading Hebrew monthly *Hashiloach*. It was in *Hashiloach* that Lubetzky's first two publications in 1898 appeared; ultimately, eleven of his essays were published in this journal.

Coincidently, Sperber had once written about Lubetzky's brother-in-law, Reuben Brainin. She recalled being moved by the photograph of Eisig in our family book and the sheer tragedy of his life. This same photo had also haunted Rhona. Our book had landed in a time and place where curiosity about Eisig's life and work was to be rekindled.

In setting the stage for her thesis, Sperber quotes a seminal commentary from her advisor, Professor Holtzman, about how we might construct literary history differently, with implications for the story we tell. Holtzman wrote:

> Assuming that a true depiction of a given literary landscape should contain not only the mighty mountains but also the humble hills that lie in their shadows, there is room to explore the more obscure paths and create preliminary monographs of unique 'marginal' characters. Such works, accumulated together, enrich and alter the story of the growth of modern Hebrew literature.

Sperber chooses the "obscure path" that Holtzman recommended, to resurrect the lost contributions of Eisig Lubetzky. In her words, the research aims "to expose the corpus of Lubetzky's work, as well as to place it within the landscape of modern Hebrew literature." She goes on to argue: "The field . . . has neglected this unique and fascinating character." . . . Lubetzky has yet to receive the place he deserves in the field of literary research . . . he has disappeared almost entirely from the history of modern (20th century) Hebrew literature." This is an omission she hopes to rectify.

Her bibliography illuminates the breadth of Lubetzky's work and his productivity, in what was a foreshortened career of some twenty-two years. As Sperber notes, in the period between 1898 and 1920, "Lubetzky published 140 texts in Hebrew, among which are eleven short stories, a single novella, and dozens of critical essays." But Hebrew was not his only language of literary contribution and his productivity did not end there. She lists ten works in Yiddish, acknowledging this as an incomplete biography. He also published in German, and in Italian and Greek, these latter two languages under the pseudonym of A. Kly. Our own foray into the Brainin Archives at the Montreal Jewish

Public Library revealed additional unpublished work in Yiddish. And Lubetzky, himself, reported that there were many articles and essays that he had destroyed or cast aside.

Sperber's bibliography of Lubetzky's writings is arranged by the journals in which he published—eleven in number. We re-ordered this list by year of publication, making more prominent his first and last publications; the last two in 1919 and 1920, just before his death. This re-ordered listing also highlights a dry period in which his publications, at least in Hebrew, came almost to a halt, from 1915-1921. What, we wonder, led to this apparent dry period, occurring close to and within the years of World War 1 (1914-1918)?

Sperber's manuscript proves to be wide-ranging and deeply analytical. She begins with one chapter dedicated to the life and death of Lubetzky, acknowledging our family book and further, that so little was known. She then appraises his work across three fields of Hebrew literature: fiction, cultural and Zionist thought, and literary criticism. Lubetzky wrote for well-known journals of the era and his creative mind addressed the fields of art, music, literature, and politics, especially Zionism and the rejection of Eastern European Jews by the Jewish burghers of Vienna. He did not languish in obscurity at that time, as his writing elicited responses from key intellectuals with whom he engaged frequently in sometimes acrimonious debates.

* * *

We were able to obtain translations of some of Eisig's fictional writings. Although filtered through "translated" words, we were moved by what we read. Not only for the beautiful images he created but also for its universal themes of striving and perceived marginality. In his writings, we saw the struggle for self-actualization as a Jew during that era, the experience of failure, and a sense of separateness apart from others. The push-pull of past and present, a loss that is mourned and a desired new life, that, in reality, is found wanting. Reading his fiction, which appeared narcissistic and revelatory, we felt we were looking into his soul, into a deep well of pain.

In his short stories, Eisig vividly explores the shtetl of his youth, even naming Gorodeja and remembering important town folk in essays such as "Samuel the Pious" and "Nehemia the Teacher, Nehemia the Heretic." And as we noted earlier, in "The Lonely Stalk of Grain (1902)," he also describes a sense of dying, caught within a narrow and ritualistic Jewish culture. Using the metaphor of one stalk of grain, which remains alone in a field approaching winter, he writes with eloquence that "I hear in its swaying the last sigh of its dying youth in the battle against mortality." But an escape and ventures in the larger world beyond the shtetl are imagined to result in failure, as seen in his first published short story "Fast After a Dream (1898)." In this tale of a failed artist, Eisig's words capture the humiliation, both private and public, of the character's inability to become "great." We read:

> I failed to listen to them and chose to tread in my own path, what do I have to show for it? I have suffered more than my strength could endure, but what good have I done? A poor Jewish man like myself will never be great; without money I can achieve nothing, even if I choose to sacrifice myself completely. I am the object of ridicule, the wild, crazy one, whose stupidity has led him to the bottom of hell.

In the veiled autobiography, we saw that marriage was also problematic as illustrated in Shuelik's description of his relationship with his wife. And in the short story, "The Lonely Stalk of Grain," the protagonist Shalom speaks of the distance between himself and his promised wife who "remains a stranger to him . . . he is lonely, forsaken, and he has nothing in this world." These are portraits of men struggling with their most intimate relationships and doomed to a life of isolation and regret.

And yet, Eisig could display empathy for women and even adopts a female voice in his novella "The Sin," published in 1910 as a serial in *Hashiloach*. Early in our search, we read the translated first chapter from this novella, a first-person account by a woman in her thirties living in a small city somewhere in Eastern Europe. Eisig's identification with the young woman is unusual, in our view, given the patriarchal nature of the era. It is the day of her wedding anniversary and she has just awakened:

> She looked around her to see whether her husband was in the room. The ticking of the clock made her feel agreeably alone. The people and the household birds disappeared, and the entire house is filled with the pleasant calm of a peaceful life. The whisper of an agreeable stillness fills the air, and the overflow of her tender feelings makes her dawdle in her bed, as she feels that she is the happiest person in the world . . . At the sight of the sun's rays falling on her bare bosom and her disheveled hair, she feels elated and ready in her happy mood, to take the whole world in her arms, the shapely arms of a fully developed woman whose beauty has not begun to fade.

However, we can also detect a man's perspective in the words he has chosen to describe how she saw herself in the mirror:

> Her . . . hair, reaching down to the roundings of her thighs, her plump arms, red from the towel's friction, her full, bright face expressing vigor and joy, her neck and shoulders, smooth as silk, her erect and fresh figure, greatly accentuated under the wide shirt, the beauty of her healthy, delicate woman's build—all this she saw in the mirror, and was filled with joy at the thought that she has retained her powers, and has not changed at all.

These images are especially poignant when it becomes apparent that after ten years of marriage, she has not conceived. She faces cruel jokes and teasing from her mother-in-law and sister-in-law, and her husband threatens to divorce her, an action allowed under Orthodox Jewish law. Ultimately, alone and in despair, she travels to Vienna to seek a consultation with a gynecologist, by whom, it is later revealed, she becomes pregnant.

It is striking that, during a misogynistic time, Eisig shows the capacity to portray the feelings of a young woman. For a man who, in his fiction (and in his life, as we were to discover) is unable to sustain any form of intimacy, this would have required almost a chameleon-like shift in perspective-taking. But, of course, there is another side to this tale. The female protagonist's adultery and ensuing deception can be interpreted as further evidence that closeness between the sexes leads to betrayal, reinforcing a belief about the untrustworthiness of women.

One of his biographers, Ungerfeld, was not impressed with Lubetzky's attempts at fiction writing which he saw as carried out with "a sense of hurry and impetuousness." In reviewing "The Sin," he wrote: "It must be said that . . . this is neither a story nor a quite a novella, but rather a psychological portrait." He went on to argue:

> The narrative content of the story is very scarce and far too corny; and its "protagonists" take the stage merely to present the tiny play of a marriage. This is nothing but a rather simple "episode" of the life of two people—without any complicated encounters between various types, and without the organic development of events that are rich in content, which might be found in a proper novel. What can be found in "The Sin" is an interesting depiction of the poor protagonist's rapidly changing states of mind as she weaves a net of doubts, fears and regrets.

He concluded that " this story does hold within it some qualities of an aesthetic literary work. However, nothing about these qualities would lead the reader to think that this is the work of a masterful author who may someday become canonical."

In contrast, Sperber sees the "psychological portrait" quality of Lubetzky's writings as the unique contribution to the literature of that era. Although as Alan Mintz has written, Lubetzky's overarching theme, the pull of modernity and the tug of tradition, characterizes autobiographical Hebrew writing in the late 19th and early 20th centuries in Europe. Lubetzky wrote about the lonely and uprooted young Jewish man whose desire for knowledge led him on a journey away from his home of origin to a new world. Once there, he found little fulfillment either in work or in his intimate relationships with women—leading to despair, suicidal ideation, and even suicide. But as Sperber argues, while other writers focused on the social context of the individual, such as the struggle with Jewish tradition or a national conflict, Lubetzky's writings were intensely introspective and psychoanalytic in nature. In her view, they represent a form of "modernist psychological fiction," moving away from romanticism and revealing a more negative and hopeless view of the world.

* * *

Beyond fiction writing, Eisig actively published non-fiction commentaries that contributed to public discourse. His many opinion pieces—feuilletons as they were labeled in Vienna—addressed the everyday issues facing the Viennese Jews, including culture and the politics of Zionism. Among a broad range of topics, he wrote about the work of Parisian artists, Hebrew artists, religion, war, music composition, and Austrian literature.

Eisig's very his first and best-known commentary was published in 1898 in *Hashiloach,* with the title "Zionism and its Opponents: An Open Letter to Max Nordau." It proved to be quite controversial.

We imagine the context in which the young Eisig wrote this piece. A slight figure, a formerly ultra-religious Jew from Belarus comes to Vienna. Impoverished and barely able to provide for his family, he is filled with a burning desire to prove himself a great writer. He begins to frequent the cafés, the centers of intellectual life, and he listens. At first, he remains on the outside, on the periphery of the ferment, but as he listens, he feels the bubbling up of disagreement.

An eminent Zionist leader, physician, author and social critic, one of the founders of the Zionist movement with Theodor Herzl, sits near him in the café, lecturing to his colleagues about the future of Jews in Europe. His name, Max Nordeau. Twenty-three years Eisig's senior, Nordeau would likely have paid little attention to this awkward outsider, but that did not stop the young upstart. We cannot separate our understanding of Eisig from the intellectual tumult around the issue of Zionism that pervaded the discourse of the Jewish intelligentsia at that time.

Nordeau had given a speech calling for an aggressive, almost militaristic movement to establish a Jewish homeland in Palestine. Eisig disagreed and his brave but rash commentary addressed the question of a Palestinian homeland for the Jews. Fifty years before the founding of the State of Israel, Eisig took a cautionary and unpopular stance, warning against an impulsive emigration to the Middle East. Of course, despite the increasing antisemitism in Austria, he did not anticipate the rise of Nazism and its horrific consequences for European Jews. But he did anticipate the complexity of establishing a Jewish state, the implications of which reverberate even into the present.

Eisig quotes Nordau as concluding "Jewry will either embrace Zionism or cease to exist" and he made himself the spokesman for a group of dissenters who had been ignored. He writes:

> But sir, there are Jews in the East—not a few in number—who have never thought of being anything but Jews, who were born with a Jewish consciousness,

> and they, too, are opposed to Zionism, although they desire and long for, as part of their nature, the continued existence of Jews and Judaism.

He asks for a deeper reflection and points to the heart of the disagreement, about timing and about universality of the choice for all:

> But sir, have you given any thought to the "aftermath" [of false hopes], when the obstacles, which, even you admit are not few in number, will prevent the anticipated realization? . . . Did you ask yourself the frightening question of what would happen in the event of failure?

As Eisig, an Eastern European Jew, was seen as inferior by the Jewish intellectuals of Western Europe, he feels the need to speak for the people, the masses, suffering for years under antisemitism, whose greatest need was to integrate into what he viewed as a more favorable Western European life. He sees Zionism as a longer-term process that would eventuate in the creation of the homeland, where some could choose to go. But he also believes that the Jewish diaspora could find success in educating their young as Jews in a European context, in achieving respect for a Hebrew literature, and being accepted as equals in Europe. His dual pathways and slower timeline contrasted sharply with that of Herzl and colleagues.

Holding this view, he was severely criticized by many of his contemporaries as too passive and indeed too naïve about the success of integration. The debates in which he and they engaged were passionate and filled with sarcastic innuendo. He was even admonished by the editor of *Hashiloach,* Ahad Ha'am, in a letter dated August 7, 1898, for the presumptuous way in which he proposed to write his response to the esteemed Dr. Nordau:

> And even its structure—an open letter to Nordau—gives a bad impression. Letters like this only take place between people who equal one another in their wisdom and in their fame. But a young man, who still hasn't made a name for himself in the world, writing a letter to a sage renowned in the entire word, the law of propriety states that he should be more humble in the presentation of his words.

Despite this admonition from the editor, Eisig's infamous letter to Nordau was published in what was seen as one of the foremost Hebrew journals of the time.

* * *

Eisig's contribution to Hebrew letters was also as a critic—in visual arts, music, and literature. Given his view that Hebrew writing needed to expand, not only with translations of European works, but perhaps, more importantly, by generating its own literature, he became an advocate for the use of Hebrew as a literary language in prose and in commentary. It was in the realm of criticism that he achieved his greatest recognition and ultimately his fiercest rebukes.

As described by Sperber, Lubetzky, the critic, developed a unique method of analysis. He proposed that artistic work must be judged on the basis of standardized criteria, not based on the subjective perspective of the reviewer. This approach flew in the face of the traditional ways in which criticism was carried out at that time. Of course, the challenge lay in the parameters of the criteria and in who developed them. He reviewed the works of many of the famous Hebrew writers, musicians, and artists of the era by examining the quality of their work and their relationship to the culture in which they emerged.

But it was the reaction of his peers that was to be his undoing. As a critic of the work of others, Lubetzky proved to be a negative force. Moshe Ungerfeld (1972) wrote that "His critiques were rather acrimonious, and even the literary greats—Zangwill, Mendel, Brenner, Barshadsky, Schofmann—were not spared." His criticisms were not constructively given but instead took the route of personal attacks on the talent or capability of the writers. In one example, cited by Sperber, he penned, "Bershadsky is not a genius. His talent does not qualify him to discover the harmony between realization and abstraction." And about Yosef Brenner, cited by Ungerfeld, he wrote, "But we also can see in this very same text, 'Out of a Gloomy Valley,' Brenner's difficult path and we witness the dying of his talent and the damnation of his abilities."

Eisig even took on such literary luminaries as Y. L. Peretz, who spared no venom of his own in his response. As cited by Sperber, Peretz wrote: "We should note that there are many kinds of artistic works that are not psychological novels . . . And now this righteous young man from Vienna has issued a decree!" Sperber suggests that it was the bitter interchange with Peretz that ultimately ended Lubetzky's career as a critic.

* * *

Sperber's master's thesis answers the call made long ago by Touroff and Ungerfeld to collect and analyze Lubetzky's contributions to Hebrew literature. And she offers a more positive assessment of his place in modern Hebrew literature:

> Upon examining Lubetzky's oeuvre, one notices the variety of fields in which he operated: the visual arts, music, politics and literary criticism, as well as the fact that he has made his unique mark in every single one of these fields. He formulated a consistent, unique critical theory, formulated unique political stances and wrote works of fiction that focus on the mind of the individual. I believe that his great talent in various areas, the breadth of his knowledge and his clear style all leave Lubetzky with a distinguished place in the realm of modern Hebrew literature.

Puzzled by how such a gifted and unique writer could virtually disappear from the history of 20th century Hebrew literature—except for a few more contemporary mentions by Holtzman (1999) and Baram-Eshel (2001)—Sperber posits an array of reasons why Lubetzky may have been discounted. Among them, he crossed fields, never wrote a book, never belonged to any defined professional group, and lived away from the literary centers of Hebrew literature, rarely interacting in person with his peers. Even today, criteria such as these play a role in the development of a reputation within a discipline. But there is more to the story.

Eisig's critical voice invited controversy, undercutting a place of prominence for him. As noted by his biographers, his verbal attacks on the elite, especially as a junior colleague, could have resulted in his being marginalized and excluded by those whose opinions mattered. While some saw his criticism as unique, others viewed his comments as greatly out of line. Gershom Bader, an author, playwright, and journalist, wrote of Lubetzky after his death in 1921 that "he was never a news reporter or a critic of the common variety, but rather a sharp critic without cowardice or deceit." He was unafraid to express views that were outside the mainstream. While Bader admired these qualities, others bristled, bringing to mind the admonition made by Ahad Ha'am about Lubetzky's letter to Nordau that, as a callow youth, he needed to show more respect.

The severe nature of his commentary created a tragic dynamic—a type of self-fulfilling prophecy—brought about by the perceptions of others and by his own expectations. Eisig held lofty aims for the development of a Hebrew literature and with a reputation as a child prodigy, he expected to be acknowledged among the great writers of the time. As Touroff (1945) described it, Lubetzky's "excessive tendency towards negativity and criticism was probably the result of a lack of satisfaction with his own personal fate, as well as of the "moral" requirement to battle his shortcomings and demand perfection both in life and in art—the very same perfection he himself was never able to reach." And as he concluded, "The 'end result' then was that by the sharpness of his criticism, Lubetzki aroused objections, and by his belletristic trials, he did not himself fulfill what he had demanded from others." A perceived failure, as seen by others and by himself, became a failure achieved.

* * *

In our many visits to Vienna, ghosts of the past were everywhere as we tried to reconstruct the world of Rhona's grandfather. And always a surprise to us, Eisig was still remembered in the present.

In a 2014 research trip, our request for a specialist through the Institute of Judaistik reached Evelyn Adunka, a historian on the Jews in Vienna. "Was your grandfather I. A. Lubetzky?" she asked Rhona, "In this case, it would be especially nice to meet because I am interested in cantors and Yiddish literature of that time." We eagerly agreed to join her at the Rathaus café and she provided us with a biographical entry in German about Lubetzky, noting he was a choir director both at the Stadttempel and at the Synagogue Kluckygasse. We could not help but notice that the biographical entry contained this oft-repeated error, "He took his life together with his son."

She also showed us pictures of the Kluckygasse Synagogue, which was very close to Eisig's apartment in the 20th district. On November 10, 1938, Kristallnacht, the building was broken into, its interior destroyed by the Nazis. A memorial plaque was erected there in 1988.

Adunka had invited Thomas Soxberger, a scholar of Jewish literature, to join us. Expressing pleasure to meet the granddaughter of Lubetzky, he gave us an inscribed copy of his 2008 book *Nackte Liede- Jiddische Literatur aus Wien 1915-1938*. Roughly translated, this means "Naked Songs: Jewish Literature in Vienna." In it, we found a Yiddish story by Lubetzky, first published in 1915 and translated into German by Soxberger. It is titled "Und ich sage euch" which in English means "And I tell you." We held this book in our hands, while sitting in the same Viennese café that Eisig had in his day frequented. And surprisingly, the chosen title of

Lubetzky's story echoed Rhona's mother's oft-repeated refrain, "Now let me tell you." This expression of strong opinions had indeed crossed the generations, from father to daughter.

Almost a century later, Sperber concludes that Lubetzky's contributions were innovative and unique for its time. Yet his life story does not reflect the success expected of a child prodigy. In fact, a sense of failure permeated his life—high expectations went unfulfilled. We, as had Nissan Touroff, mused about what makes some people succeed and others remain in obscurity, never to fully achieve their potential. We soon learned how the dark clouds under which Lubetzky lived ultimately sabotaged his dreams.

Chapter Seven

The Darkness Within

Because we are not God, our narration of another's life is a pretense of knowledge— simultaneously an attempt to know and a confession of how little we know.
—James Wood, 2017

Even as a young man, Eisig appears to have been haunted by demons. Buried in the boxes labeled Lubetzky at the Montreal Jewish Public Library, we found the following letter. Undated and unsigned, this letter, in translation, begins with the salutation, "Dear Mother." It reads:

> What am I lacking? But this is my misfortune, that I don't know what I'm lacking. If it was something palpable I would know what this life is all about. Then, [but] this right life consists of imperfections [failures, blunders] and straits [extremities]. A dead person isn't lacking in anything because he doesn't need anything, but a living person who has a [life's] path knows what he's lacking, and the more he is lacking the greater is his chance to be dissatisfied.
>
> . . . I don't have an appetite. I want to be by myself. I run away from people. This is what I have. Thank God, I'm alone in my room but the ___ is oppressing me like a heavy load, and there are times when I want to run out of my room because the mute walls and the

> air irritate me. I want some peace of mind and I don't have enough of it so I wander around all day without being disturbed, but I'm going meshuggah [crazy] from the deathly silence, lying and counting the long seconds, which is even worse than working as an organ grinder. I'm not lacking in anything. I have everything I want but this is my misfortune, that I see all the things that I don't want [and it's not] what I hoped for.
>
> And like this the days go by and in my heart everything is devastated and destroyed; everything feels dead. . . . For days long I lie on the sofa and I hear how it gnaws and is rushing inside, and I feel in my heart the promenade of the Angel of Death. I just want only one thing, that no one should move me, and no one should bother me, and I should lay like this until the last sensation. The knowledge of boredom should also die down in me. Other than this I want nothing, absolutely nothing.

But as Eisig continues, he also writes of the joy that he, as a preacher, experiences in front of his congregation. When he sermonizes, he knows moments of exultation—feeling himself to be "burning like a fire":

> I bellow asunder a great and powerful "Hear O Israel" and place great emphasis on stretching out [the vowel in the word] God is Oneeeee so that it ___ ___ in a state of great ecstasy, and I'm even more worked up in a lather [feverish] and I roll up my sleeves and I intone the Jewish oath, "If I Forget Thee, O

> Jerusalem, May My Tongue Stick to My Palate." I've become a Lover of Zion, a Zionist. I ride around in the cities and shtetlech [Jewish villages] to gather the Jews and give fiery speeches.

And yet, when the sermonizing is over, his mood changes drastically:

> But when I am by myself in my room. . . . The ideas and hopes with the congregation don't really concern me. The seer and the sum of these sermons with all the rapture . . . This has absolutely no connection with the love of Zion and the Life of Israel. The words of the fiery sermons creep inside the thinned out __ head, which is full of anxieties. These feelings don't warm and can't warm the dead and frozen hearts. But, what then? . . . The spirit is broken . . . The burdened heart will always be extinguished.

These words depict a paralyzing depression, grandiosity, a flooding of anxiety, and spiraling moods—leaving its author "dying off day by day . . . without a single thought or single glimmer of hope." If this were indeed a letter to his mother, was it ever sent? And if it had been sent, how did it find its way back among his personal papers? Or was this an unpublished fiction piece, drawing upon his own inner life as as an adolescent, when he served as a traveling preacher and before he left Gorodeja for the Milan Conservatory of Music?

Not only the shifting moods but also the characteristics of the handwriting conveyed emotional upheaval. As with the veiled autobiography, our translator found the text difficult to decipher—in part because the writings were in a version of Deutschmerisch (a hybrid of German and Yiddish) and in part because of the disarray on the pages. The missing words and obscure meaning of some terms in the text rendered many sentences unintelligible. Tiny writing, circling around the edges and filling the entire page with print, proved almost impossible to read. His letters often lacked punctuation, added later by the translator to better uncover their meaning. Did this style of writing result from the high price of paper at that time or did the disarray reflect something else—a frantic process of expression and the rush of exhilarated state? We found other pages with the same kind of tiny script in circular form and similar content that revealed a cycling of emotions.

Did Eisig, himself, experience these alternating periods of profound depression with manic episodes of productivity? If only we could understand what, at that young age, oppressed Eisig like a heavy load and what the perceived lack was within him that caused him so much pain. Was he railing against the hopes of Jews for redemption in Zion—a false path as he later wrote about in his infamous letter to Dr. Max Nordau? Was he losing faith that he could be among the religious prophets for his congregation and did this loss of faith precipitate his dreams for a more secular life and his flight westward?

* * *

In his early years as a writer, evidence about Lubetzky's vulnerable mental state appears in the letters of submission he wrote to Ahad Ha'am, the editor of the journal *Hashiloach* (The Messenger). At that point, Lubetzky was in his later twenties and Ahad Ha'am was his senior by almost two decades. From this archived correspondence of three years—January 2, 1898 through June 25, 1901—we were able to obtain and translate twenty-four letters sent by Lubetzky to Ahad Ha'am. And, in a book about the editor's work, we found five of his responses to Lubetzky.

These letters are addressed to Herr U. Ginzberg (the given name of Ahad Ha'am), with the salutation "Dear Sir!" and signed I. A. Lubetsky, "with admiration" or "with respect." The postmarks place the editor in Odessa, Ukraine and Lubetzky in France, Poland, and Austria, where he resided either in hotels or private homes. The 1898 letters (ten in number) are sent from Hotel Flotters at 3 Rue Flotters or from the home of Theophane Chipoulinsky at 15 Rue Claude in Paris. Two letters are from Tarnow, Poland and the remaining twelve letters are sent from Vienna addresses, from the homes of Herr Dr. J. Kohn and Herr A. Klager, as well as from Hotel Bauer.

Lubetzky's very first letter to Ahad Ha'am (January 2, 1898) sheds light on how he spent his time during the years 1891 through 1898, following his flight from Vilnius and conscription. He has been actively writing, noting that the story he was submitting, "Fast for a Dream," was finished three years earlier. As well, he has at hand a large body of completed work, including chapters for his book *Jewish Music in Relation to the Music of the Nations and its Future Prospects*, parts of which were already published in the magazine *La Critica* in Rome. He offers to send Ahad Ha'am additional critiques about music, painting, and sculpture, and stories about the Salon, a circle of Jewish men and women who embrace culture and the arts. He tells Ahad Ha'am that he has also continued his education as a composer and music educator.

While Lubetzky's letters demonstrate his intellect, breadth of knowledge, and the challenge he has taken on for himself—to translate artistic terms into Hebrew equivalents—these letters are also poignant to read. Sometimes, his communications are clear. But at other times, they are lengthy, disorganized, and difficult to follow. Lubetzky's letters reveal a volatile nature and a troubled mental state. He even admits to hospitalizations for nerves that occurred during this time period. In response, the letters from editor Ahad Ha'am are measured but sometimes critical, expressing irritation with Lubetzky at both his ways and his work. The back and forth exchange between the two men is a testy one at best. Yet Ahad Ha'am continues to engage with Lubetzky, hoping, perhaps, to shape his behavior. And indeed, he publishes some of his work.

We carefully read the editor's judgment of Lubetzky's submissions and can appreciate the expected cycle of revise and resubmit—an exchange that characterizes the review process involved in publication decisions. But the underlying tension is surprising. An author, pushing boundaries and challenging established writers. An editor, chafing at a young author's boldness and even arrogance for overstepping the boundaries. For example, while pleased about some of Lubetzky's submissions, Ahad Ha'am also expresses his displeasure with several other essays:

> Yesterday, I received your letter with the attachment of the feuilleton and I am very sorry that I will not be able to make room for it. . . . It contains a very crude allegory . . . when you present it in such a foreign form, it is bound to make a very bad impression—

> don't you understand that *The Messenger* simply cannot print such things. [January 10, 1899]

> To my great disappointment, I cannot make room for your article. While even radical ideas have the right to be heard, it has to be done in a different manner, a manner which on one hand doesn't intend "to anger" and on the other hand has good enough supports and not just general assumptions. [January 29, 1901]

In turn, Lubetzky's balking at any criticism made it difficult to engage in dialogue. We get a flavor of Lubetzky's extreme reactions to Ahad Ha'am's judgment of his work—passionate, paranoid, and angry—out of keeping with the formal and polite interactions that characterize the era as well as the norms that govern a junior author whose reputation is not yet forged. Lubetzky responds:

> Hence I intended to pass on your last letter in silence, but now . . . I see I cannot restrain myself. . . . Indeed it is possible that I had too much naivete to believe that with my manners I would be accepted into the society of the reader of *The Messenger* . . . I came to challenge the accepted spirit . . . Let me confess that it might not be polite to come in poly-tonal manner to a person with whom one is not well-acquainted. But, if you wouldn't have paid so much attention to the manner in which I express myself but rather to the content of my words, then, I predict, you would have found there many things worthy of response. And if, in many places I behaved arrogantly, that is, without supporting my arguments, it is because I thought that I may do

> so because you would yourself understand the foundation upon which my words are based. [May 3, 1898]

> Despite having found in your letters many hints which proved to me that you put in a special effort into your wish to humiliate me this time, nevertheless, I am appealing to my good manners, and I answer you on account of the respect which fills my heart for the writer Ahad Ha'am [yet] in the person, as it seems, there can be found not a small measure of meticulousness and punctiliousness, which occasionally brings him to pettiness. As obviously understood, I will respond to you, that by your rudeness—with which you cursed me, with silence and with hints—it is impossible, nor do I wish to be harassed. [February 12, 1899]

Believing that Ahad Ha'am had little talent himself for literature, Lubetzky perceives the editor's corrections as worthless. He angrily refuses to have his work edited while at the same time, he desires the publication of his writings:

> My stories I also won't send you until you promise me that, aside from the language, you will not correct a single thing. I do not want to argue with you, and to talk too much, for I see that I cannot control my temper, but I will say to you briefly that if you behave like that with the other writers then you are destroying the shoots . . . you have no right whatsoever to correct the stories, for this requires . . . a special talent, and that you lack. I tried to show you in simple terms but you do not wish to argue about things of taste, and therefore I am telling you briefly here that your

> taste is quite questionable . . . I already told you in the beginning of my letter that I won't give you a single line of my story unless I know for certain that it will not suffer from the interference of your pen. [September 30, 1898]

As editors serve as gatekeepers for what will make it into print, the submitting author is always placed in a vulnerable position. The extent of Lubetzky's vituperative accusations, the degree of paranoia and rage expressed to the editor, demonstrate how little control he had over his sharp tongue. He threw caution to the wind, seemingly unaware or uninterested in how these words might affect the chances of his work being published. And yet, within these ill-tempered exchanges are surprisingly open disclosures by Lubetzky about his private life.

The letters underscore Lubetzky's desperation over money as he pleads for advances on his submissions, acknowledging how hard it is to support himself as a writer. This poverty is likely why during these years, he stayed in the homes of others and moved frequently. He explains: "In my current situation, I don't have the ability to allow myself the pleasure of writing for free" [January 2, 1898]. Lubetzky persists in his press for payment, but in this case, with humor: "Now that my health situation has gotten better I am going to be an established starver [instead of established writer]" [July 5, 1898]. In another letter, he asks:

> If you could send me advances for twenty-five rubles, then I would thank you from the bottom of my heart. Even though it is very difficult for me to ask you about financial matters, my situation right now is very

> bad. It has been some time since I made a single penny. [January 5, 1899]

Ahad Ha'am's response is firm: "Your request about the advances I will fulfill when you send me something that I can actually receive [that is, publish]. We have a rule to pay writers only after their articles are printed" [January 10, 1899].

But it becomes clear in the ensuing letters that the editor goes out of his way to help. And Lubetzky acknowledges Ahad Ha'am's kindness with appreciation: "You did me a great favor that you agreed to print something of mine this month so that I will have sustenance for the first while after I will leave the hospital" [undated, but likely 1901].

Ahad Ha'am also becomes embroiled in Lubetzky's private affairs when contacted by the family of Lubetzky's first wife, abandoned ten years earlier in Belarus. She was left an "agunah," a chained wife unable to remarry according to Jewish religious law. Lubetzky is frantic and asks Ahad Ha'am not to reveal his address under any circumstance, but only the address of his father in Goredeja, noting that "it's not due to robbery or murder that I desire to conceal my address but because the issues of my family force me to be so careful" [August 3, 1898]. In this same letter, Lubetzky becomes increasingly incensed with Ahad Ha'am's concerns and defends his honor:

> Hence, because of this woman, I asked you not to notify anyone about my address, but not because I wanted to hide from her but because she has no connection to me. Her desire—for me to live with her—I could not, nor want not, to fulfill. . . . .

If I hindered the doings of my wife, then in any circumstance, they cannot punish me for it because I was then a lad of seventeen which even according to the law, I was not of age to be punished by law more than she was, who was by then a woman in the full sense of the word, who was according to her years, old enough for reason and punishment.

I do not want—because it is impossible for me—to live with her, but my well-being hasn't crossed her mind. Many times it was suggested, I and my parents, by the in-law who came to us in her name and in the name of her family, that if she wants to receive from me a bill of divorce that we should also give her a sum of money. Now I don't know if it will ever be in my power to give her anything because I myself am poor and also my salary I am earning in great constriction. I am earning with great difficulty, and to my parents, if they want, I can barely give anything. But nonetheless, she can try to speak to them and I, will do my part, and will try harder. And with regards to my son, familial feelings do not connect me to him either way, I traveled from there even before he was born and afterwards I saw him only once.

The only thing remaining is the feeling of responsibility, or rather. . . . the coercive responsibility that I'm, too, responsible for his birth. This responsibility I would be ready, and even now, to fulfill according to my strength when she hands him over to me, but not in the same time as she is bringing him up. If it is too hard for her to keep him, she can send him to my parents and when it will ease for me I will take him to me. [December 5, 1898]

While some accounts have suggested Lubetzky left his first wife after his child was born, here he acknowledges that he fled during his wife's pregnancy and had seen his son only once. Feeling coerced into this marriage at a young age, he writes of little feeling for his wife or son. That the "get" (a Jewish divorce decree) was tied to a payment is likely the reason that a poverty-stricken Lubetzky could not comply. He was, however, willing to assume full responsibility for the boy, financial and otherwise, but only if the son would be raised by him outside the Hassidic shtetl community—a proposal likely unacceptable to the boy's mother and implausible due to his poverty. Rhona's mother Lotte never spoke of a half-brother and she may not have known of his existence. But without a given name, we were unable to track what happened to Lubetzky's first-born son nor could we determine the fate of subsequent generations.

In these exchanges with Ahad Ha'am, Lubetzky's fluctuating emotional states comes through most clearly. Periods of withdrawal and anomie as well as repeated hospitalizations for this condition interfere with his capacity to complete the work:

I cannot do such a thing because I am now sick and it is six weeks that I have been in the hospital, but soon I hope to be released. [January 1,1898]

Due to my illness I am imprisoned all day in my room. [January 25, 1898]

> Soon I will leave the hospital and from the looks of it, will need to change my city of residence. [May 3, 1898]

> Due to the health situation, I must now travel to Switzerland, but my financial situation will not allow me at this time to execute the doctors' recommendation and thus you would do me a great favor if you wanted to pay me my entire salary in one installment. . . . It is now some time that I left the hospital, after I rested a bit, I started working. [June 29, 1898]

> When I sent you "Fast for a Dream," I didn't have a chance to go over it due to the agitation of the nerves. [July 21, 1898]

Lubetzky also acknowledges that his outbursts towards the editor are a reflection of his emotional upheaval and offers an apology. In an undated letter, perhaps written in 1901, he admits to another hospitalization ("after I will leave the hospital") and concedes that his words might not make sense:

> My heart is beating me up about the harsh things I said against you in my last letter. Either way, I had no right for this. . . . The one reason behind these words was my illness. I am a sick man, and your corrections so angered me that I ripped up the manuscript of "The First Kiss" and "The Fast of Generosity" which I begun to prepare . . . Now, that my spirit has rested within me I realized my transgression, and I am asking for your forgiveness. [October 31, 1898]

> Due to my suffering, I had to stop my writing several times, but today, when I felt better, I sat down to finish this letter, and when I now reviewed it, I'll say that due to the frustration of the nerves, my mind wasn't at ease and therefore my words aren't clear nor properly organized, and also, in many places I digressed from the goal which I set for this letter. [undated, perhaps in 1901].

These letters, written when Lubetzky was in his late twenties, disclose that he suffered from what he called "nerves." Symptoms of depression, disorganization, and agitation of such magnitude that he was unable even to leave his room. Hypomanic episodes that resulted in racing thoughts and an inability to write in a logical fashion. Similar to the shifting mood states of the traveling preacher, as depicted in his "Dear Mother" letter, here Lubetzky admits that this emotional state is his own and to his need for hospitalization. While mental hospitals in the 19th century were mostly warehouses with little in the way of treatment, the Burghölzli Hospital in Zurich, founded in 1870, ushered in the modern era of psychiatry, including psychoanalytic treatment. We do not know where Lubetzky was hospitalized or whether he benefited from a more enlightened approach. It is also unclear how much his Vienna family knew about this early history of hospitalizations or whether such hospitalizations became necessary in later years. Because of the stigma of mental illness, any history of psychiatric hospitalization likely would never have been acknowledged by the family.

In the last letter that we have from this correspondence (January 29, 1901), Ahad Ha'am writes that he has lost patience with Lubetzky. He has had enough:

> I will note to you, Sir, as I have already written to you, I think, once before, that I cannot accept manuscripts which have deletion marks and scribbles.

There is a surprising twist to the story, lying beneath the surface of this fascinating exchange of letters. While Lubetzky openly disclosed his own bouts with nerves, depression, and agitation, Ahad Ha'am remained silent about his own condition. As described by Hebrew scholars Yossi Goldstein and Steven Zipperstein, Ahad Ha'am, himself, experienced alternating periods of depression and euphoria, which was for him, a life-long affliction. He appears to have endured a particularly difficult time during 1899, when he wrote to a colleague, "My nervous disorder is now so bad that I haven't been able to write a simple letter and it has been about three weeks since I have abandoned my work entirely and I have done nothing at all."

Thus, during this correspondence, both men were in the throes of profound depression. Lubetzky does not appear to have been aware of this nor did Ahad Ha'am acknowledge this affliction or explicitly empathize with Lubetzky's plight, except, perhaps, to make early payments and publish some of his work. What is also striking, however, is that Lubetzky never totally succumbed to the deadening shadow that hung over him. He kept writing!

* * *

While a home life might offer a sanctuary and temper the stresses of his work, in Eisig's case, it did not. "She has no connection to me," he had said of his first wife and he fled that relationship. And it appears that his second marriage was also fraught with conflict and disaffection—in part, because of his absence, both physical and psychological. As noted earlier, after meeting the beautiful Musa at the home of her brother, Reuben Brainin, the literary lion in Jewish circles, he asked for her hand. Their marriage took place in 1903 when Eisig was thirty-one and Musa was twenty-seven, already considered by many as an old maid. While we found a record of their marriage in the archives of the Jewish Community of Vienna, we wondered whether his first Belarussian marriage had ever been legally dissolved, with the "get" finally given. Their three children followed in rapid succession: Max Herzl in 1904, Lyja (Lotte) in 1905, and Helena (Hedy) in 1908.

Interviews with Rhona's Aunt Hedy illuminated life in the Lubetzky household, from her perspective as the youngest child. Although she faltered at the start, later, over many cups of tea together, Rhona's questions began to open the floodgates of her memory. Hedy told us that Eisig and Musa were greatly mismatched as a couple. Musa had a temperamental and hysterical personality, and although she possessed a natural intelligence, it had not been developed. She never attended school, but instead had taught herself to read and to appreciate art, whereas Eisig frequented a different world and experienced life on a much higher intellectual plane. Well-traveled, he had lived in many different countries and, as Hedy acknowledged, he had been married before, when he was sixteen. It interested us that Hedy had known about this earlier marriage, but had kept silent, as did all three siblings about so much of their Vienna life. In her words, "He must have been around a lot. . . . whereas my mother was a very naive woman."

As remembered by Hedy, Eisig had "no idea of life or . . .

he was in the clouds" and he was mostly absent from the household. Musa would cry out, saying "Every woman on Sunday, on Saturday, goes in the park with the carriage, with the husband." But as Hedy noted, he was never there: "She wanted a normal husband. . . she didn't understand it." Hedy also saw her father as very remote, even aloof: "Thinking back now, probably not knowing what it means to have children, to be with children, and to talk to children. At that time I didn't understand it, so I didn't understand him. He wasn't like a father, like other fathers." She recalled that her father never talked to the children about anything of substance and that there was no physical affection between her parents nor between Eisig and his offspring.

Her mother was very unhappy, frequently in tears, and the house was filled with their constant arguments, largely about Eisig not spending time with the family. Hedy wondered whether he was simply uninterested in them or preoccupied with other things. Musa even accused Eisig of having an affair and another family. Hedy recalled: "She approached him that there's another woman. It might have been true. I don't know." She went on: "I'll tell you something. I wouldn't be surprised. It would fit into this picture. He was never home. And he had somebody, but he said that it's a business dealing."

Their marriage was one of harsh words, followed by silence. Hedy felt caught between her warring parents, remembering that they went around for months not talking to each other. They would use her as an interlocutor: "Tell her, tell him, you know, this sort of thing. . . . My mother replied with just hysterics. There wasn't such a thing as discussing or explaining."

But as Hedy reflected on her past, she also acknowledged

what her father may have lacked in his choice of a wife: "I don't think he had any understanding at home. I don't think he had any discussion at home, and . . . thinking back, they were not equal. I didn't understand it at that time."

Thus, home was not a refuge for Eisig or for his family. We searched for evidence that he had another family in Vienna but were unable to find any trace. Although Hedy was unaware of his life outside their home, Eisig was likely at work much of the time, either directing synagogue choirs, composing and giving music lessons, or writing. As a writer, he spent time in the cafés, away from the quarrels, where he read, engaged in conversations with the cultural elite of the time, and prepared manuscripts.

And yet, for all his efforts, Eisig was exceedingly poor. While rich in intellectual life, his daily circumstances were a constant struggle. He was both a participant and an onlooker in the richness that was Vienna. There is no doubt that grinding poverty had taken a toll on his well-being. Even when he returned to Vienna, a city that was prosperous, cultured, exciting and the center of the Austro-Hungarian Empire, his world was split between a public persona of talent and a private home life of impoverishment, both in emotional closeness as well as in financial means.

Although Hedy did not speak of it, Eisig and Musa were deeply preoccupied with concerns about money. Among the letters we found in Montreal's Jewish Public Library, we came across one poignant note from Musa to her brother, Reuben, written in 1910. It detailed the depths of their financial and physical distress, and appealed for help in the form of literary work for Eisig. This letter is our only insight into the inner world of Musa and how she experienced the circumstances of her life at that time. She writes the following words to Reuben, signing it "from your sister who loves you":

> You must also be curious to know how things are going with us . . . If the truth be told, on the material plane, things are not going well, and from a health standpoint also not good. My three children, may they live, are __ and tall. All three are very pallid and weak. The boy Max is in the second grade and is doing well at school, and he plays piano well. His piano teacher is giving me much hope . . . He has a very good teacher. If God will help me I will be able to pay for him. The teacher tells us that he will soon need a professor. And you can imagine how difficult it is for us to come up with twenty kronen because we barely have enough to struggle through the day.
>
> Aizel [Eisig] has a small office and it's not comfortable. His parents are not sending us anything anymore in the mail. Aizel is not lazy and he wants to make some money . . . I became ill from worrying so much. He has great headaches and internal pains. Aizel is also weak in health. Throughout the winter my children were getting sick. The doctor says they are all weak and they should not stay in Vienna in the summertime . . .
>
> As you can imagine, my dear brother, my illness is due to the fact that I can't endure all this anymore. Believe me, my dear brother, I'm not grieving to you because I want something from you. The only thing I want from you is to empathize with your weak sister

> and do something for us this time. You have promised many times to find Aizel some journalistic work, and I've been waiting and hoping, and now that you are yourself the owner of a prominent newspaper so I am begging you a thousand times to help Aizel get a job. Aizel will write what you want and where you want and how much you want. Aizel has become a different person. I hope that this time you will hear what I'm saying and you won't turn us down. Be well and successful.

In reading this letter, we wondered whether Eisig's physical symptoms reflected an ongoing depression. In fact, the reality was that their financial circumstances were quite dire—a reality of which Hedy was not fully aware. She did remember the flat in which they lived, in the 20th district of Vienna. It was primitive, with a single bedroom and kitchen, and a shared toilet outside the apartment. Ultimately, they were able to secure a second flat in the same building, one that was nicer and had a bathroom with toilet inside it. It still was very far from middle class comfort.

At the time of this letter, Reuben Brainin had already left Vienna behind, as he moved between Berlin, New York, and Montreal. During this period, he edited a number of journals, both in Hebrew and Yiddish, including the Montreal Yiddish newspaper, *Der Kanader Adler*, the newspaper to which Musa was referring, but which he did not own.

In the same archive, we found fourteen largely undated letters (likely from 1912-1914) from Eisig to Reuben, appealing to his brother-in-law for assistance. As had Musa, he was not asking for charity but for the opportunity to publish and receive prompt payment for his work. And Musa was ailing, with worry about the finances but also inflicted with severe health issues, such as pneumonia and kidney problems.

Brainin acceded to the entreaties of his sister and brother-in-law and secured some writing opportunities for Rhona's grandfather. But as the correspondence suggests, many of Eisig's letters went unanswered and the payment was either very slow or not forthcoming at all. Eisig finds himself in a humiliating and inferior position in relation to Brainin and ultimately holds him responsible for their predicament. He laments, "To be perfectly honest, I did not want to send you these articles, but my family pressured me." He goes on:

> My state has gotten so much worse this past winter, and we were counting on you to send me my salary, but you did not keep your promises. . . . In the end, I was left without any money to pay my rent. This lack of money you have caused me has led to many fights between Musa and myself, things are so bad now, it is as though my house is in a state of war. My house has not been able to find rest, and this is all caused by you.

In another letter, Eisig mentions twenty-two articles that he sent to Brainin—none of which were paid—and he notes that he cannot forgive his brother-in-law. He feels as if "the money issue is like a stone in my throat." He writes with rising anger:

> By the time you receive this letter you will understand the importance of these contributions of mine . . . But you should know that I do not envy your lot in the next world: I believe that no hell would serve

> as sufficient punishment for the harm that you have caused me and my family. I ask you again: do not lead us to commit actions we both might regret.

What those actions might have been, we cannot fathom. Eisig, in another letter, alludes to a growing distance between the two of them, laying the blame on Brainin:

> My dear brother, Reuven,
> How are you doing? How are things going with you healthwise? You must surely be wondering, dear brother, why I haven't written to you for so long. But it isn't my fault— if you wouldn't distance yourself so far from us. We get the sense that you don't want to hear from us. You don't want to know us anymore. And how sad this is, and it lies under the heart.
>
> . . . In life, so similar and yet so alienated one from the other. When one is such a great renowned brother who plays a great role in the world and doesn't want to have anything to do with his siblings or know them, this is very sorrowful. You'll pardon me, dear brother, for my preaching.

We find two clues that might explain the unanswered letters, delayed payments, and apparent emotional distance of Brainin. The first concerns the negative force of Eisig's behavior and his sense of entitlement—similarly revealed in his relationship with Ahad Ha'am. About a letter, allegedly sent from Reuben's wife Masha, Eisig writes this to Reuben:

> Yesterday, Rivka handed to me a letter from your

> lady [wife Masha] in which she writes that they would have sent me money already if it weren't for my rude letter. She adds that Reuben does not deserve this kind of attitude for taking an interest in his relatives. I was very upset about this letter, but today I am relaxed and utterly amused. This punishment of yours is extremely classy, as is your Masha's attempt to extract gratitude from me; really, it should be engraved in gold letters. I would thank you deeply if you could inform me of the content of my rude letter, as I do not remember offending your honor in any one of my letters.

And second, in keeping with the cutting nature of his literary criticism aimed at all the luminaries, Lubetzky had also taken on the work of Brainin, prior to this correspondence of 1910-1914. In a 1908 article titled "From the Book Market," Lubetzky sarcastically accuses Brainin of arrogance as well as incoherence in his essay. He writes "Reuben Brainin's 'The Musings of a Biographer' are not the musings of the heart and of the mind; they are rather musings of the pen." He describes Brainin's writing as "a pompous poetic piece; but despite its floweriness, you won't find in it any unity of thought or idea." He goes on, "What is hard to forgive is the manner in which he explains this: just like an advocate in front of a crowd of judges, or like a public speaker who wishes to show off his great rhetorical skills."

This "great and renowned" brother-in-law, ten years his senior, proved to be Eisig's nemesis. Both were competing in the same field. Likely envious of Brainin's reputation and success and yet beholden to him, Lubetzky struck back. In all likelihood, this public criticism from Lubetzky did not further endear him to Brainin. Given this attack, why would Brainin be generous towards his brother-in-law? The only answer is the love he felt for his younger sister. And surprisingly, Brainin kept these letters from Musa and Eisig among his personal papers.

Lubetzky's own literary reputation would never match that of his brother-in-law, nor would his persona. He was argumentative, unwilling to be edited, and sharp in his criticism. In contrast, Brainin, as described by Hebrew scholar Stanley Nash, "was praised for the clear and palatable Hebrew style with which he graced hundreds of feuilletons and stories, as well as for his personal charisma, engaging conversational ability, and selfless efforts at attracting other talents to his vision of an aesthetically refined and Europe-oriented Hebraic renaissance."

However, Reuben Brainin was not a man without flaws. Family lore and a book by Carole Balin and Wendy Zierler, titled *To Tread on New Ground* (2014), attest to Brainin's infidelities, in this latter case, about his extramarital relationship with the Hebrew writer Hava Shapiro. Evidence is provided about his failure to respond to his alleged lover's letters, over decades. Later, his support for the controversial plan to settle Jews in Birobidzhan, Russia, cost Brainin his following among the Hebraist-Zionist literary circle. Interestingly, he too was hospitalized for six months in 1902, due to a nervous breakdown, prior to the marriage of Eisig and Musa.

Yet Brainin was larger than life and the accolades he received from far and wide were many. We have wondered whether Eisig sought out Musa because a relationship with Reuben Brainin might open the door to the Jewish intelligentsia of Vienna. While Musa was beautiful, the difference in their intellectual life undoubtably made them an unsuitable match. And how hard it must have been for Eisig and Musa to compare their lives to that of Reuben—in reputation and, perhaps, in financial security.

* * *

Eisig faced still more obstacles that cut away at his ambitions. One should not paint a one-sided a picture of Vienna during these times. It was not the Land of Oz for the Jews, as antisemitism was prevalent in the city, a precursor to the ideology that developed under Hitler and the Nazis. The municipal government was clearly antisemitic and the city had elected a mayor, Karl Lueger, who was overtly so. Many doors were closed to Jews and so for those who wished to get ahead, conversion to Christianity was an option and a minority chose this pathway. And yet, the Jewish community persisted, but against tremendous challenges.

Eisig had to confront the discrimination against Jews that was endemic in Austro-Hungary as well as the discrimination practiced by Western European Jews against the Jews of Eastern Europe. First, he lost his position at the Music Conservatory in Budapest because he was a Jew. And second, Eisig felt that the Jews of Germany, the literary and intellectual center of European Jewish culture, in particular, looked down on him and the other Ostjuden whom they saw as peasants, uneducated, and ignorant. He believed that the Zionists under Herzl had little understanding of the experience of life for Jews in the shtetls of Eastern Europe where daily existence was a challenge. His very survival was under continual threat.

There also lurked an underbelly to this gilded world. Vienna was at the forefront, not only of culture; it also was a city plagued with depression and suicides. As the writer Frederic Morton has described in his book *The Nervous Splendor,* Vienna in the late 19th century had "more suicides than most European cities, but a particularly high incidence among the upper bourgeoisie." It was no coincidence that psychoanalysis emerged in this milieu. The most famous suicide was that of Crown Prince Rudolf in 1889, shot by his own hand; his mistress dead by his side. Was suicide an honorable way out of the stifling bourgeois existence of fin-de-siècle Vienna, rising antisemitism, looming wars, and personal failures?

* * *

Eisig's biographers attributed the tragedy of his life to an irascible and difficult character and to the severity of his tongue—personalized attacks and disrespect—that ultimately dried up his publication outlets, as his peers turned against him. But his critical nature appeared to have far deeper roots, as Ungerfeld (1972) recognized: "His excessive anxiety and mental tendencies prevented him from nurturing his talents." Further evidence is found in his unpublished writings, in his letters to Ahad Ha'am and Brainin, and by his own admission. The striking descriptions of highs and lows suggest that he was grappling with a bipolar disorder, also called a manic depressive illness. In the 19th century, this kind of disturbance was recognized as "circular insanity," with effective treatments not yet available. His over-determined responses to the editor and his brother-in-law—manifested by aggression, paranoia, and rudeness—were likely symptoms of the hypomanic states. And if, in fact, his writings were autobiographical in nature, such as in the "Dear

Mother" letter and in his "Fast After a Dream" essay, then the low periods presaged the depression that would ultimately lead to his suicide, a struggle in which he may have felt "the promenade of the Angel of Death" in his own heart. How much that mental struggle played out in his home life, we cannot say, as Hedy did not speak of it. Yet something kept Eisig "in the clouds" and drew him further afield from the day to-day-life of his family—be it what he called his nerves, concerns about financial support for his family, and/or the conditions he needed to write and to compose music.

* * *

On a return visit to Vienna in 2014, we looked for the streets where Eisig had walked, trying to picture the world in which he had lived. We stayed in the 2nd District, Leopoldstadt, at the lovely Hotel Stefanie, the oldest hotel in Vienna. As we looked out the window, we could hear the chimes of the Carmelite church and as we walked the Taborstrasse, we could imagine life in the Jewish quarter. Once obliterated and now alive again, as Jews from the former Soviet Union had moved to Vienna, there were Jewish shops, kosher restaurants, and even Chassids, men with long beards, the fringes of their undergarments hanging outside their jackets. When we checked in at the hotel, we were asked whether we desired a kosher breakfast. We were surprisingly moved. While Eisig and family first lived in the 20th district called Brigittenau, it was within walking distance to the center of Jewish life, Leopldstadt, of which it had been a part until 1900.

We visited the apartment building that Hedy remembered growing up on Karl Meisel Strasse, its address found in the registration records of the Vienna Jewish Archives. To reach it, we walked through the nearby park, the Augarten. Early autumn, the air was warm with the incipient crispness of October. Once on the street, we searched for the building, climbed up two steps and into the gloom of a dark entrance hall. A young man let us in behind him, after asking what we wanted. Rhona told him that her family had once lived in apartment #2 and he took us around. Unfortunately, no one was at home and we could not get in to see it. As Eisig's brother Gabriel had lived downstairs in another flat, we also searched for it. Our guide to the building opened that door and told us that now it was a storage area for bicycles. It was indeed small, dark and cold. And, of course, there was no longer a toilet down the hall. We tried to imagine what it was like to live there at the turn of the 20th century—a life very far from the splendid mansions of Imperial Vienna and the Ringstrasse.

We came to realize that Eisig had been on a path of destruction for most of his life. Although he tried to make use of his innate and remarkable talents, the combination of mental illness and external stressors proved too much. Even this marginal existence, of writing and music, was slipping out of his hands. More challenges lay ahead with the advent of World War I (1914-1918) in a city under siege and impoverished. Eisig soon lost his job as a choir director due to a scarcity of funds and the war prevented access to publication opportunities outside Austria. Something else had to be done to survive and support his family.

Eisig Lubetzky was to take another giant leap forward, before he fell again.

Chapter Eight

By His Own Hand

And when the wheel of fortune suddenly turned against him and he lost his means overnight, he could not recover from his condition and disconnected the thread of his life.
—Gershom Bader, 1921

As challenging as Eisig's life had been, both the best and the worst were yet to come. Despite his disappointments, he delighted in the café culture, the intense dialogues between the Zionists and anti-Zionists, the music, and the genteel life that made up for his borderline poverty. However, with the outbreak of World War I, the rhythms of the everyday were totally disrupted.

While never subject to direct assault, the city was slowly strangled by lack of food and the supplies that maintain a comfortable existence. Strikes, riots, and political turmoil convulsed the country while starvation and malnutrition became rampant as rationing began. War fever was transformed into despair as conscription took hold, the wounded returned to Vienna, and refugees poured into the city. Along with the refugees from the East came anti-immigrant anger, and ominously, an increase in antisemitism. Within two years of the war, in 1916, the Emperor Franz Josef of the Austro-Hungarian Empire died. The Hapsburg Monarchy, under his beleaguered successor Karl I, fell in 1918 and Austria was declared an independent republic. Along with the socio-economic turmoil, inflation rose precipitously. By 1921, the rate of inflation was rising 50% monthly.

Desperation ruled the day. Employment was difficult to find.

Once again, Eisig found his way—a remarkable rise it was!

In an article that appeared in the *Yidishes Tageblatt* (The Jewish Daily News) in 1921, the Vienna correspondent Y. Krepel described in great detail how Lubetzky lived during this challenging period and the economic straitjacket in which he found himself:

> With the outbreak of the war, he became as miserable as a stone in the water. He had to stop his literary activity because exchange with foreign countries had ceased. The temple could not continue the choir and so no longer needed him as director. And on top of all this, Lubetski was a Russian citizen and it took great effort to keep him out of internment. The Zionist organization, for which Lubetski had worked for years made no effort on his behalf and only Dr. Bloch of the *Austrian Weekly News* [Österreichische Wochenschrift] vouched for him with the Austrian police.
>
> He received permission to remain in Vienna, but under the conditions that he should not appear in public places, should not write, and could not engage in politics. The Kultusgemeinde [Jewish communal organization] gave him a monthly support fund of fifty crowns and Dr. Bloch also gave him small amounts from time to time. And so, the well-known writer spent the first year of the war in a state of great need . . . He decided to try his luck at trading, which at the time was beginning to become very profitable.

> Against the prohibition of the police not to show himself in public places, Lubetski began to peddle flour, sugar and similar things in cafés. Very soon he became known as a smuggler of groceries, from whom one could get anything. His luck held, from day to day he became richer and by the end of the war people estimated that Lubetski was a millionaire.

Thus Eisig, described as "miserable as a stone in water," rose from pauper to millionaire. His windfall of earnings eased the relentless burden of poverty he carried for so long and allowed him and the family to move to a better address, a larger flat in the 18th district of Vienna. This move to Messerschmidtgasse occurred sometime in 1918, according to the registration records. And it was this flat that we had hoped to see in 1969 and on subsequent visits but were unable to gain entry beyond the front hall of the building. His brother Gabriel, with his family, also joined Eisig on a neighboring street, Bastiengasse.

Lubetzky then took even greater risks, as Krepel noted, by engaging in currency speculation, "one of the plagues with which poor Vienna was [now] being punished":

> Once it was the capitol of a great empire, the center of trade for fifty million people, but since the end of the war [World War I], it has fallen in standing and lost its previous glory. Only in one respect does it remain the old Vienna. It is the center of currency trading for all the new countries of Central Europe . . . Thousands and thousands of people make their living from it, thousands have become millionaires from it, hundreds have even become billionaires. But it is also true

> that hundreds and thousands have been brought to ruin; more than one has found a rope, a bullet from a revolver or a flask of poison, his angel of death. This is because the business of currency trading brings with it the chance that one may become very rich very quickly, but one may also become a beggar overnight.

Krepel went on to say, "The currency rush that came over Vienna in the last two years also sucked Lubetski in and he very quickly became one of the biggest speculators whose wealth people assessed at many millions."

We could not have envisioned the extent of wealth he amassed during this brief period of his life. Aunt Hedy had never mentioned it, leaving us to wonder how these earnings might have changed their circumstances at home. Eisig had made a bold but dangerous leap forward into business (his father's merchant livelihood) and then finance, after a longstanding literary and musical career. As in so many aspects of his life, he aimed for the heights, which he apparently achieved in this domain. His rise was "meteoric" according to Touroff (1945) and his success "legendary" according to Ungerfeld (1972). At first glance, trading seems out of keeping with the introspective focus that writing demands. And yet, denied a livelihood by the war and the Viennese authorities, he resisted this decree, pursuing opportunities, often illegal, to make money for his family. He pushed against the boundaries of finance in the same way that he pushed the boundaries of Hebrew literature.

Those halcyon days did not last and, ultimately, the tides turned against him. Krepel continued the story:

> In recent weeks he had started to lose out, the dollar

> had suddenly begun to fall and Lubetski had sold a million dollars at a certain price, under an obligation to deliver them by a certain date. The day came, but meanwhile the dollar had climbed steeply, so that Lubetski would have been out of pocket at least eighty million crowns in order to fulfill his obligation. He did not have enough money and was not willing to declare bankruptcy, so he took poison and ended his life. . . . This is what has happened with the well-known Hebrew and Yiddish writer, Yitskhok Eyzik Lubetski, who poisoned himself because of the uncertainty caused by a sudden drop in currencies.

It was on September 3, 1921, a Saturday in Vienna, that Rhona's grandfather, Eisig Lubetzky, killed himself. He was only forty-nine years old.

Krepel's article (published September 28, 1921) identified currency speculation and the fall of the Austrian kroner after World War I as the precipitants for Lubetzky's final act. From what we learned about Eisig's life, death by his own hand seemed almost inevitable.

* * *

The response to Lubetzky's untimely death was widespread, perhaps because of the range of his contributions as well as his engagement with the larger world. Krepel bemoaned the fact that the first newspaper accounts of his suicide saw Lubetzky primarily as a currency trader, ignoring his rich literary past. He wrote that "Among the circles that had known Lubetski as a writer, his tragic death raised feelings of great sorrow." Indeed, an article in *Ha'aretz* (The

People of the Land) by Gershon Bader, published on the 7th of October, 1921 brought "sad news of the passing of the Hebrew author Isaac Lubetzky . . . an important figure in Hebrew journalism."

Within the stock exchange, acccording to Krepel, Lubetzky was seen as a modest and generous man, "giving greatly to charity, supporting all of his near and distant relatives, and . . . known as one of the most upstanding of people." Upon his death, his colleagues were reported as having responded generously in kind: "In a letter left by Lubetski he made clear that he was leaving behind his family without support. The currency traders collected a million crowns for his widow."

In contrast, despite the sorrow upon his death, more mixed feelings were expressed by the literary community. "He was cruel in life and cruel in death as well," wrote Shalom Streit (1921), in a searing indictment of Lubetzky's cutting words. He emphasized the lashing of Lubetzky's tongue, which ultimately had led to closed doors in the literary and journalistic world:

> The strength of his work was mostly nourished by this cruelty of his. He was a critical surgeon, as it were, and used to analyze living, trembling literary works with great passion. His "surgical" analyses were often charming and captivating; he would mostly cut-off a living organ, but rarely would he remove any unnecessary tumors. He was a well-developed man of reason who followed a set of rules; he had a kind of Procrustean bed, in which he placed all artistic works in order to decide whether or not he approves of them.

In the political realm, Gershom Bader (1921) made a similar case for backlash against him from his peers. He noted that Lubetzky's astute but "bitter" prophecies regarding the future fate of the Jews never saw the light of day in print:

> In the year 1903, I met Lubetsky in Vienna. Those were the days of the dispute between Nordau and Ahad Ha'am and the days of suffering after the Kishinev pogrom. Devoid of all counsel, lacking all hope was he, as he walked with me through the streets of the crowded square. The disasters in Kishinev—he told me then— were just the small beginnings of the calamities which are about to befall us in the future years, and soon it will be impossible for a Jew to exist and live even a minimal existence or a life of slavery. We must, however, awaken, as a result of this, the Jewish ear. So that Jews will know to be on guard for future calamities, and will not allow the conformists to lead them astray on journeys both vain and repulsive.
>
> Upon hearing his words, I suggested to him that he should arrange his thoughts in writing and publish them in the *Wachter* [Watch Dog]. Lubetsky then presented his bitter words in a collection of articles which were never printed because not a single paper made room for them.
>
> Thus, Lubetsky was forced to swallow his prophecies or hide them in his collection of unprinted articles, because he was not permitted to express what was on his heart—and that heart was full of love for his people, and full of pain and worry about all that was

happening around him, until he fell completely silent in his last years.

This same critical nature of Lubetzky was seen also in the world of music, as described by Avrom Reizen (1927):

> He knew vocal theory, and he not only knew it, he had actually discovered a new method for placing voices . . . He belittled all the other [music] professors in Vienna, unhappily demonstrating and going on at length how each one had with their research methods destroyed the voices of otherwise great singers who had accidentally fallen into their hands. Of course, A. Lubetski believed only in his own theories and with the strength of his faith he was proven successful in song.

Reizen went on: "It was extremely interesting to sit in on one of Lubetski's lessons with his students, there were four at the time. Among them there were two with truly great voices, one of them a young cantor in a temple in Vienna whom Lubetski was preparing for the grand opera."

Reizen was to meet that same cantor years later in Berlin, and asked him, "Do you sing in the opera here?"

"What opera?" the former student complained, "I am a cantor in Budapest now." And that question led him to share his negative opinion about Lubetski, whose "methods," he believed, "had destroyed his voice."

Upon Lubetzky's death, the final judgments about the quality of his work were also mixed—some favorable and others less so—underscoring his failure to reach the standard of greatness he set, the very heights to which he had aspired. These were among the judgments at that time:

A man of great musical talent. . . . Lubetski was a very sharp-witted journalist, but also wrote very many good feuilletons and stories, which were reprinted in German newspapers. [Krepel, 1921]

A dry Talmudist, inclined to interpretation, he nevertheless possessed many positive qualities and even spiritual beauty. An authority on music, although without a foundational knowledge of the theory of music, he composed some melodies for Yiddish poems. To my poem "The Young Proprietress," he composed a truly wonderful, lovely and fitting melody. He composed the melody extemporaneously, in the veranda of our hotel. [Reizen, 1927]

His own stories, of which he wished to make an example, fit well into this framework of his; and yet, they are not considered to be among the masterpieces of our literature. [Streit, 1921]

[Lubetzky] wrote with great skill, stories and critical articles. In the content of his stories, it is impossible, however, to observe his unique personality because he did not rise, in this discipline, to his aspired height. But we find in [his stories] a unique style, a wide and rich narrative voice. [Bader, 1921]

And indeed, Lubetzky tried to take his place among the great artists and authors, but to his great sorrow, he did not quite succeed. . . . Lubetzky' stories are not very impressive, and so we can say that the sharp critic did not manage to uphold in his stories that

> which he demanded of others . . . His works did not resonate as much as he hoped, either in singing halls or in literary journals. [Ungerfeld, 1972]

Lubetzky was well aware of this harsh assessment about his personal style and his writings. He apparently tried to restrain his overbearing nature. Early in his career, he wrote to editor Ahad Ha'am about his wish "not to force upon them [the readers] my opinion like Moses at Sinai" but he could not help himself. And he was also angry and bitter at his lot. Reizen recalled his rage, disturbed about the lukewarm reception of his work: "One evening Lubetski returned home from Vienna, where he spent the days in cafés, furious as always. He was furious because he observed and felt that his novel [*The Sin*, 1910] was being ignored and not appreciated according to its great value."

That he never met with the success he felt he had earned was crushing to him. He thought he deserved better. Imagine how difficult it must have been for Eisig, striving for recognition as a Hebrew writer and critic, to live in the shadow of the assertive and apparently charismatic Brainin. At the same time, he was dependent on Brainin, both for writing opportunities and income.

Reizen's memories of the two men make it abundantly clear how differently these individuals were appraised by others. And this is our only picture of how Eisig's physical presence appeared in the eyes of a peer—the very sound of him. Reizen, who lived with Lubetzky for a couple of months, at a summer resort outside of Vienna, remembered him as "a notable, interesting type" who wrote in Yiddish and Hebrew and yet "was not able to speak any one language properly." He elaborated that "his German was grating and he would salt every sentence with a Hebrew word." And as we too discovered, his unpublished writings also intermixed these languages. However, Reizen was more than awed to meet for the first time Lubetzky's visitor, Reuben Brainin, whom he described as having a "fiery gaze and an energetic appearance, and he made a powerful impression on me." And he noted, "When Brainin calls, one must follow."

Yet, in light of Lubetzky's subsequent suicide, Reizen remained haunted by one particular encounter he had with Rhona's grandfather, where he had made a threat—a prophecy about the conditions under which he would be forced to end his life:

> His life ambitions were very grand. Despite the fact that he was a spiritual man, he thought very highly of this world [a euphemism for enjoying worldly sensual pleasures, trans.]. As if it were today, I remember his words as he once complained to me that he must live a limited life, not according to his ambition. I carefully replied to him, "You live a full life, you sit in beautiful cafés . . . "
>
> "Well, yes, if I couldn't allow myself to spend a few crowns a day for my pleasure, I would have to commit suicide."
>
> And regretfully this generally richly gifted man— left with a pack of worthless paper money—carried out his threat. The news of this shook me greatly. First, for Lubetzky himself, and second, when I remembered his own intimation of this.

Eisig Lubetzky could not stop the train wreck that was unfolding. His reputation (in finance, literature, and music) tarnished and his "grand ambitions" never to be met. Vulnerable, because of his status in Austria as an alien, and alone, as his marriage was filled with strife. His ruined fortune placed his family at economic risk. He, unable to face those whose fortunes he had lost beside his own, and he, unable to afford his precious time at the café. As Moshe Ungerfeld suggests, in the fitting title of his 1972 essay "The Man Who Escaped Himself, " it was from his self that he had to cut the cord. And Lubetzky knew that he had brought it on himself.

What of the letter Lubetzky left behind, the letter that sought support for his family as first mentioned by Krepel? Shalom Streit described that same letter in his essay, stating that it was written to a friend—an unnamed individual—and he had read it. Streit shared a picture of Lubetzky in his final moments:

> During the hectic days of the [Zionist] Congress, a rumor came from Vienna to Carlsbad about the death of the critic Isaac Lubetzky. He committed suicide . . . I have read the last letter he wrote to his friend only one hour before his death. He was suffering through a great deal of difficulty, and the letter paints the portrait of a soft, sad man. He simply could not bear the heavy burden of living. In his letter, he asks his friend to care for his wife and children.

Like the colleagues of the stock exchange, Streit suggested a way for meeting Lubetzky's appeal to aid the family he left behind: "Perhaps some future savior might publish his writings that are scattered in various journals, and such publication should serve both as a monument for Lubetzky and as a means of providing for his wife and orphaned children." Perhaps Rhona became the "future savior" whose curiosity about him helped fuel the present day collection by Sperber of Lubetzky's "scattered" writings—a monument for the man, but too little, too late, to provide for his wife and children.

* * *

Despite the rich detail we uncovered about Eisig's last years and his fateful act, there were still questions to answer. There now appeared to be two final letters that Eisig penned—one to an unnamed friend and the other to Musa and the family, its envelope in our possession. As Streit had read the letter to a friend, perhaps it lay among his personal papers. What else did it say?

Curious, we began a search for Streit's descendants and learned that his daughter, Esther Streit-Wurzel, a renowned children's book author in her eighties, lived in Israel. We soon found her contact information. Rhona made the call and Streit-Wurzel's husband answered the telephone. After she explained the reason for reaching out, there was a long pause. "My wife is in her final days," he said, "but because this concerns her late father, I'm sure she would want to speak with you."

Tired and strained, but with great excitement in her voice, Esther exclaimed, "Do you know my father? Do you know my father?" Rhona told her that she had read one of Shalom Streit's articles about her own grandfather, that quoted a line from his suicide note. She asked whether

Esther's family had kept Streit's correspondence or perhaps donated these materials to a library. A long silence ensued and Esther revealed that upon his death, her mother had burned all of his papers.

Disappointed, Rhona thanked her for the opportunity to speak together at this difficult time and wished her well. Both of us were shaken by this exchange so close to Esther's passing just days later. But we were astonished that the memory of deceased family members, interconnected in the past, could in the present create such a heartfelt bond between two strangers.

The trail to this second suicide note ended with the call. We never learned who this friend was, how Eisig's letter had gotten into his hands, how widely it been shared, and what it said. We imagined that it might have been addressed to Dr. Bloch of the *Austrian Weekly News,* who vouched for Eisig with the Austrian police or Dr. Kohn, whose address Eisig had used in his extended correspondence with Ahad Ha'am. But what we do know is that Eisig's act—appealing to a friend to care for his family at a time of his utter desperation—demonstrated his concern about the future welfare of Musa and his children, and underscored his awareness that he failed at doing so himself.

There were still more questions about Eisig's last moments and the intent behind Max's presence in the apartment while Rhona's grandfather prepared for and carried out his suicide. Krepel's article noted that Lubetzky had died by taking poison and others followed suit in naming this as his method. It also had been reported that he took the life of his son Max as well, which was not true. In an effort to reconcile the differing accounts, we visited the archives of the Jewish Community of Vienna, the Israelitische Kultusgemeinde

Wien, to search for Eisig's death certificate. After passing a checkpoint where passports and purses were examined, we stood for hours in a very long line, surrounded by Holocaust survivors and their next generations. Emotions ran high as people shed tears—poignant tears about lost lives, happy tears upon finding remnants of the past in their family story, or frustrated tears that the information they sought was nowhere to be found.

At that time, a single individual, known to so many—the long-time and now retired archivist Mag.Wolf-Erich Eckstein—oversaw the small warren of rooms, with shelves lining the walls that were packed with large leather-bound books, each dated and alphabetized. At the front sat a long and low counter, where the books were opened and the citation found, upon which Eckstein carried the book away to copy the entry. From long experience, Eckstein could painstakingly retrieve each handwritten record and we could see the records of Eisig's life in Vienna—births, deaths, marriages, and addresses of family members listed.

In a sense, this anachronism in an age of digitized records reflected the hold that Vienna's history has on the present. Touching the books, seeing the ink, the scrawled dates and names, pulled us back in time in a way that information on a computer screen or even in a printout never could. With his help, we examined the record of Eisig's death. There, the cause of death was clearly written, by "kitchen gases" not poison, verifying the account of Max.

It appears that Touroff sought further information from a family member for his 1945 article on Lubetzky. It was Max, Lubetzky's son, "who inherited his father's musical talent" with whom he had a conversation or an exchange of letters. How he located Max, then residing in New York, remains a mystery. Learning from Max's perspective, Touroff wrote about Lubetzky's growing agitation that was not seen by the family as unusual or lethal:

> Lubetzky was extremely agitated for several days before his suicide. He would arrive at their beautiful summer home near Vienna in the evenings, and his entire demeanor would reveal a great discomfort. He was also unable to sleep at night. His family, however, were used to his state of agitation and did not sense that a tragedy was encroaching. Lubetzky suggested that his family's wish to move back into their apartment in the city was "premature," and asked them to remain in the summer home a little while longer.
>
> On one of those days he suggested that the son, who was a young boy at the time, join him in his trip to the city and spend the night with him in their Vienna apartment. That night, he turned on the gas-pipes and ended his bitter, disappointment-filled life.
>
> What is most surprising about this last act of his [and his son himself has expressed his wonderment] is that the father, in preparing for the act of suicide, wanted his beloved child to be nearby, without considering the possibility of risking his life as well.

Touroff concluded that Lubetzky's intent—in placing his son in danger—could never be ascertained.

But perhaps there are answers buried deep in Eisig's first published Hebrew story "Fast After a Dream," which was printed in the journal *Hashiloach* when he was twenty-six years old, more than two decades before his suicide. As we have described it earlier, this is a dark tale of a failed artist. Interestingly, Eisig gives the protagonist his father's name, David.

David has fled the constraints of his religious shtetl life to embrace a new world as an artist in Paris, a life not understood by his father nor his rabbi. Instead, identified as a "wild talent," he receives beatings at their hands for his passion to draw and is deemed "a heretic, for making pictures." And yet, having pursued his dreams of an artistic career in Paris, he achieves only failure.

The protagonist experiences an inexorable slide towards suicide, asking himself, "Why did I leave the Torah school for the sake of pursuing the arts?" He rants about his destruction, aware that it is self-inflicted:

> You alone are to blame for all the torments you have undergone so far. You should know that art is not a stage for preachers and thinkers; those belong in the Torah schools, which are multiplying every day. You must remember that the purpose of art is to achieve beauty. But you are keen on finding destruction and ruin wherever you look; you always choose to depict the bad aspects of life rather than the good, and you forget that the masses for whom you paint demand tenderness and pleasantness rather than poison.

The details of this early story very closely mirror the arc of Eisig Lubetzky's life—his dreams and his dark soul. Its title refers to "the fast" that an individual undertakes to seek atonement from God and others for their transgressions—a religious ritual in which Jews engage at Yom Kippur, in preparation for a new year.

It was very important for Eisig to dedicate this work to his father. But the dedication ultimately printed by the editor Ahad Ha'am, read simply: "Dedicated to my father, Rabbi David Eliyahu." However, revealed in the correspondence between editor and author, is Lubetzky's desire for a longer and more complex dedication—one that Ahad Ha'am either failed or refused to publish. Lubetzky writes: "Please see to print these lines at the top of my story 'Fast After a Dream' [undated letter]":

> To my dear father the Rabbi David Eliyah Lubetsky,
>
> For the pre-fast meals in which you criticized me, dear father, during my many fasts, the fasts that I fasted for my dreams which I dreamt against your will and knowledge, I ask you, dear father, to receive from me as an atonement, my story "Fast after a Dream."
>
> Please accept it, father, and read it and maybe you can console yourself in that it would prove to you that the miserable one who thinks his dreams are the reality is happier than the ones whose lives pass them by like dreams. For it is better to live in a dream than to dream in real life.
>
> Your son, the author

In this proposed dedication, Lubetzky asks his father's forgiveness, to accept his artistic dreams and this first story as a gift. Dreams that he hid from his parents, dreams against his father's will, dreams that that took him away from a holy life in Belarus. This dedication also reveals Eisig's bitterness at the criticism he received and perhaps beatings as well, as in David's tale. The tone is accusatory, suggesting that his father's own choice was of lesser value. It also contains a self-assertion, that despite his unhappiness, his efforts have been worthwhile because he tried. It is interesting that Eisig chose his father's name for the protagonist—a failed man who seeks to end his life. Was this an underhanded way of directing criticism toward his father?

The desired dedication was never printed. We wonder whether his father ever read this story and his other published work, and whether Eisig sought atonement from his father in different ways? We will never know.

As the protagonist David never reaches the heights to which he aspired, he plots his suicide. In reviewing this story, Ungerfeld (1972), raised the question: "Did the young teller of this tale [Lubetzky] have the feeling, that he, too, would be seeking a way out of his situation by ending his own life?" In this story, as in Eisig's "Dear Mother" letter that described a paralyzing depression, we, too, wondered whether these writings reveal a premonition about his own suicide to come, many years in the future.

But delving still deeper, it appears that Eisig was ambivalent as he wrestled with what was to be the outcome of the suicide attempt in his story. In a letter to Ahad Ha'am [January 2, 1898], he describes his thinking about the character: "Originally, I had condemned my protagonist to death, afterwards, however, I regretted it, and I intended to save him and to return him home to the little town inside the Pale, and to describe the tension between the nature of the thinker-artist who has already seen the contrast between a fuller life and the life of poverty and congestion of the Pale, and in doing so, to illuminate . . . the whirling winds of this world."

So, ultimately, he decided that the protagonist was to be saved. In the climactic moment where David's life hangs in the balance, we read:

> No! I cannot go on like this. This needs to end. Only this handkerchief could set me free. He leaped out of his bed, and quickly, as though he was afraid someone might catch up to him, jumped up on the chair and began to tie the handkerchief around his neck. The knot had been tied; everything was ready. All he needed now was to tighten the knot and kick down the chair, but . . . Right then, the landlady entered the room with a loud cry. Her voice rose the neighbors, and many people gathered around him, including the police officer who will take him down to the station, that "crazy" painter who disturbs "the order" at night.

The attempted suicide is thwarted and David survives. His protagonist fails at suicide, due to the unexpected visit from his landlady. Perhaps, Eisig was similarly ambivalent in his intent and brought his beloved son Max home to save him from the horrendous act he was about to undertake.

Could it also be possible that he needed to expiate his guilt about the financial losses by taking his own life? In his mind, public knowledge of his despair would have saved him from the inevitable anger and scorn from those whose money he had lost in currency speculation. An act of suicide, even unsuccessful, would have demonstrated his remorse. Perhaps, through a redemptive act of self-destruction—interrupted—he could go home, back to the security of Gorodeja where his family still lived, just as he had proposed for his protagonist David. It may be that after all, he wanted to be saved.

And if Eisig was in the midst of an agitated depression, he may have wanted his son with him for support when he returned to Vienna. Given what we know about his emotional states and Max's report about his father's agitation in the prior days, Eisig may simply have acted impulsively, giving no thought to the danger facing his son.

But Max was too late. If he had known that his father did not wish him harm but rather that he was invited there to become the savior, this interpretation might have provided some comfort. Yet that he failed as a savior might have inflicted even greater pain.

What became of the letter addressed to Musa and their children? Perhaps it was read only by Max, who brought it to Musa and then, it was destroyed. And if it were destroyed, why was the envelope kept and never shared? Is it even possible that a letter to the family was never written, beyond the preparation of the envelope?

Ultimately, neither letter, to the friend or the family, was ever found.

While left with an empty envelope, reflecting a historical void in Rhona's family narrative, its very emptiness propelled us to fill it—to acknowledge Eisig's existence in the family and his place in the worlds of literature and music. Even without these final letters, the multiple traces we found enlarged our understanding of Rhona's grandfather, his state of mind and his life, more than we had ever imagined possible and more than his own children ever knew.

We think about Rhona's grandfather's last night. We

picture the flat, the darkness and the sorrow. And in our imagination, we speak for him, the words arising from the found fragments we have pieced together about this moment. We imagine his desperate thoughts as he paced and paced:

> I cannot go on. I can no longer take the pain. I see no way out. They are after me, coming for their money, and I have lost it all. I cannot escape. I know they will find me. What will they do to me?
>
> Where will we go? How will we live, what will we eat? A pauper all my life until now, and so few precious years of comfort. Never knowing when, or even if, I will have money to feed my family.
>
> What humiliation, what shame, for a man who left behind what would have been an honorable life in Gorodeja, reading Torah, preaching to an adoring audience, the people of my youth. A child wonder, they called me, and what did I become?
>
> I tasted wealth for a moment. And that pleasure was ripped from my heart. I cannot face the world. I cannot face my family.
>
> I have tried to succeed, to leave my mark. To show that Jews can achieve at the highest level, to live in the Western world, in a world that will respect them. It was not to be. Everything turned to ashes; I never reached the heights I had imagined for myself. Not my voice or my music. Not my writing, not my commentary. Not

even in the world of finance, one moment a millionaire, the next moment all is lost. I am the ruin of myself. I drove my failures. I cannot change my situation.

Cycling always, always so fast to the depths of despair when I could not rise out of my bed, and then the surge. Such productivity, writing reams of prose, of music, working throughout the night, only to crash down, distraught again. I never knew peace. I cannot find my way.

How I have let you down, Father, I disappointed you, but there was a fire in me, burning, burning. I needed to act on my dreams, needed to flee.

Musa, once you were a beautiful young woman, this first glimpse of you in your long white nightgown at the home of your brother Reuben. He, leading an intellectual circle to which I once aspired. I know I was better than him, yet he was the famous one. And now, there is anger between us. You, my wife, disappoint me. You do not understand my dreams. You dream of material things. You make demands on me that I cannot meet.

Mordechai [Max], my son and oldest one, how much you are like me. A talented musician, with a worldly view, and you, too, cycle as I do, between highs and lows. Lyja [Lotte], you took from me my sharp and critical nature, questioning, pushing, always with an opinion, and never backing down. And Helena, my little Hedy, the sweet one, the youngest, you sit quietly, such a pretty child.

I cannot go on. Max, Max, save me.

***

Max did try to save his father. He ran down the hallway. Years later, after our many failed attempts to see where Eisig died, friends, on their first trip to Vienna, took a taxi to the family address on Messerschmidtgasse and found the front door of the building open. Walking up the stairs, they saw that the door to what was formerly the Lubetzky apartment was open as well. The flat was undergoing renovation for new owners. They walked in, wandered around, and returned with grainy photographs of the living room and the hallway. These images and Max's own words—"He was dead and there was nothing I could do to save him"— still haunt Rhona.

As we reflect on why Eisig took his own life, we see both in his writings and also in his personal notes that he saw himself as a failure. As a prodigy, so adored in his shtetl environment, he felt destined for greatness but in the larger world of Western Europe, this was a pinnacle he would never reach. Marginalized, professionally isolated, and incapable of sustaining intimacy, he stood largely alone.

In the words of Hebrew literary scholar, Einat Baram Eshel (2001), "His [Lubetzky's] story ends with his suicide, very much like that of the literary heroes who were so common in the literature of that period, and he can be said to have continued in his life, the experience of the uprooted." And yet, within his professional world, he was never entirely forgotten—many would long remember his character and would puzzle over his suicide.

What if he had gained the recognition he sought, what if

the world had acknowledged his unique voice? Would it have been enough to change the course he was on? Or would it never have been enough to fill an insatiable emptiness that consumed him and the biological demon that lay within?

We cannot reverse his final act. Now, more than one hundred years after his premature death, buried knee-deep in the words he left behind, Rhona still harbors the fantasy of saving him—changing his tragic trajectory and undoing the sadness he left in his wake.

What then was the aftermath of his suicide? What was to be his legacy?

Part III

LEGACY

Chapter Nine

Aftermath

In tales of loss, we can always fill in the gaps with more detail, more stories. The process goes on even when the old tellers and the old actors are long gone.
—Christina Marsden Gillis, 2017

Each of Eisig's children offered slightly different details about the circumstances around their father's suicide. Lotte, age sixteen, and Max, seventeen, remembered that the family had been together at a hotel in the country, prior to the departure of Eisig and Max for the city. Hedy, twelve, recalled that she and Lotte had been sent to a boarding school in the country and were called back from there, returning to Vienna by train. She did remember that Max was in the city with their father. Hedy also confirmed that the family did not own a country house as Turoff had reported.

However, Hedy could not recall how she learned about the actual cause of her father's death. Instead, what her mother told her turned out to be a lie:

> It wasn't discussed. I didn't find out too much. I didn't see anything. I have no memory that I went to the funeral. But I do remember my mother sitting shiva [the Jewish mourning ritual], and saying that this was a heart attack. And I always felt her story was wrong, not right, you know.

> Max knew of this. Maybe he told me but I don't remember that. I found out what happened. . . . That he committed suicide, that he played the stock market, but there was no talk about it. There was a feeling of fear, of unhappiness. I didn't understand it, this I remember. I couldn't comprehend it. I didn't know that you could do such a thing. I was, after all, not yet thirteen.

And so, the secret about the suicide began here—initiated by Musa. A secret she kept from her two daughters until Max, perhaps, revealed the truth to his sisters. A secret not to be discussed and one that would cross over to the next generation.

Although Eisig was a spiritual man, given his early love of the Torah, his Viennese home was largely secular. In Orthodox or traditional Judaism, taking one's own life is considered a violation of Jewish law. The body is viewed as belonging to God, so in a sense, the suicidal act steals what is of value from God. It is also true that death by one's own hand carried enormous stigma—still true today—for the victim and for those left behind. In embracing the lie, Musa may have been in denial, protecting herself and her younger children from the bitter truth. She may not have known that the details of his suicide were made public in newspaper articles and in the Hebrew and Yiddish journals of the time. And given the circumstances of Eisig's death, perhaps there was no funeral at all.

At the funeral of Reuben Brainin in 1939, thousands lined the streets in Montreal to honor his works. Ultimately, Brainin was buried with great pomp and circumstance on a verdant green mountain in Montreal. In contrast, in 1921, the decade-younger Eisig Lubetzky was buried privately, his resting place marked by a small stone plaque in a now overgrown and forgotten cemetery in Vienna. The striking differences in the lives and reputations of these two men—brothers-in-law, writers, Hebrew scholars—remained to the end.

What did Musa tell the extended family, his and hers, those in Belarus and Vienna, those who had left for London, Montreal, and New York? Did she communicate the news by telegram to her brother Reuben, then living in New York, and what was his reaction, given their difficult relationship? When we learned that Brainin's personal diaries were housed in Jerusalem, we arranged for a graduate student translator to visit the National Library of Israel. Searching through the diary entries for September-October 1921, she came upon the relevant passage and sent us its translation from Hebrew into English. It was at 4 a.m. on the morning of September 29, 1921 that Brainin wrote this entry, private thoughts at the time, but revealed to the public after his death:

> Last night I visited the theater on 27th St. with my wife, to see Ansky's *The Dybbuk*. After the first act, I was approached by the Hebrew author M. Lipson. He called my attention to a letter from Vienna that was printed in yesterday's *Yidishes Tageblatt*. I happened to have this newspaper with me, and as I began to read the aforementioned letter, I was immediately horrified: the title read in big letters that the Jewish/Hebrew author Isaac Lubetzky had ended his life in Vienna [at the age of forty-nine] by drinking poison. And this Lubetzky is my brother-in-law, husband of

> my sister Musa. Apparently, it happened over a month ago, and I heard nothing about it. This dreadful news horrified me. Lubetzky had become rich these past few years—a millionaire-times-ten; and now, after losing his money in an unsuccessful affair, he ended his own life. The fate of my sister and her three talented children saddens me to my core. Eighteen years ago, I led him to the chuppah [wedding canopy] with my sister in __. It was in my home that he met my sister and fell in love with her. Their eldest was born in Vienna on the same day Theodor Herzl died, and I was his godfather. My brother-in-law, Isaac Lubetzky, was a very special man. I introduced him to Hebrew literature as well. I have been thinking about him all evening, and my heart aches for my sister, Musa.

Perhaps out of shame or their estrangement at that time, Musa had not told her brother of Eisig's death. Given the fiery letters Eisig had written Reuben and the public castigation of his brother-in-law's writings, we were surprised by the affection Reuben expressed. Surprised also by his characterization of Eisig as "a very special man." While Reuben wrote about having mentored Eisig in his field of Hebrew literature, he left unsaid Lubetzky's own legacy in the field. He left unsaid the hard feelings that must have existed between them. Instead, he expressed his deep concern for Eisig, his sister, and their three "talented" children.

* * *

To understand the aftermath of Eisig's death, life before

his passing proved to be as important as the suicidal act itself in shaping what followed. Whether observed or remembered, whether brief or long-standing, there were signs of a turbulent family life, signs that Eisig's mind was not at peace. Max had mentioned to Touroff that the family was used to Eisig's states of agitation and his inability to sleep—not seen as unusual or a cause for worry. How frequent were these states, we wondered, and might some of his absences from home resulted from hospital stays for mental distress?

We searched the family pictures for clues about life in the Lubetzky household. There were a number of formal portraits, and as mentioned earlier, three of these were present in the bedroom of Rhona's parents, but there were others. Professional photographs of families in early 20th century Vienna were highly stylized. Smiles were absent and the faces looked straight at the camera, feelings obscured. And yet, we could not help but wonder whether beneath the stiffness of the images, emotions were raging, suppressed and hidden from each other and the world.

Three of the family photographs especially intrigued us. The first depicts Eisig and Musa and their first two children—a dashing Eisig, high collar, an intense look, lightly touching his son's wrist. His wife, Musa, her hair in a chignon, long beads cascading down the front of her patterned dress, looking distant and forlorn. In the front is Lotte, perhaps five or six years old, a hand on each parent's knee, not touched by either parent and ready to leap out of the photograph.

In a later photograph, all three children are present. Lotte is about sixteen years old, Max a year older, and seated between Eisig and Musa is Hedy, the youngest, holding flowers, bow in her hair, her hand covered by that of her mother. Lotte's hands are on Hedy's shoulder. In this scene, Eisig is leaning to the side in his ornate chair, suit with a vest and cravat, looking straight at the camera with a somewhat self-satisfied air. He looks like a successful Austrian businessman, confident and proud. He does not touch anyone of his family members. Musa, older now, heavier, in a fancy dress with a lace front, a fringed purse over her arm, seems pensive, again somewhat distant. There are no smiles, no warmth. And finally one more photo taken at the same time, focuses on Eisig and Musa. Here, Eisig in the same chair, cigarette in his right hand, once again looking content with his lot. Musa stands at his side, elbow on her husband's shoulder, a soft expression on her face.

What we see is that Eisig dominates the family, that Musa is his handmaiden, and that the youngest, Hedy, is the darling. Admittedly, these kinds of family photos are characteristic of the genre of the time but there are also hints of disaffection and differential expressions of love toward the children. Ironically, the later two portraits of this affluent Austrian family were taken just a few months before Eisig killed himself. This last family photo hung in Lotte's bedroom for the rest of her life.

Drawing upon the interviews with Hedy, we have described some of the painful tensions within the household that pervaded daily life. Among them, was the marital strife between Eisig and Musa, especially around Eisig's frequent absences and his failure to assume the "normal" role of husband and father. Also, the letter written by Musa to her brother Reuben in 1910 (when their children were six, five, and two), painted a picture of the family living in dire financial straits, with the health of Eisig, Musa, and their children threatened. To outsiders, like Avrom Reizen (1927), Musa was seen as a supportive wife. In writing about Lubetzky, he extolled Musa's virtues as a partner who met her husband's every need: "His young and gentle wife . . . took great care through her attention and loyalty to him that he should want for nothing. She gave in to all of his whims as those of a genius."

But whatever Eisig's whims were, Musa's patience with them began to fray. Eisig's stories revealed men who could not tolerate intimate relationships, men who expressed feelings of repulsion toward their wives and the desire to flee, and men experiencing torment, loneliness, and isolation. We have suggested that these were Eisig's own feelings as he appeared incapable of affection. Instead, at home, a sharp and critical tongue was his mode of expression.

Marital conflict can spill over into parents' expectations for and interactions with their children. And so it was with the Lubetzky family. Within families, siblings live quite different lives. Such differential treatment can arise from their birth order, their individual characteristics and resemblance to either parent, and the unique circumstances (time period, marital history), into which they are born. Hedy revealed how differently her parents treated their three children.

Max held a special place in the family as the eldest and a male, not an unusual preference at that time and in certain cultures. Indeed, Max was named Mordechai-Herzl, as he was born on the day that Theodor Herzl, the famed Zionist and friend of Eisig, died. The highest of expectations were held for him, their first-born. He too, like his child prodigy father, had a special talent in music. Eisig and Musa sought out the best of music teachers for Max to shape his career as a classical pianist, but alas, the assessment of his potential fell short. His teachers pointed to "an inborn talent" but a lack of willingness "to work with it." Unlike his father, Max was known for his sense of humor and an exhuberant, fun-loving spirit. But he seemed to lack the disciplinary focus necessary to improve his skills. Hoping to change this trajectory, Eisig and Musa even sent Max to the famous Viennese physician Josef Breuer, who had developed the talking cure for nervous disorders. But as Max had once told Rhona, the psychoanalyst failed to help him. "I was smarter than Dr. Breuer," he jokingly used to say.

Once Eisig became wealthy, Max was enrolled in an upper class "gymnasium" as academic high schools were called in Vienna. This was not a Jewish school. As it was open to the entire community, the student population differed greatly from the background of the family. While the choice of school surprised Hedy (as in her words, "My father was a Zionist and Jewish-oriented"), it appeared to reflect the assimilationist dream of Eisig, to prepare his children to live in a broader secular world.

For Lotte, less than a year younger than Max, friction characterized her life in the household, especially between her and her mother. Hedy could remember little of Lotte's relationship to her father, except that he acquiesced to Musa's entreaties about Lotte's misbehavior. Hedy recounted:

> My mother couldn't handle Lotte and she was a normal child. As far as I can see, she was temperamental, vivacious. She was curious. I don't think it was anything serious. She had dates, or she went out, or she wanted to go out a lot. But they didn't understand. My father was never there, and probably my mother complained to him, that Lotte didn't listen to her.

Hedy went on to point out a characteristic of Lotte that Lotte shared with their father: "Your mother always said the truth." In Rhona's mind, Hedy might have added this phrase, "even when it hurt." In sharp contrast, Hedy chose not to follow in Lotte's footsteps when it came to truth-telling. In her words, "I learned my lesson. It's no use." Hedy recalled that "Lotte told her [Musa] when they were fighting that she's wrong, she's this and she's that, but the way she put it, certainly wasn't the right way."

There was one painful memory about Lotte that Hedy described as pivotal to her own incapacity to take joy in life. As Rhona was to discover, it proved pivotal in Lotte's life as well. This was a very public event in which Lotte was extruded from the nuclear family. It occurred at Demel, a famous Vienna patisserie on Kohlmarkt, close to the Graben. On what must have been a rare occasion, given Eisig's frequent absences, the family went out for pastry one Sunday afternoon. Hedy could not recall their ages at the time. Punished for speaking out, Lotte was made to wait outside the café, where she stood with her face pressed to the window. Max and Hedy were instructed to pick out the dessert they wanted and then, without Lotte, the family sat down at a table by the window to enjoy the afternoon tea and sweets. Under the woeful gaze of her sister, Hedy recalled being unable to swallow her pastry. This inability to take in the sweetness of life became a core element of Hedy's being.

We have visited this bakery many times, admiring and tasting the luscious pastries. Each time, Rhona's heart breaks for her mother—denied the treats that she loved and forced to watch her siblings so favored by her parents. Is this Rhona's attempt to savor what her mother could not taste? Or is it an attempt to undo this very same pattern—

the denial of sweets—that Lotte would later impose on her. So often, we repeat that which we cannot repair. This need to visit Demel on each visit to Vienna was an attempt to rework the past. To rectify a gross injustice, both for Lotte and Rhona, and thus to assuage the pain of having been denied.

Hedy concluded, "My mother couldn't handle Lotte. So they sent her away."

For one year, Lotte was sent to live with a frugal, elderly couple who lived outside of Vienna and ran a boarding house in the summer for guests—a place that the Lubetzky family had frequented.

> For some reason they thought that it would be good for Lotte, which I also don't understand. The owner was very strict and didn't give Lotte enough to eat, and it was probably wartime, I guess. Or right after the war. She wanted Lotte to dress warm and not attractive, and your mother used to cheat and take off the things when she went out. . . . I don't think it was the right atmosphere for a girl either. She was alone with an elderly couple.

Then, with the rising financial means of the family, Lotte was sent away for several years to a residential high school, which Hedy viewed as another exclusion. Hedy again noted the oddity of her parents' choice of schools for her siblings, which failed to recognize that Lotte was an avid reader, with a high intellect:

> She was sent to a boarding school because my mother, and apparently my father, couldn't handle her. And they thought she would get a good education, which

> she did. But it was, to my surprise, which I only understood later, a boarding school which had aristocrats from all over the country. Girls were trained . . . to have a good marriage, and know how to behave socially. Very superficial, you know? They took them to museums, to theatres, to opera. It was interesting, lectures and school. But I don't think that was the right atmosphere for her.

One legacy of this experience was Lotte's desire for the finer things of Viennese cultural life but, as she learned, these were to be attained not through her own ambition but through marriage. Left out of Hedy's narrative was an acknowledgment of the antisemitism that likely was present in the school. Antisemitism must have colored the experience of the three children in the wider world of Vienna at that time but none of them spoke of religious discrimination.

Evidence for Lotte's less favored place within the family could also be seen at an even younger age, in a letter Eisig wrote his brother-in-law Reuben, dated April 20, 1912. Eisig shared the family news: "The children are growing up. Mordechai-Herzl and Leah are both in school. Also, Mordechai-Herzl studies music and he is very talented. The young girl Helena is extremely smart and beautiful."

Striking to us is Eisig's omission of Lotte's special qualities, in stark contrast to her siblings who are uniquely praised. Was this the fate of a middle child or was there something else? Perhaps it was the unsettling similarity to her father's own habit of truth-telling—his truth and now her truth—that upset the household, her forthrightness perceived as provocation. Lotte's identification with her father's manner would become her undoing, with her mother and likely, with her father, who was trying to change that same harsh voice within himself.

Lotte's expulsion from their household was made very real to us when the required household registration forms we had requested from the Stadt Wien, the Municipal and Provincial Archives of Vienna, arrived at our home. In the heavily stuffed brown envelope postmarked Wien, we found eight such registrations, handwritten in German, that tracked the residence of Eisig from before his marriage through 1918. This was evidence of the Lubetzky household growing, successively adding Musa, Mordechaj-Herzl (Max), Lyja (Leah or Lotte), and finally, Helena (Hedy) to the family. But by 1918, coinciding with a new address on the more upscale Messerschmidtgasse, there were only two children listed, no longer the three siblings. The name of Lotte, now thirteen-years-old, was nowhere to be found. This visual evidence of her mother's extrusion from the family brought Rhona to tears. Among the most emotional moments of our search, it fueled a growing empathy for her mother's painful childhood.

Ultimately, Hedy became the favorite of Musa, despite her mother telling her that at the start she was not wanted. Because Musa had given birth to Max and Lotte within one year, she felt she could not handle a third child. But when she went for an abortion—criminalized at that time with few exceptions—she could not go through with it.

As noted earlier, Eisig was rarely there and never talked to the children "outside of little things." There was no physical affection expressed between her parents or toward the children—no hugs, no kisses, no comfort provided. Hedy cherished one sweet moment, when her mother had made a celebration for the Jewish holiday of Purim, one week too early. She said, "My father started laughing, in a nice way. It was funny, a week before the holiday." When asked what she thought about her childhood, she replied, "Not a happy one."

Hedy often felt like an only child in her home. Her two siblings were out of the house, "sort of far away from me, you know, older and not reachable," she remembered. She did not mind being alone. She was favored by her mother and by her father, in his way, as the youngest, a quiet and good child, "a goodie-goodie child, which I really wasn't." About her father, Hedy remembered his telling her: "As little as it was, he always used to say that the husband I will meet, you will bless him . . . So there must have been some love or something, you know?"

In contrast to her own lot, Hedy carried a special burden—that her sister Lotte received little love from her parents. And as the favored and youngest child, she suffered guilt about her comparative advantage.

Most importantly for the sibling relationship, Hedy was the only one of the three children who had the capacity to handle Musa: "She was very excitable and I sort of quieted her down. . . . So my mother had quite a lot of love for me, in her way. My mother was very kind and sweet to me, as the youngest or being always home."

* * *

This was the family constellation—a distant father, an accusatory mother, a prized son, a doted-upon youngest, and an outcast, both figuratively and literally. While life had improved materially for the Lubetzky family during and after World War I, the luxuries were not destined to last and all came crashing down, the point at which Eisig ended his life.

A suicide unleashes a complex chain of events. Every family copes with the loss in its own way and in the Lubetzky family, much was unspoken. The fabricated story prevented the family from dealing with the determinants of Eisig's death and its meaning for each of them. The actual facts became repressed or lost in the shrouds of memory, as evident in Hedy's faltering recollections of the details. When a warring mind cuts the cord of life, the finality of that act destroys the opportunity to resolve any ambivalent feelings that may predate the suicide. And so it was with Eisig's survivors. His wife and children were left deeply unsettled, overcome with mixed emotions, perhaps rage, guilt, relief, and grief. But ambivalent feelings of his survivors, with no opportunity to explore them, were also part of his legacy.

After Eisig's death, Musa, widowed at age forty-five, appeared to unravel. Described by Hedy as dependent, hysterical, and prone to tantrums at the best of times, she now felt utterly abandoned and proved barely able to function. We wondered whether Eisig and Musa had ceased speaking to each other before Eisig's return to Vienna that fateful evening. And whether Musa felt rage over his desertion or perhaps regret that her demands and accusation may have driven him away. But with the suicide, their turbulent marital relationship—mired by long periods of silence—would never be resolved.

Hedy described the aftermath as a time of enormous sadness and great change: "Change in everything, and my mother not capable of handling things financially and emotionally, and couldn't cope with three children . . . . She was left without anything overnight. No means. And she, herself, wasn't capable of earning anything. So that was a big readjustment."

Among the consequences of Eisig's suicide for his children, none of the three siblings was able to complete the graduation requirements of high school. And none had the opportunity for a university education.

Hedy recalled that Max "got completely out of hand" after their father's death. While Max shared Eisig's talent in music, "Max [also] had some [other] things from my father—a restlessness and not speaking . . . He had no sense of responsibility even when he got older . . . there was something lacking."

Forced to leave his elite school following his father's death, Max attended a program in commerce and accepted a job, but found himself ill-suited for the world of business. Hedy laughingly recounted this tale about him, contrasting his behavior to that of Lotte and herself.

> He was on a job. And it was the Depression time, and they were told whoever gives up the job first, gets a special bonus. So our Max put his hand up, and he was the first one. He got some settlement. I don't know. . . . He took me out and bought me something. I don't remember what. He had no understanding of the seriousness of the situation.

At work, Max was known to be invisible and always disappearing, as one employer described it to Hedy: "I never saw if Max was ever there . . . and if I sent him somewhere, Max just didn't come back." Given Max's profligacy and unreliability, Hedy was forced to go to his office weekly to try to get his salary to cover his debts. In the ensuing years, she also had to go to court to resolve his financial difficulties.

Perhaps his mind was on his music, life style, and relationships with women as he was known to have had many girlfriends. According to Hedy, Max's passion was his music. Whether he was not sufficiently talented to become a concert pianist or whether he chose not to pursue that path, he channeled his musical abilities into playing piano in the Yiddish theatre in Vienna and in the provinces. He also composed music and directed a band. And he was known to be generous to a fault. Cousin Hugo Brainin, younger than Max by twenty years, fondly remembered the times that Max took him and his brother Norbert Brainin (later to become a violinist in the eminent Amadeus Quartet) to Yiddish musicals on Praterstrasse, 60, in Vienna, where he performed as the pianist. Max would place his young cousins in the rear of the theatre, standing room only, and then, during the interval, he would move them into empty seats at the front.

Max, of course, carried the weight of finding his father dead, not knowing his father's intent in bringing him back to the apartment on that tragic night, and not being able to save him. He was deeply scarred for life. Did Max also feel remorse that he had failed to meet his father's expectations that he pursue a classical musical career? This disappointment was never to be resolved and perhaps was similar to Eisig's remorse over his failure to meet his own father's expectations for his genius son.

When Lotte returned to Vienna from boarding school, their father had already died and in Hedy's words, "It was a very hard time for everybody to adjust to different circumstances." But Lotte, a young woman who possessed great intelligence and strong opinions, had experienced her father's rejection long before the suicide and had been absent from the family home for at least three years. With her father's suicide, she was spurned again—this time, the finale. And perhaps too, she felt disappointment at Eisig's complicity, even his passivity in not defending her in the constant struggles with Musa. And she may have felt guilt that her sharp words had driven him away.

Lotte attended a local school for a time, and took a side job to earn money. Although a dedicated worker, she loved to socialize with friends and she had many of them. As Hedy put it: "She did everything what she could to get out and have a good time." But she still could not get along with Musa. Hedy described her mother's lack of understanding of young people in this way: "My mother used to think that if you don't stay home and be a good girl, then you are not a good girl." Lotte also faced great disappointment around the family's abrupt loss of money and status. Hedy recalled this unhappy scene:

> I remember she was invited to a New Year's party, and she didn't have anything to put on, and she borrowed from other friends, everything—clothes and accessories and everything. And I think she even sold something. She thought that she was very beautiful and was very excited, but she came back very down because she noticed that she didn't fit in at all. She wasn't dressed right, and everybody was in ball gowns, and she didn't feel good about it.

After Eisig's death, Hedy began high school but, as she explained, without a maid in the house, she was the only source of help: "I used to do washing and ironing and things like that when I went to school, so I didn't study very much." For her, it was very trying, and so "she stopped early, also took a course, and tried to find a job, which was very hard in Vienna, at that time."

The family received some support in the aftermath of Eisig's passing. We had learned that Eisig's fellow currency traders raised some money for the family. Musa's relatives, the Brainins, also stepped in with financial help, especially Musa's nephews Max and Leo. Hedy remembers that every Sunday morning, Brainin family relatives would faithfully visit for tea, sandwiches, and Musa's famous Bishop's Bread, a Viennese fruit and nut cake.

The savior role of cousins Max and Leo in Lotte's life was made vivid in the reunion we arranged for Lotte in 1989. At age eighty-four, after so many declined invitations to travel to Vienna, she finally agreed to visit London with us. The purpose of this trip was to reunite with Max and Leo, whom she had not seen since her youth. Like her, they had fled Vienna early, in their case, to England to work together with their older brother in the furrier business. During World War II, Max Brainin, as a German-speaking Jew, was interned in Australia for a period of time, and housed with Nazis. We found the paperwork showing his internment, when we visited the Jewish Holocaust Centre in Melbourne, Australia. When he returned to England after the war, the brothers founded two successful stores, Brainin Brothers Furs and Cashmere, on Bond Street in London and on Bauermarkt 2A in Vienna.

Their reunion, spread over many days, was the most emotion Rhona had ever seen her mother express, not only in the tears shed, the embraces shared, and the rapid

German exchange of stories, but also in the laughter around the photographs they examined. Their meeting sparked many happy memories. When it was time to leave, it was wrenching to tear them apart, as it was to be the last time they would see each other.

Both before and after Eisig's suicide, his younger brother Gabriel and his wife Vera also provided a safe haven and much emotional support. Gabriel had left Belarus to join Eisig in Vienna. He had always lived near his brother, first, in the same building on Karl Meisel Strasse in the 20th district and later, with his wife Vera, on Bastiengasse, which was a short block away from Eisig's flat on Messerschmidgasse. Among the family photographs, there were pictures of Eisig and Gabriel, with assorted family members in the park, sharing a picnic on the grass. Lotte was deeply attached to them, especially so to Aunt Vera. Hedy also remembered how much she loved her aunt and uncle and how she enjoyed the many overnight visits she made, before they had a child of their own. Given her mother's lack of understanding, Lotte learned not to go to her mother for support but rather to seek out Uncle Gabriel and Aunt Vera. Clearly, they became the good parents who filled a void in Lotte's childhood. Later, Gabriel and Vera had a daughter whom they named for Hedy, and these two cousins, born nine years apart, came to be called grosse (big) Hedy and kleine (little) Hedy.

Gabriel and Eisig could not have been more different. Although close to each other, Eisig was intensely introspective and a loner while Gabriel was outgoing and loved to socialize. While both sought out the cafés, Eisig used them as venues for writing while Gabriel sought out the warmth of convivial conversation. Gabriel liked to meet for theatre and late evening meals and Vera joined him in these soirées. For both Lotte and Hedy, their aunt and uncle modeled a marriage and a loving partnership that was so lacking in their own home.

Vera died of cancer in 1924 at the age of forty-four, leaving behind her husband and daughter, kleine Hedy, only seven-years-old. For Lotte, this second loss, so soon after her father's death, proved too much to bear. And Gabriel, distraught by the loss of his beloved wife, turned inward in mourning and devoted himself to his daughter. When Lotte did speak to Rhona about her reasons for leaving Vienna, a rare occurrence, she mentioned only the death of her Aunt Vera—never alluding to her father's suicide that had preceded it.

As Hedy told us, soon after Aunt Vera's death, Musa's youngest sister Liesl wrote that perhaps Lotte should come to Montreal, giving her the opportunity to get away from Vienna and also from the struggles between mother and daughter. Within four years of Eisig's suicide, Lotte, at the age of twenty, fled Vienna for a new life in Montreal, Canada, arriving on August 26, 1925. She was never to return to her birthplace. By doing so, in the decade of the 1920s, she was able to pull herself out of harm's way, far from the threat of the Nazi annexation of Austria, the "Anschluss" which would engulf Vienna in March of 1938 and culminate in the Holocaust. Lotte would leave behind her mother Musa, and her siblings, Max and Hedy, but they were not to be forgotten.

Eisig's suicide and her mother's flight gave Rhona the gift of life.

In Vienna, Hedy became the fulcrum around which the house revolved. She did the housework and sought employment, while Musa did some simple cooking. Max was unavailable. Lotte kept in close touch and she sent money monthly. Hedy was extremely grateful: "We depended on that a lot, as we made very little money in Vienna." And so, for Musa, Max, and Hedy, life continued. Educational opportunities were lost and life was more constrained because of lack of funds.

Eisig was gone and it was almost as though he had never existed. No one, in Rhona's presence, ever expressed grief at his loss. Perhaps too many years had passed since his death, perhaps he was never mourned.

Chapter Ten

Lotte—Vienna to Montreal

Stories have to be told or they die, and when they die, we can't remember who we are or why we are here.
—Sue Monk Kidd, 2002

In 1925, Montreal was a bilingual French-English metropolis and the most populous city in Canada. A report from the Canadian Council for Refugees in 2000 noted that in the first two decades of the 20th century, more than 138,00 Jews from Eastern Europe were admitted to Canada, many of those settling in Montreal. When Lotte arrived, the city was thriving post-war and so was its Jewish population. Yet, the new life that the twenty-year-old Lotte found there did not ultimately bring her greater happiness.

Incorporated into the family of her Aunt Liesl (Reuben Brainin's youngest sister) and Uncle Sam Ortenberg and living in their flat on Willowdale Avenue, she became a nanny, caring for the house and their two children, Judy and Benzion. Judy was the child of Sam's first marriage to Reuben's daughter, who tragically died in the 1918 influenza pandemic. Lotte was especially close to her sweet Aunt Liesl. Within two years after Lotte's arrival, Benzion, the younger child died of a cerebellar tumor at just four years of age. A second daughter, Vita, arrived one year later. The tragic loss of Liesl's son left her in a deep depression, and to cope with her state, Liesl and her husband went away often, leaving Lotte to care for the two girls. The three of them became sisters-in-life, but their relationship, while caring, was also mixed with rivalries and hurt—in part, as Judy said, because of "Lotte's sharp tongue and her tendency to speak what she called the truth."

Among the Montreal family, Eisig Lubetzky's nemesis, Reuben Brainin, would loom large. Rhona's great-uncle was idolized. Many in the family have a bronze bust of this man in their homes, sculpted by Judy, Reuben's granddaughter, and passed down to the next generations. In this striking sculpture, he is a stern-looking patriarch. The lines on his face are carefully etched to create an impression of strength and wisdom. Ironically, as we write this book about Eisig's life, it is Reuben's visage that stares down on us—the bronze bust living in our California home for more than two decades, passed on from Rhona's mother.

Hedy remembered Reuben as very handsome, with blue eyes and black beard, and as a womanizer, who "exercised his good looks." She remembered as well that Reuben never forgave her father, who had little patience for this idol and criticized him severely. Lost in the admiration that surrounded Brainin, Eisig faded in the background—his own contributions to the literary canon unknown to the family.

Judy would regale Rhona with stories about Lotte as a young woman. She described her as "the product of a European young ladies' private school, elegant, sexy, and artfully made-up." We have a photograph of Lotte sitting at Liesl's dressing table, brushing her hair, sophisticated and beautiful in a long black silk dress, preparing for an evening out with friends. Judy saved one of Lotte's lace dresses from this era that she gave to Rhona before her death. It still hangs in our closet—Rhona, unable to part with it. We have seen many photos of young Lotte in her early years in Canada, posing mostly with male friends, among them a social psychologist who was to become world-renowned and whose work Rhona would ultimately read, but whose advances Lotte rejected. And then there was an ardent fiancé, but the engagement was broken at her initiation.

Lotte met Rhona's father, Dr. Alec Strasberg, at a weekend gathering at the Greenberg's Hotel Vermont, one hour north of Montreal in the Laurentian Mountains of Ste. Agathe. Owned by Alec's older step-sister and her husband, this Jewish hotel provided a lively respite in the country—at a time when antisemitism was rife, even in their new world of Canada, and many of the Laurentian hotels were restricted. Signs read "No Dogs or Jews Allowed." The Brainin family, including Reuben, visited the hotel often and Rhona has childhood memories of picking fresh peas from its beautiful vegetable garden. Hedy suggested that Lotte was attracted to Alec's good looks, his intelligence, and quiet ways, as well as the fact that he was a doctor. Lotte and Alec married in Liesl's living room in 1933, when she was twenty-eight and he was thirty-eight. Musa collected a few things to send to Lotte from Vienna, linen and silver, of which she had very little.

* * *

During those early years, Lotte's heart turned to Vienna. She wanted to have her family with her in Montreal. At first she could afford to bring only one of them and begged Hedy to come. While desperate to join Lotte, Hedy could not leave Musa behind, as Max was of little help. As she described it, her mother was not capable of living on her own and further, "she just wouldn't let me go." Crippled by panic attacks, Musa would sit by the window when Hedy went out for the evening and watch for her return. Musa would ask Hedy, "Did he kiss you?" After once saying "yes," her mother's negative reaction was such that Hedy learned her lesson and subsequently always reported that "nobody kissed me." Lotte would repeat Musa's pattern of waiting by the window or the door—first for Rhona, during her adolescence, and later for Hedy, at the point when her own cognitive capacities were diminishing.

As Hedy reflected on her more than a decade-long caretaking years in Vienna, she would say, that despite opportunities for dates and marriage proposals, those years robbed her of a carefree young adulthood. As she told us earlier, she was robbed of her childhood as well.

Living a continent away, Lotte was able to see more clearly that Austrian citizenship would not protect the Jews from the rapidly approaching threat of the Nazis. She read about what was happening in Germany where increasingly onerous restrictions were being placed on Jews. And she saw that the threats from Hitler were receiving a positive response in Austria. She continued to pressure her family to leave Vienna and worked relentlessly to raise money for visas and boat passage to North America. Hedy remembered that it was Lotte who feared for their lives, whereas they, the small Lubetzky family living in Vienna, went on with business as usual, restricted as it was, but surprisingly unaware of the noose tightening day by day. Despite the fact that antisemitism was rife in Austria, the Lubetzky family lived as though it was irrelevant to their lives. That naivete, common to Jews who identified strongly as Viennese, would have led to certain death, were it not for Lotte's actions.

Thanks to her heroic efforts and a somewhat responsive

Canadian government at that time, Lotte was able to secure visas and funds for the passage of two of her family members. Musa and Hedy left Vienna by train and then sailed to Canada, arriving on November 17, 1936. They carried with them only a few precious pieces of china and silver as well as some family photographs. Musa, age sixty, and Hedy, age twenty-eight, joined Lotte and Alec in an apartment around the corner from Liesl's family. Lotte had finally succeeded in bringing her mother and sister to safety. But left behind, always on her mind, were her brother Max and his bride Olga, and her Uncle Gabriel and his daughter kleine Hedy.

* * *

Lotte's caretaking role was to continue long into her marriage. As Alec had lived with his widowed mother, he brought her with him into the couple's first apartment in the heart of the Jewish immigrant community. According to family lore, she was not delighted with Lotte, seeing her as a competitor for her son's feelings. She died not long after the move. One of Alec's sisters also joined their cramped living quarters for a time. And it was soon after, that Hedy and Musa arrived in Montreal.

Hedy stayed with Lotte and Alec for six years until her marriage to Benno Hecht in 1942. With a beginning weekly salary of $7.00, soon to rise to $15.00, she could not afford an apartment of her own. As Hedy described those early years to Rhona, "It was very hard for your parents, it was very hard for me . . . and it was hell on earth." The stress in the home brought her stomach trouble and other physical ailments.

This "hell on earth" was no doubt due to Musa's excessive demands, family tensions over her care, and the close living quarters. And Hedy and Musa missed Vienna and their lives there. After Hedy's death, among her papers, we found seven carefully preserved letters, tied together with a frayed ribbon. Dated from 1936 to 1939, these letters came from Uncle Gabriel, written to Hedy (in German) and Musa (in Yiddish).

In one undated letter, likely the first, Gabriel expresses concern about Hedy's adjustment to Canada and underscores just how much he missed his niece. He also reminisces about the richness of their Viennese world—evenings spent in the theatre and cafés of their beloved city—a life lost and one that she mourned:

> Whether it is mere habit, or rather some deeper cause—I often pass by Messerschmidtgasse. And every time, as if by a higher will, I have to lift my head, look up to the windows. Maybe in the hope that everything was only a dream, that I will catch the sight of you in one of the windows. Or even hear your cheeping voice. Yet apart from that, the lane hasn't changed, only the poor doggy of your neighbors got older. And weaker.
>
> Normally we . . . used to dress up already at 6 p.m. and head, without a care in the world, and full of beautiful hopes, to the "Reklame." There, after a short mandatory mocha, we enjoyed the presence of all the new friends we had made. . . . Around 8:30 p.m., we resort to the "Kunst-Tempel." And after the show to the "Duxl," as it is known to the intimate circle, or the

> "Duxbaum," as it is generally referred to. There we sit, smothered in harmony and comfort, eating chopped liver with radish or fish in aspic, in the circle of close friends: Nachbar & Co [to this date I do not know her name], Olga, Liesl, sometimes also Max, who has never enough patience nor money . . . . If we enjoyed ourselves? This I will leave to your and my own fantasy.

And to his sister-in-law Musa, Gabriel reassures her that she will soon overcome her homesickness: "Very shortly you will forget that there is a city in this world that is called Vienna." He also sends news about the welfare of her son: "Maxel seems good, kein ahora [a Yiddish expression not to tempt the evil eye with praise], really very good, if you don't consider the fact that he sleeps to 4 p.m. every day. . . . He and Olga live like two doves . . . And he is loved by everyone . . . actually the entire second district of the city [December 29, 1936]."

But as to his own life in Vienna, Gabriel alludes to changes, especially with regard to his freedom: "As for myself, as you can imagine, there is absolutely nothing new. Only the scope of my moving-about becomes yet smaller and, accordingly, also the diversity, the colorfulness of my being [December 29, 1936]." Although not named in this letter, what Gabriel described as a narrowing of his movement likely resulted from the implementation of the Nuremberg Racial Laws that were extended to Austria in 1935, and began the process of restricting the rights of Jews.

We, too, had looked up at those same windows on Messerschmidtgasse, thinking not only of the family life within those walls, but also about that fateful night when

Eisig ended his life. We visited the Café Recklame, one of Eisig's favorites. Across the street from the former home of Theodor Herzl, this café, later to become a theatre, was once the center for the Jewish intelligentsia. We smiled at Gabriel's description of Max—impatient, sleeping late, no money, but cherished by all— matching Rhona's experience of him. Also touching was the love expressed between Max and Olga, about to be or newly married at that time. But just one month after Hedy's and Musa's arrival in Montreal, the constriction of Jewish life in Vienna became inescapable.

Musa and Hedy, however, could not so easily forget Vienna. A year later, it became clear that Hedy was considering a return to the city. In a letter dated November 23, 1937, we learn about Hedy's change of heart and surprisingly, that Gabriel encourages her to return:

> In case that you cannot bear being there any longer and intend to return to Vienna by all means, then you have to hurry up the journey. . . . So, my fine Hedi, you hold your destiny in your own hands, you can gorge on movies and coffeehouses, you can stuff your pockets full of Viennese treats, and if you want it, then the wild dream can come true.

Only four months later, Hitler's army entered Vienna in March of 1938. How close Hedy came to returning, we will never know, as she never mentioned to us her desire to do so. Had Hedy acted upon that wish, her fate would likely have mirrored that of Gabriel.

The Lubetzky family in Belarus was also facing threats to their survival. Gabriel writes of their efforts to help him but underscores their own dire straits:

> I have no positive things to tell you about the people from Gorodeja. Due to the general crisis in Poland, their financial situation has worsened severely. Health-wise too, all of them have suffered. [November 23, 1937]

> I often receive letters from Gorodeja, but these letters as well aren't very bright either. The Pater is weak, Motel ill, and the income is scarce. [November 15, 1938]

Gabriel's only child, kleine Hedy, had married Jacob Picker in 1938 in Vienna. Fortunately, the young couple was able to escape but most tragically, they had to leave her father behind. In his letter of November 15, 1938, less than a week after Kristallnacht, Gabriel reports that he moved out of his apartment on Bastiengasse which he owned, to lodgings on Krummbaumgasse in the second district. While he does not acknowledge that this was a forced relocation, he admits that, "it was just difficult for me lately to write letters, I simply cannot gather my thoughts on paper." The reality was setting in:

> I belong, as you most likely know, to the selected few who are in possession of an affidavit, but do not know when the happy hour will come for them too, when they will be able to stand up there on board of the ship. The American Consulate gives no further information about this. My Hedi and Jakob are still in Italy. They also have affidavits but meanwhile they do not know what to do with themselves since so far all attempts to go to Palestine or Egypt have failed.

In his last letter to Hedy, on January 13, 1939, there was no longer any subterfuge, to which he had clung, perhaps to quiet any worries she may have had:

> More desperate is my situation with regard to the emigration. If no miracle occurs [which doesn't happen nowadays] I will have to wait very long. My affidavits are even very good, but unfortunately, I fall under the Polish quota that belongs to one of the worst. In the opinion of people that are informed about everything, I have to expect a waiting time of two-three years. What this means for a person who hasn't been doing anything at all the last eight months and who will not be able to do anything throughout this waiting time, this can only be understood by someone who is in the same situation.

In this letter, he captures his increasing aloneness, an image that sears our hearts. The losses are apparent, as he notes: "Almost all of the friends and acquaintances have left already, to various directions, to all corners of the world. Forever. It was a last hand-shake. It is like an epidemic. One after the other. And the circle around oneself gets ever emptier and emptier."

But for this gentle and caring man who called himself a "sworn pessimist," there continues to be a sliver of hope expressed in his very last letters. To Musa, he writes:

> I hope that the times will come once again, that we will be, if God agrees, everyone together again and you will show us again all the tricks that you knew and maybe even new, better ones. Stay strong. [January 13, 1939]

These last two letters, written in early 1939, were the final communication from Gabriel to his Montreal relatives. No matter what entreaties Lotte made to the Canadian government, she could not obtain a visa for her uncle. During and post-World War II, only nuclear family members were considered for refugee status. The category of "uncle" failed to make the cut and the number of visas grew even more limited. A Canadian immigration officer, Frederick Blair (1939) was famously quoted as saying that, with respect to the Jews, "None is too many." As we read Gabriel's words, we could feel Lotte's anxiety and even her guilt, in the face of her fruitless quest to save her uncle.

These visa limits also impacted the prospects for Max and his wife Olga as Lotte's applications for their entry into Canada were also declined. Yet with her persistence and the help of Brainin relatives in New York, Max and Olga were finally able to gain entrance to the United States. Leaving on one of the last transports out of Vienna, they arrived in New York on November 24, 1939 on the SS President Harding—three years after Musa and Hedy had fled Vienna. They came without any financial means. When Jews left Austria, they were required to declare all of their property. An asset form filed in 1938 by Olga with the Vienna Ministry of Finance noted that she was "married to a Jew" as specified by the Reichsgetsetz Law of 1935, and that by then, was an unemployed typist, with assets of a few pieces of jewelry valued at twenty-five Reichsmarks.

Four years after their arrival in New York, Olga died of cancer—a profound loss for Max, but one he never talked about. A brief second marriage ended in divorce. Max earned his living as a pianist and comedian in the Borsht belt of New York, the Catskills, that was filled with hotels catering to Jews. It was ten years later, in 1949, that Max was finally able to join his immediate family in Montreal.

That a number of the Brainin relatives, including Reuben, had left Vienna far earlier—fleeing to London, Montreal, and New York—proved critical to the survival of their entire family by providing a lifeline of visa sponsors. But the extended Lubetzky family was not so fortunate and only a handful escaped a certain death. Eisig's untimely death at his own hand saved him from experiencing the horrors of the Holocaust. With Lotte's early emigration, his nuclear family was rescued. Gabriel's daughter, kleine Hedy, finally managed to escape to Israel with her husband. But Gabriel and the rest of the Lubetzky family in Belarus ultimately perished at the hands of the Nazis.

A reunion with Gabriel, as was hoped for in his final letter, was not to be. But the details of what had happened to him and to the others were not known to Rhona's family. Among her mother's papers, Rhona found the reply to Lotte's inquiry about the whereabouts of Gabriel after the end of World War II. In a letter from the United Jewish Refugee & War Relief Agencies, dated July 17, 1946, it was written "Lubetzky Gabriel—deported on 9.6.42 to Minsk and has not returned to Vienna." This devastating news was received shortly after Rhona's birth.

Lotte loved her Uncle Gabriel unreservedly. From the little she shared with Rhona about her life in Vienna, Gabriel and Vera emerged as the most positive figures in her childhood and adolescence. If Lotte had any capacity to nurture, it grew from the seeds planted by her uncle and aunt. Her inability to save Gabriel might have contributed, in part, to the undercurrent of rage that sabotaged her intimate relationships. And so, within her, she carried her own legacy of the Holocaust.

* * *

For Hedy, after six years of living with Musa in Lotte and Alec's apartment, meeting Benno was a breath of fresh air. But early on, he made very clear that he "didn't much care for Musa." For Lotte and Alec, Musa was to live with them for twenty-two years of their marriage. While one husband, Benno, refused to take her in, the other husband, Alec, had already allowed it. But, as Hedy described it, Alec greatly resented Musa who came with "unsolved problems" and was excessively dependent upon Lotte, a dependency that Lotte apparently fostered.

As Rhona was to learn, this living arrangement emerged from a bargain, agreed to by Lotte and Hedy, that was never spoken of. Musa, childlike and dependent, had been the responsibility of Hedy for many years—a period of fifteen years following Eisig's death. She carried the burden along after Lotte's departure from Vienna in 1925. It then became Lotte's turn to shoulder the load, a responsibility so overwhelming that she periodically would beg Hedy to take Musa for a time. This proved impossible.

Complex and painful dynamics underlay this agreement. On the one hand, the herculean efforts and frugal living of Lotte allowed her mother and two siblings to escape the Nazis. On the other hand, her siblings felt that Lotte had abandoned them, leaving Hedy trapped in her mother's house. Rhona grew up in the midst of a complex web of myths—the good sister (Hedy), the bad sister (Lotte), and the damaged brother (Max) who proved incapable of caretaking and was absolved of any responsibilities. This tacit bargain also came to color the lives of the next generation. And so, two generations lived out a script that was first written in 1921 in Vienna, another part of Eisig's legacy.

Hedy mused about her sister's marriage: "It turned out that she [Lotte] was more ambitious, and she would have liked success with a doctor with a good practice . . . She wanted a little more than she got. And she never had it." Hedy saw them as "misfits," immediately noticing this upon her arrival in Montreal. Lotte was very dissatisfied—she was more social, she wanted material things, and he [Alec] did not care for "appearances." "Maybe I'm wrong," Hedy said, "but I don't think that she really appreciated his fine qualities."

As an adult, Rhona came to value her father's many attributes such as his commitment to caring for the immigrant poor, the enclave of Chinatown, in Montreal. It was not until 1984 when Medicare was adopted in Canada and Lotte took over the billing, that he was able to earn a modest but stable living. Alec was a dreamer like Eisig, always living in his head, but he had a sweetness that eluded Eisig. Sadly, he was not demonstrably affectionate. Alec preferred to write poetry, read philosophy, take long walks, and observe the beauty of nature. This gap in expectations between husband and wife led to dissension in the marriage, compounding the reality that Musa lay between them. Both Lotte and her mother Musa led marital lives marked by disappointment, critical of their husbands for not meeting their needs.

Thus, over those years, Rhona's family lived in rented flats, with Lotte, like her mother before her, expressing constant worry about money. Hedy and Benno struggled for a long time to develop a successful business in the face of financial and health challenges. But its ultimate success afforded them a house in an upscale neighborhood and opportunities for travel. They even employed Max for a few years, an arrangement that did not work out due to his poor work ethic.

As we now understand, this was the family context in 1946, post-World War II, into which Rhona was born and raised. A family mired in losses and secrets, discrimination and financial pressures, and a host of failed expectations. Rarely expressed in words but evident in how life was lived, day by day.

It was in one of the interviews that Rhona first talked with Hedy about how painful her own childhood had been. Rhona told her about Musa's paranoia, about her refusal to accept care from anyone other than Lotte, and how there was little couple or family time that was not ruined by Musa's needs. She believed that her mother was trying to gain acceptance from Musa, to do everything so right that Musa would finally say, "Thank you, you're a wonderful daughter." But even as a child, she could see Musa's face light up when either Hedy or Max visited—in stark contrast to the stone-faced anger Musa expressed toward Lotte. And Hedy, too, reported this, the differential treatment that spurned Lotte, evident to her since her own earliest days.

As Hedy listened to Rhona's memories, she noted that she felt "removed." It was as if she was talking about someone else, not her family. "Is it because, I am old or because it's so long ago?" she asked.

Rhona responded, "Is it because this is how you learned to cope, holding yourself somewhat apart, both from the pain but also from the pleasure?"

Hedy, in the face of her mother's helplessness, learned

"not to rely on anybody. I always had to carry on." She continued, "Lotte tried to cope, doing whatever she could, and Max ran away from everything."

Hedy spoke about the enormous guilt she carried, both for what she received from her mother that Lotte did not and for her loving marriage: "There was definitely a relationship between my mother and me that your mother didn't have, and that was also something she always missed. She [Lotte] was hurt, you know. . . . There was also a deep-rooted jealousy about me, about my marriage, about everything. I understood that she never had love in life."

As Hedy talked, Rhona came to understand something profound that she had not fully understood before. Lotte believed that she could redeem herself by saving Musa's life and by caring for her in Montreal. Yet the redemption never came. In this quest, Lotte saved not only Hedy's life but also Hedy's marriage, to the detriment of her own. But Lotte did not get the love she sought. For Hedy, this reality resulted in a debt that she was to pay back in spades. Denying her own needs to join her daughter in California, she watched over Lotte's decline, dutifully caring for her until the very end.

***

Reflecting the birth order of their family, Max died first in 1988 at the age of eighty-four, of an overdose—painkillers mixed with alcohol. It might have been accidental, but we always wondered about his intent. He was living with his third wife Cecile in Palm Beach, Florida, when he died during the night, as he, in a sleepy state, sought more medication. He was found unresponsive on the floor the next morning. Like his father, Max suffered from depression and mania. He drank heavily, forsaking his earlier musical promise and spent much of his life unemployed. But like his father, he went out for coffee daily, engaging in banter with customers and waitstaff. For Rhona, he remained her imaginative and caring uncle, whom she adored for his stories and the unconditional love that he freely expressed to her.

As described earlier, demented at the end, Lotte died ten years later in 1998, at the age of ninety-three, with Hedy and Rhona by her side, in what they both experienced as an unsettling death.

Hedy, the last of the three siblings to leave us, died peacefully in 2005, at the age of ninety-six, on the second day of a hospitalization, with her mind fully intact. Soon after Lotte's death, with great courage, she left Montreal for her second emigration, this time to San Francisco to spend her last precious days close to her daughter, Hannah, and family. After long years of hard work, the untimely death in 1977 of her husband, Benno, when she was sixty-nine years old, and the years of caring for Rhona's mother, she seized the opportunity to finally care for herself.

At her death, reflecting her wishes, she was lovingly surrounded by her daughter, son-in-law, and grandchildren, as well as by us and our two sons. It was after Hedy's death, when we gathered in her apartment, that we found our family-made book about Eisig Lubetzky at her bedside, its pages open and well-worn, she re-reading it until the very end.

Chapter Eleven

In the Shadow of the Holocaust

To forget the dead would be akin to killing them a second time.
—Elie Wiesel, 1960

Lotte's life was marked by loss—her father, Vera, Gabriel, her birthplace Vienna, and the love of her mother. Her failure to save Uncle Gabriel haunted her throughout her life. Given these losses, it was not surprising that she never returned to Vienna. Never learned about the final days of Gabriel and the extended Lubetzky family, nor was she in touch with Gabriel's daughter kleine Hedy and her family in Israel. So much about the Lubetzky family was kept silent.

To find out what Gabriel's family knew about the Lubetzky history, we set out on a journey that Lotte, Max, or Hedy never took, to follow Gabriel's forced march out of Vienna and to learn more about his fate as well that of the Belarus branch. We also wanted to meet kleine Hedy's descendants in Israel. As noted earlier, Gabriel's only child kleine Hedy and her husband Jacob Picker were able to escape Austria. Following a short period in a transfer camp in Italy, they arrived safely in Palestine and raised two sons there—Dan and Gabriel, the youngest named for his late grandfather.

Hedy kept in sporadic touch with the elders of the Picker family by letter. And her daughter Hannah was the only one in our immediate family to visit kleine Hedy in Israel in 1972, shortly before kleine Hedy's death at the age of fifty-five.

In 1999, Rhona wrote kleine Hedy's sons, noting the family relationship—their grandfathers were brothers and their mothers, first cousins. She also sent a copy of our recently completed family book on Eisig Lubetzky. This led to an extended correspondence between Dan Picker, an architect in Jerusalem, and Rhona. She was eager to meet him, as they each had pieces of a large puzzle that perhaps could be made whole again.

In 2008, we visited Jerusalem for the first time to discover new family. On a sunny December day, we met Dan, two years older than Rhona, and his adult daughter Sharon, in a lovely café in the Rehavia section of Jerusalem. There, we enjoyed good coffee and pastries, and a relaxed and warm conversation. Very casually, Dan mentioned that this café was bombed in 2002 and he had barely escaped with his life. While oriented to the distant past in Vienna, we could not escape talking about the events that colored Dan's youth and his adult years in Israel. Dan and Rhona—through the happenstance of when their mothers fled Austria—had lived very different lives. His, a life of greater privation and danger.

Dan proved to be the spitting image of Rhona's Uncle Max and even had the same sense of humor. There were eerie similarities in the jokes they told—about Jewish foods, wives, and marriages—and even in the letters they wrote. Rhona had kept one of Max's letters, written when she was away at summer camp, which ended with, "So enjoy your life out there and shmile." And similarly, Dan always told us to "keep smiling," his final words in our email exchanges. Max and Dan, different generations, different countries, yet so much the same. It was as if Uncle Max had returned from the dead.

In our conversations, we learned more about the life of the Israeli branch of our small family. Dan waxed eloquent about the Viennese recipes he loved, the same nusstorte, the liptauer (a Viennese cheese spread), the gurken salat (cucumber salad) that we also enjoyed. And Sharon shared the observation that "a part of Vienna lies in me, too."

Dan described his mother as always dressed in a suit, adorned with a strand of pearls, even in her visits to the corner store. It was an improbable sight, kleine Hedy in formal attire, shopping for the little food available in the early years of the State of Israel. This Viennese way of dressing was an exact match of the style of her older cousin Hedy, as Rhona knew her in Montreal. In their youth, the two Hedys—Dan's mother and Rhona's aunt—looked like identical twins.

For kleine Hedy, it was a life of extreme hardship—the early loss of her mother when she was seven-years-old, the death of her father at the hands of the Nazis, and her hard existence in Palestine living through three wars. Dan told us that she never spoke of the family. Her life was "a riddle to him" as she raised her two sons with "the typical silence regarding her personal history, in order to save us the pain." This silence was a familiar one for Rhona.

Yet traces of our shared past remained. In our exchange of family photographs, Dan and Rhona possessed the same Lubetzky family photograph taken in Gorodeja, when Gabriel and kleine Hedy had visited from Vienna. Unlike Rhona's copy, Dan's photo was dated, the year 1934, with the names of the relatives listed. This was the only photo Rhona had of the entire Belarussian Lubetzky family (missing Eisig, of course), captured in front of the house of David Eli, the patriarch. Finally, she could match names with their adult faces—David Eli, Motel, Feitel, Peschke, and Gabriel—

and with the next generation of children, Mirele, Itale, and kleine Hedy.

Sharon had prepared a special book about her great-grandfather for a high school ancestry project, a copy of which she gave to us. And bound within this book were photographs of Gabriel and family, copies of seven letters (originals in German and translations in Hebrew) that he had written from Vienna to kleine Hedy and Jacob in Italy and Israel, and documentation of his death. We learned then that two sets of letters from Gabriel existed—one set addressed to his daughter in Palestine, another for his niece and sister-in-law in Canada. When the letters stopped, his family on both sides of the world frantically searched for him.

It was Dan who first acknowledged the elephant in the room. He told us that his grandfather Gabriel had counted on Rhona's Uncle Max to get him out of Vienna and save him from a certain death at the hands of the Nazis.

Rhona explained how hard her family had tried, but they, like so many others in Canada and the United States, frantic to free loved ones, were unable to secure the necessary visa for Gabriel. The ultimate failure resided, not in Lotte or Max's actions, but in government policies that limited the resettlement of Jewish refugees. Rhona could not say what Uncle Max felt about this failure, as he never shared that part of his life with her. But she could speak of its impact on her mother. "It was a great sorrow to her," Rhona continued, "a burden she carried lifelong, not being able to save her uncle." She went on: "It was the Brainin lineage, Musa's family, settled in New York, who ultimately saved Max and his wife, but under the immigration regulations, a visa could not be allocated to an uncle and especially not to a relative from the Lubetzky side." We could not help wondering whether the two mothers had ever exchanged letters or talked about this fatal reality, about blame or regret.

We met again at another café, bringing Sharon's son Ori together with one of our sons, Jeremy and his wife, and our two-year-old grandson, who were on sabbatical in Israel. Our time together was coming to an end. Not surprisingly, it proved difficult to say goodbye to new cousins who lived so far away. Before we left, Dan described the pilgrimage that he and his son Tamir had made to Vienna to see the outside of buildings in which his grandfather had lived. But their trip stopped short of visiting his grandfather's birthplace in Belarus or the site of his final march. "It was too emotional for me," he recounted to us.

And so, we carried this Israeli family in our hearts as we followed Gabriel's last days.

* * *

We now had in hand a second set of letters from Gabriel, who was trapped in Vienna. Our last letter, dated January 13, 1939. Their last letter, December 2, 1939. Almost a year apart and the latter, just on the heels of Max and Olga's safe arrival in New York. Gabriel's letters to his daughter and her husband appeared more forthright, more despairing, than those he wrote to the Montreal family. Yet, despite the tightening noose, Gabriel still worried about his children who, after months in Italy trying to arrange transport, had finally arrived in Palestine. He wrote about the Gorodeja family, who had become increasingly impoverished and were no longer able to help kleine Hedy and Jacob with some money to start a new life. And, as a father, he made suggestions as to how the young couple might move ahead in their new land.

These letters detail the sheer extent of his efforts to escape and the frustrating roadblocks he encountered at every turn—all to no avail. Sustained over many years, these efforts included hiring a lawyer, camping out in the consular offices of numerous countries, investigating low-cost housing in different countries, and reaching for help from every relative or friend he had outside of Austria. The ironclad bureaucracy that impeded his escape is evident:

> I was already almost on my way to London, but I am luckless, and unfortunately there has been another deferral. This is because the British government has issued new orders, according to which I must send in a document that confirms my stay in the United States. These new orders are strict. Since the American consulate in Vienna refuses to issue this document for me and I must obtain it on my own, I suppose there will be another deferral, and it will be at least several months until I can leave the country. [November 10, 1938]

> There is no possible way for me to approach the American consulate. They only see people who have already been summoned for an interview. Others can only ask for information in writing, which I have tried to do. I contacted the consulate several times, asking them to provide me with a copy of a signed document confirming my stay in the U.S, as that is the condition for my entire existence. I'm afraid the answer is

> always the same: the consulate does not provide copies, nor does it provide original documents. [November 28, 1939]

It has been well demonstrated that the U.S. Department of State placed roadblocks in the path of the Jews trying to escape Europe.

In rising desperation, Gabriel pinned much hope on his nephew Max to be his savior. On March 6, 1939, he writes, "Max and Olga have already received their visa and are now preparing for their departure. I now hope that from there, Max will be able to change my own situation." But months later [August 16, 1939], Gabriel admits to his daughter and son-in-law his fear that "later" may indeed be too late:

> I'm afraid there are no changes in my situation, and I am extremely desperate. Max has been trying to comfort me by saying that my visa should arrive very soon, but since I have been hearing this chant for five months now, I am not influenced by its spell. There is something rotten about this whole business, and I don't know what it is! I only know that for most people, it takes about four or five weeks without any intervention on their part; it has been eight months for me, with plenty of intervention on my part. This is no longer a lack of luck —perhaps it is fate . . . It could very well be that "later" will already be too late. Almost all my acquaintances have already left.

In his last letter [December 2, 1939], Gabriel's mood is almost euphoric, holding out a thread of hope that Max will be able to help and that he might make it out of Vienna one day:

> The last few days have been quite productive. Max, newly arrived in the U.S., writes that he has received the document I need, and he hopes to send it to me within four or five weeks. As a sworn pessimist, I shouldn't be affected by this shining ray of light. Nevertheless, I tell myself that it could be that just this once, my lack of fortune won't keep up with me and I'll still manage to squeeze myself in. I hope so.

Unknown to us, Max had received the U.S. document that Gabriel needed. Did Max follow through and mail it to Vienna? And if he did, was it perhaps the forced relocation of the Jews that had prevented Gabriel from receiving this potentially life-saving piece of paper? Or if it was received, was this paperwork insufficient at this late date to ensure his departure? So many different narratives might explain why Gabriel's escape was blocked, lifting the blame off Lotte's shoulders. And such a scenario would paint Max as a savior, instead of an irresponsible soul, whose efforts proved futile.

This was the last time any of the surviving family members heard from Gabriel Lubetzky. Letters to him, written from Palestine and Montreal, went unanswered. Letters to and from the Red Cross, were found in the papers of Lotte, Aunt Hedy, and Dan's mother kleine Hedy, each frantically trying to locate his whereabouts.

By May of 1939, the exodus that Gabriel so vividly described had stripped Vienna of approximately 130,000 of its 206,000 Jews (63% of its Jewish population). By October of 1941, the mass deportation of the remaining Viennese Jews was underway, with over 65,000 Jews exterminated. Against a past in which Jewish culture and education had flourished, "expulsion, deportation, and murder" became the history of the Jews in Vienna.

Our search of asset forms, required of all Jews at that time to appraise their private property, uncovered two filings by Gabriel Lubetzky with the Ministry of Finance: in 1938 and in 1942, respectively. These documents were obtained from the Osterreichisches Staatsarchiv and translated. Gabriel listed himself as a Jew, a widower, and an office worker, who had lost his job without severance pay by June of 1938. He reported his address on Bastiengasse and meager assets of some jewelry, valued at one hundred Reichsmarks. Poignantly, he asked for consideration given his delay in filing, as he did not realize the obligation to file without receipt of any income.

By the time of his 1942 filing, Gabriel had been moved to an apartment on Lessinggasse, to be housed with multiple families awaiting deportation. His name was now listed as Gabriel Israel Lubetsky, with the "Israel" required for males and "Sara" for females, so that the authorities could more easily identify Jews. And, as we were to discover, there was an escape-tax to be paid by Jews leaving the country, even for those who were to be deported for extermination. At the end, Gabriel had sixty-one Reichsmarks to his name—even this pittance would be robbed by the Nazis.

In Sharon Picker's family book, we found the undated confirmation of Gabriel's death, obtained from the Central Database of Shoah Victims' Names and filed by Holocaust survivors at Yad Vashem in Jerusalem. At Yad Vashem, the full record for Gabriel Lubetzky noted his birthdate as 22/8/1892 and his wartime address as Wien 2, Lessinggasse 8. This survivor-reported birthdate differed from Gabriel's own filings with the Vienna authorities, where he indicated an earlier birthdate of August 11, 1882. This record also noted his deportation on June 9, 1942, as prisoner #556, taken from Vienna to Maly Trostinec, a Nazi extermination camp just outside of Minsk in Belarus. Gabriel's final 1942 asset filing was also stamped with the date of his deportation, a copy of which we now hold in our hands.

Three years after the family last heard from him and just six days after his deportation from Vienna, Gabriel was murdered on June 15, 1942. He was fifty-nine.

* * *

Retracing Gabriel's last steps, we are in Vienna, having engaged the assistance of a knowledgeable guide, Walter Juraschek, with whom we walk through the historical sections of the old Jewish Quarter. On earlier trips, we had visited the Bastiengasse address in the 18th District, around the corner from the flat of his brother Eisig on Messerschmidtgasse. Now we stand outside the apartment building on Krummbaumgasse in Vienna's second district, where Uncle Gabriel lived for a short time. It is a stately building, under restoration when we visited, with its outside walls covered in a black protective covering. Our ears are assaulted by the deafening sound of jackhammers. Gabriel was then moved to the deportation house on Lessinggasse—the building no longer there, torn down with no visible marker remaining.

Gabriel's letters helped us imagine his life and the young adult lives of Hedy and Max, during better times—the cafés, the music, the debates, and the gossip among the Jews of Vienna. And through his words, we think about the net closing in, as the Jews became increasingly limited in their options for living, and about his desperate attempts to escape.

Walter takes us to the site of the deportations of the Jews—a school in the second district where present and past merge—in photos captured by us and photos that Walter brings of the roundup. The Sperl School, hidden away, fronts on an alley that leads to the street. It was here in deplorable conditions that the Nazis gathered the Jews prior to their being taken to the Aspangbahnhof train station for transport to Eastern Europe. We walk down the same alley that Gabriel once walked. Walter shows us photos of those who were caught in the dragnet, despairing and yet unaware of what horrors lay ahead. And we examine the iconic photograph of a large cart onto which Jewish deportees pile their suitcases, supervised by a member of the SS.

As we look up at the brightly painted school, yellow in color, and peek into its windows, we see active and happy children and their teachers. It seems unreal and yet, the very stones of the building and below it on the ground, inscribed with names of the dead, testify to the atrocities committed there. These commissioned "Stolpersteine" or stumbling blocks (in English) are brass memorial plaques, created by the artist Gunter Demnig. They are scattered through the streets of Vienna and many other cities in Europe, drilled into sidewalks or walls to remind us who once lived there, to remind us of their persecution. We are both on edge and close to tears, as we explore Gabriel's last moments in Vienna. From there, we go to the station where thousands boarded the trains for their final journey.

Happenstance, as we stop in Prague on our way to Belarus, we discover a pivotal exhibit at the Jewish Museum. It is titled "Since then I believe in fate . . . " Transports of

Protectorate Jews to Bylelorussia, 1941-1942. It recounts the less well-known deportations to the Baltic States and to the Nazi-occupied territories of Poland and Belarus. Inspired by the four-part documentary *Forgotten Transports* by filmmaker Lukáš Přibyl and in collaboration with Přibyl, this exhibit pieces together testimony about the Maly Trostenets Camp, from the twenty-two survivors, from local inhabitants, and from German soldiers. In Prague, we hear their voices, see photographs of the camp and of the killings, although much of the evidence has been destroyed. We look for Gabriel's face, but we do not find it.

The country of Belarus was especially devastated by World War II, with more than two million of its citizens killed. Of these, some 800,000 were Jews. We visit Maly Trostenets, which was built by the Nazis on the site of a collective farm in a village about twelve kilometres to the southeast of Minsk. On May 10, 1942, it became an extermination camp and Gabriel arrived a month later, sent back to his homeland to die. As the mass exterminations of prisoners within the camp began only in 1943, it is likely that Gabriel was among the detainees killed outside the camp in the outlying forests, within six days of his deportation. These prisoners were lined up in front of large pits and shot in the back. The Soviets claim to have discovered thirty-four grave-pits of enormous length and width after the war's end. In 2019, a monument was erected that listed the names of those who perished at this site and a book of essays by their descendents was published.

As we walk through the site on a chilly day, all we see is a pleasant park with a stone monument to the "Soviet citizens" who were killed by the Germans. "Soviet citizens" it reads, but, once again, there is no mention of the Jews. We had reached Gabriel's last stop, and at the base of the monument, we place small stones to remember him, as we had done at Eisig's grave.

As evident in the letters, Gabriel and kleine Hedy had lost touch with the Gorodeja family. The names of our extended family members were not recorded in the Yizkor book on *Tooretz-Yeremitz* as having died in Turets, nor were their names found on a list of victims in Gorodeja provided to us by the mayor. Instead, confirmation of their deaths came in the documents filed at Yad Vashem in the Central Database of Shoah Victims.

Filings made between 1956-1957 by Khaia Levin, listed as a cousin, confirmed the deaths of Eisig's siblings. These include Mordekhai (Motel) and his wife Batia; Fajtel (Feitel) who was divorced; and Pesa (Peschke), a widow, her daughter Miriam (Mirele), and a one-year- old grandson Avraham. These family members may have perished in the killing pit high on the hill in Gorodeja on which we had stood, carrying the last photo of the Lubetzky family. Yet another notification by Yehuda Gesik, listing himself as a nephew, reported the death of David Eliahu, Eisig's father, also of Motel and Batia, and two children, Yehudit (Itele) and Matilda (Mirele), all at Gorodeja. These two filings made by distant relatives do not match in their entirety but are confirmatory about their deaths. If the reported birthdates are correct, the birth order would place Eisig as the eldest (1872), followed by Motel (1881), Gabriel (1882), Feitel (1884), and Peschke (1887).

The fate of Eisig's first-born son, his name unknown to us, could not be determined. Assuming that Eisig's first wife and child had not left Gorodeja, it is likely that they, too, would have perished there at the hands of the Nazis.

And so it ends, more than half of a family whose members had once lived vibrant lives were wiped out. The cold words on the filing pages fail to capture the tragedy of their extermination, carried out simply because they were of the Jewish faith. Because there were survivors, there exist descendants of this small Lubetzky family, who live on. Their numbers growing larger with each successive generation.

* * *

One Lubetzky, in 1921, by his own hand.

Ten Lubetzky family members, between 1941-1942, at the hands of the Nazis.

What marks their presence on this earth? When we remember them? What remains, when we, with our memories, are gone?

In Gorodeja, Turets, and Maly Trostenets, the killing sites are memorialized, thanks, in part, to the efforts of Frank and Galena Swartz of Voluntas. A black iron sculpture depicting the bent window frames of destroyed homes or a cement pillar signifying the destruction. Here, those lost are not named, nor even mentioned as Jews. It is the individuals who reported their deaths to Yad Vashem in Jerusalem, who named them one by one.

In Vienna, we return to the crumbling and weed-covered monument that marked Eisig's gravesite in Vienna, his name barely legible. Entrusted by Hedy to care for his grave, we, Rhona and Hannah, Eisig's only grandchildren, along with husbands Harvey and Michael, erect a new monument in Eisig's memory. And now it stands, shiny and bold, his name clearly displayed.

An enormous wall plaque can be found in the Stadttemple,

the Great Synagogue of Vienna on Seitenstettengasse, which lists, one by one, those lost to the Nazi deportations. There we find Uncle Gabriel's name. Can a name on a memorial plaque capture the existence of a man who had a full life, who loved and was loved? Yet, we find comfort in seeing his name on a wall within the vast beauty of a Jewish holy place.

Past and present merge again, as it has throughout our journey. Other reasons had brought us to Vienna at this time—an invited address that Harvey gave at a conference on trauma, held to celebrate the 20th Anniversary of ESRA, a Center for Psychosocial Care. This organization, its name meaning "help" in Hebrew, was forged as a cooperative project between the Jewish community of Vienna and the city, and it is located on the very site that before 1938 housed the great Leopoldstadt Temple. As Harvey speaks about his work in the aftermath of the Bosnian genocide, we search for Rhona's past, in the wake of a Viennese suicide and the Holocaust.

A dinner that evening takes place at the Rathaus, the City Hall of Vienna, its magnificent architecture neo-gothic in style. Dressed for the event and accompanied by our Brainin cousins, we climb two flights of red-carpeted stairs to enter a grand hall, filled with 500 people seated around multiple tables. At the elegant dinner, we are moved by a videotaped address from the President of Austria, lauding the wonderful work of this Jewish organization—a German phrase here and there translated for us by our cousins. And then, bringing tears to our eyes, we hear the refrain of a familiar and beautiful Hebrew prayer "Oseh Shalom" (He Who Makes Peace) and of a Yiddish folk song, with the words and transliterations displayed on large screens. Led by ESRA staff members, the entire hall joins in a rousing chorus.

Hebrew and Yiddish, two languages that Rhona's grandfather and great-uncle once spoke. Two languages and the cultures they represented, snuffed out in Austria. We find it painful to take it all in. In the early 21st century, we now sing out these ancestral languages in "official" quarters but in 1942, Gabriel Lubetzky was deported to his execution, just because he was a Jew.

However, we are roundly cautioned in our reverie about the meaning of this event. "There are multiple layers here, anti-semitism is still very much alive," we are told. Despite the presence of 6,000 Jews in Vienna, we see vigilance in the guard boxes outside locked synagogues, with no name identifying these religious organizations. Our attendance at a synagogue is possible only with a recommendation from a member and passport clearance by security. We learn about protests against Israel, against Jews, and the desecration of holy places. And we cannot help but remember that the Brainins, returning after the war, felt they could not, without consequences, identify themselves as Jews. Vienna, a city that Max, Lotte, and Hedy, could never visit again. Vienna, a city that draws us back. Vienna, a city in which we despair.

We gather all the pictures from our long journey, bringing them back to share with Hannah and Michael, and our families in California, and we send copies to Dan and Sharon in Jerusalem. Upon our return to California, a gift from Israel awaits us. Inside the package is our very own copy of the cherished Yizkor book on *Tooretz-Yeremitz*—the last second-hand copy available in Israel at that time. It was sent to us most lovingly by Dan Picker. A symbol of our shared heritage and of the grandfathers we never knew.

Chapter Twelve

From Generation to Generation— L'Dor V'Dor

Our parents, of course, and our children; our grandparents and our grandchildren. We are caught in the dance of life with them and, however tedious that dance can sometimes seem, it is the music of our lives. To deny it is to deny our heritage and our legacy.
—Jon Carroll, 2014

All of us have ghosts in our family closets. With age, we become even more curious about what family members kept secret, a silence seemingly impenetrable. A silence that arose out of memories too painful to share or a silence that sought to shield us. A silence that emerged out of dehumanizing policies designed to destroy populations, obliterating their very existence. Yet much of our identity and place in the world is shaped by the past. A past that lies within, sometimes quiescent, sometimes raging, shaping or undermining the choices we make.

Thus, many hunger to discover their familial heritage and to find their place within it. This is evident in the public's fascination with the U.S. television series *Finding Your Roots*, created by Henry Louis Gates Jr., and with the ever-growing genre of *family* memoirs. Historian Jeremy Popkin describes these memoirs as "the painstaking quest for information about a family past that they [the children] did not know." Secrets can emerge around identifying parentage and the existence of other siblings, an altered identity (religious, racial or ethnic), a war or genocide past (as victim, perpetrator, warrior, resister, or savior), a criminal act, and more. And as described in this book, secrets can be about an ancestor or intimate family member whose mental illness and suicide were hidden.

Humans are complex, family relationships even more so, and the ways in which legacies are passed to successive generations represent relatively uncharted territory. Families constitute an intricate system, made up of far more than a sum of individuals or of dyadic relationships. Rather, families are nested within layers of social context, where inner and outer worlds collide. Psychologists Ross Parke and Glen Elder, in their edited book *Children in Changing Worlds: Sociocultural and Temporal Perspectives*, provide a rich understanding of how human development takes place within historical, cultural, and life-course contexts. They highlight how interactive influences frame who thrives and who falters. These influences can reach across generational time, the transmission of past to present, affecting the lives of individuals and families.

A key to Rhona's heritage lay in the world of her grandfather. No longer just a name, Eisig Lubetzky became a vivid presence and the central figure around which this book was built. Although we never found the suicide note addressed to his wife and children, we filled the empty envelope with far more than a letter of farewell. What we learned revealed a fascinating but troubled man and his impact on the family. What we learned illuminated the roots of Rhona's mother's character and revealed a multigenerational mother-daughter conflict that ultimately colored their lives. In part, this complex history framed who Rhona became. Eisig's act of suicide was to reverberate far beyond the immediacy of death, touching successive generations.

This story began with a revelation, but its fullness emerged years later from a paper trail, published and unpublished, secured by legions of librarians and archivists. It was deepened by the recollections of Aunt Hedy who was finally able to speak about the past, by a connection made with surviving Lubetzky relatives in Israel, and by an acknowledgment of those family members who were murdered in the Holocaust.

The story we tell fills a knowledge gap about the life of Hebrew writer and critic Lubetzky, especially of his family, and looks beyond, into the next generations. Our inquiry also precipitated a 21st century collection and re-appraisal of Lubetzky's writings, belatedly fulfilling Eisig's wish as expressed in his suicide note to a friend and in the call of his biographers. Finally, we broke the silence and returned Eisig to his rightful place in Rhona's family tree. While aspects of this transgenerational tale may have been missed, misunderstood, or lost in translation, there is value in new storytellers who were intimate witnesses to part of this history and in newly-found materials.

How do we make sense of the forces that Eisig confronted in his life and how could the actions of one man transcend generations? A story that played out across 150 years, in different countries, historical periods, and societal structures— supporting or constraining family life. The writer James Wood acknowledges that as much as we learn of the past, we must also accept how little we understand. So many interpretations are possible.

We came to know Rhona's grandfather in ways that his own children never knew him. It was as if he stepped out of the photograph that Rhona had passed by every day of her childhood. No longer an enigma, he came alive in his written words. We were moved by how he saw his world, the imagery and his eloquence. Struck by his fierce intellect—striving to depict the culture of Western European life, to create standards for a Hebrew literary tradition, and to ensure a place for contributions by Jews to be valued in Viennese society. We saw resilience in how he remade himself—as a writer, choir director, and financier—in order to materially support his family. And we found evidence of caring, in his plea to colleagues to help the family he was soon to leave behind.

Yet he also was a tragic figure, unlikeable, ever an outsider. In his words, a "lonely stalk of grain," who withered in the chill winds of autumn. He wrestled with demons—the highest of expectations for achievement never met, mental illness, and a sharp tongue. He lived in a society that he deeply loved but one that discriminated against him and relegated him to poverty for most of his years. He distanced himself from his wife and children. His final abandonment of the family was not an act of cruelty, as one critic suggested, but instead the actions of a despairing man. This is the grandfather Rhona claimed and as with all human beings, strength and vulnerability live side by side.

Eisig's life story illustrates the tyranny of excessively high expectations for self and others. His identification as a child prodigy fostered grand dreams that proved to be unattainable. Indeed, in an analysis of the participants in Lewis Terman's longitudinal study of the gifted, psychologist Carole Holahan shows that there is variation in whether such expectations of early genius in childhood become confirmed or disconfirmed in adulthood. While expectations can be powerful, as Rhona's own studies have demonstrated, they also require a supporting social context and/or intervening actions that can translate such prophecies into reality. For intellectual achievement to be fostered, a community of gate-keepers must provide opportunities for development and expression, and these gate-keepers also serve as the final arbiters of accomplishment.

Eisig not only changed his cultural context but also the disciplines in which he worked. His thirst for learning took him from a small Orthodox Jewish community, where he was exalted, to a more worldly but antisemitic Western European society that found his critical demeanor and his writings wanting and ultimately scorned him. Left bitter and angry, his negative view of the talents of others and a sharp tongue undercut his literary reputation and tainted the relationship with his family. The cultural world in which he lived did not support his talents or ambitions. The plummeting of his self-appraisal was not surprising. Holahan also found that those individuals identified early as gifted were more likely later in life to believe that they had *not* lived up to their intellectual abilities. And at midlife, they had poorer psychological well-being.

Perhaps, even more critical, Eisig's inability to reach his aspirations was profoundly undermined by severe mental illness, evident even as a young adult, that periodically robbed him of vitality and coherence, and unleashed his grandiosity and the bitter critic in him. And at that time, existing treatments were not effective. Mental illness casts a long and unrelenting shadow, tormenting not only the afflicted but also those in the inner circle and beyond. If not successfully treated, such illnesses can interrupt the realization of dreams and if culminating in suicide, can also shatter the lives of those left behind.

Recent statistics on depression, bipolar illness, and

suicide show just how widespread these mental health problems are. Studies from the National Institute of Mental Health suggest that the lifetime prevalence of mood disorders in the United States is about 1 in 5 individuals; of these, about 4% are of the bipolar variety, involving both depression and mania. And while highly variable by age group, sex, and race/ethnicity, suicides for men occur at the rate of 22.8 per 100,000 of the population. In 2020, in this country, suicide claimed the lives of 49,316 individuals. It is also estimated that even today, despite all the scientific advances, about half of these afflicted individuals remain untreated. As we have seen, mental illness, as with a physical illness, impacts not only the individual but also the family, workplace, and the community. These prevalence statistics underestimate the larger impact of these disorders. Indeed, all of us in some way share the experience of mental illness, whether in the present or the past, within our family or community, or within ourselves.

Until the first half of the 20th century, severe mental illness was largely viewed with fear all over the world. In his book, *Stepchildren of the Shtetl*, covering the period from 1800-1939, Judaic Studies scholar Natan Meir describes the dire conditions of the squalid poorhouses of the East European shtetls and the insane asylums of Warsaw and Odessa, where individuals experiencing madness were incarcerated. In the U.S., warehousing of those with severe mental illness continued well into the 1960s, at which point large institutions were shut down and psychiatric care was shifted to community settings with briefer stays.

The stigma of madness ensured that families would cover up these disturbances as much as possible. Given the need to maintain their status in Vienna, it is no surprise that

Musa hid Eisig's difficulties and the fact of his suicide from her daughters and others. That orthodox Judaism required those who committed suicide to be interred in separate sections outside of the cemetery proper also underscores the isolation of these sufferers in death as in life.

Despite shifts in our understanding of the causes of psychiatric illness, moving from demonology to a more sophisticated understanding, mental illness remains a convenient scapegoat for many of society's ills. Ignorance breeds mythology, fear breeds rejection. Psychologists Stephen Hinshaw and Dante Cicchetti describe the complex interplay of "genes, neurobiology, environment, and self," that characterizes mental illness. Their analysis further suggests that the continued stigma exhibited towards those with aberrant behavior not only undermines the willingness of individuals to seek treatment but also limits the further development and availability of mental health services. Effective treatments for serious mental illness now exist and for many, these psychiatric disorders can be managed and its sufferers can live a full life. But stigma still plays a key role in keeping services in short supply—through lack of parity in insurance coverage for mental as compared to physical illness, limited hospital beds, lack of access tò care, poor coordination of services, and insufficient research funding to advance understanding and treatment.

Despite increased knowledge about mental illness and widespread availability of suicide hotlines, the stigma continues. Positive steps forward include a growing literature of first-person accounts of mental illness by afflicted individuals, movingly depicted in such books as Kay Redfield Jamison's *An Unquiet Mind* and William Styron's *Depression*. And public acknowledgment by prominant individuals who have experienced mental health challenges may become a powerful driver in the reduction of stigma.

What other forces contributed to Eisig's downfall? It is impossible to tell his story without acknowledging the poverty which permeated his existence and his marginalized status in Vienna as a Jew from Belarussia. He saw himself as an "established starver" until the last three years of his life. The contrast between his meager existence and the wealth of Viennese society must have been intolerable, especially as his intellectual contributions did not achieve the acclaim he expected.

While he aspired to be part of Viennese culture, the overt and covert antisemitism which characterized Viennese society relegated him to the ghettoized Jewish community. As we have noted, job opportunities were limited to certain fields and Jew-hatred was found in all segments of society, perhaps, even more so in the upper classes. Although the Jewish community flourished in the arts, music, literature, medicine, and other professions, Jews were faced with the choice of assimilation in order to belong and some converted to Christianity. But for many, this was anathema and so they walked a fine line between identifying primarily as Jewish or Viennese, limiting opportunities for success. Eisig tried to belong to two worlds but he faced antisemitism many times, from non-Jews and Jews alike. And so, the ambitions of the child prodigy were thwarted.

Compounding these societal constraints, Eisig's family life was in a shambles. Domestic stress was evident well before Eisig's suicide. The Lubetzky children grew up with depressed parents, engaged in marital warfare. A largely absent and critical father. A helpless and angry mother, whose expectations for a happy life were never fulfilled.

And a family history of sadness, dashed expectations, and despair. Further, a destructive pattern of differential treatment toward the children led to untoward consequences for each child. The eldest, Max, having inherited his father's bipolar disorder and musical talent, faced criticism for not meeting the high expectations set for him and, from adolescence on, left home as frequently as he could. The middle child, Lotte, who shared her father's intellect and modeled his critical nature, asserted herself by speaking out and was literally banished from the household. The favored youngest, Hedy, with the sweetest nature, did all she could to promote harmony and dealt with her inability to be a peacemaker by retreating into herself. Research on expectations and their effects suggests that even young children are aware of differential treatment, in the family and the classroom. This awareness can carrry consequences, not only for a negatively-targeted child, but also for a favored one, who may suffer guilt over the special treatment and anxiety over losing one's coveted place in a contested hierarchy.

To varying degrees, all three of Lubetzky's children shared their father's critical nature, focusing on what was missing in others and in themselves, rather than what was present and positive. And as with criticism, the three siblings also carried their sadness in different ways but none led a fulfilled life. How much of this was biological, how much was the legacy of a deprived upbringing, we do not know. However, there is no doubt that they suffered a large number of what physician William Felitti and colleagues have called adverse childhood experiences (ACEs)—the effects of depressed parents whose marriage was filled with pain, their father's suicidal act, struggles with poverty, and the loss of a culture that had abandoned them. These traumatic experiences impacted their ability to thrive.

Born in Vienna, the children, also embraced the same goal as Eisig— to move beyond the confines of the Jewish immigrant community into the larger society. The viability of Jewish survival in Europe was a major concern of Viennese Jewry but the impact of antisemitism on Eisig's children was less clear. For them, the idealization of Viennese culture likely served to obscure the limitations placed on them as Jews, until Hedy and Max were caught in its net. Suddenly, they and all the Jews who had identified primarily as Viennese were horrified to find themselves stripped of their rights, livelihood, and eventually lives during the Nazi occupation.

As with so many others, the impact of the Holocaust was never discussed in Rhona's home. While the tragic death of Gabriel was shared as fact, details about him and the sorrow of the loss were barely acknowledged. That was part of the darkness, the secrets not confronted. And by leaving Vienna, this next generation suffered what has been called, by psychiatrist Maurice Eisenbruch, a cultural bereavement, a loss they would mourn for the rest of their days. It may also be a form of what family therapist Pauline Boss has described as an "ambiguous loss," where resolution never occurs and unresolved grief undermines quality of life. For Max, Lotte, and Hedy, nostalgia for Vienna in the first three decades of the 20th century was a fixture of their lives.

While all these forces were at play in the life and death of Eisig, ultimately it was the stigma and shame associated with the suicide that led the small Lubetzky family to erase him from the family history. In contrast, the larger world—diverse communities of writers, financiers, and Holocaust survivors from his Belarussian birthplace—memorialized him. Those communities kept his memory alive. Eisig's suicide closed the door to reconciliation and sent the family on a downward spiral. He left his teenage children to care for a dependent mother, ultimately for thirty-two years, and to earn their way, interrupting their schooling and impacting their lives.

Despite the many traumas, there was evidence of resilience in the children of Eisig Lubetzky. Inadvertently, his suicide also paved the way to the family's survival, through Lotte's early departure for Canada. What we came to appreciate was Lotte's fierce agency in saving her small family from harm. To leave Vienna in 1925 at the age of twenty and forge a new life in Canada, while supporting the family back home with her meager earnings. To raise funds, obtain Canadian visas, and ultimately rescue four lives (her mother, sister, brother, and sister-in-law) from the death-knell of the Holocaust. To persist against great odds in efforts to save her uncle—a defeat that left her unable to set foot in Vienna again or to face his surviving descendants. Still, she was able to carry on, as a daughter, a wife, and a mother.

Ironically, Lotte, the rejected one, became the savior and, indeed, the fulcrum of the family, keeping its generations secure and closely tied together. Despite the darkness of the past and the challenges of their adult years, the family made new lives in Montreal, each in their own way. What never wavered was their love and caring for each other. From these three Lubetzky siblings came the two cousins, Hannah and Rhona, who in turn brought into the world four children and seven grandchildren between them—the fifth generation and the great-great grandchildren of Eisig and Musa.

Every family confronts serious challenges—some more, some less than others. We pass on to the next generation our genetic vulnerabilities and strengths. We choose to share or not share with our children details about ourselves, our lives, and the barriers we may face. But even if silent, we model in nonverbal ways and in our actions how we experience the world, the sadness as well as the joy, and how we cope with adversity. While our parents are the most immediate transmitters of our family legacies, the roots also go backwards in time.

Much has been written about the transmission of trauma effects within and across generations—be they a result of genes, gene-environment interactions, and/or the modeling of thought, emotion, and behavior. We cannot speak here to the role of "inherited" familial trauma, where trauma exposure may result in alterations in the genes that are passed on to the next generation. The epigenetics of trauma transmission, as described by trauma researcher Rachel Yehuda, is a promising field of research but its mechanisms are not yet definitive and a fuller exploration of this area is beyond the scope of this book. However, in our view, it is likely that a propensity for a bipolar illness, musical talent, and keen intellectual ability was inherited by some of the Lubetzky descendants, that multiple and interactive environmental stressors especially impacted Eisig, Musa, and their children, and that protective influences that could have mitigated the stresses were far more limited in their generations than for the succeeding ones.

Most importantly, that the trauma associated with Eisig's mental illness and suicide lay buried kept its impact on the family active but always beneath the surface. Already vulnerable, Eisig's children experienced still more loss, both before and after their emigration to Montreal. The Lubetzky inheritance included a dark, fearful, and critical view of the world, with its effects inevitably seeping through to the next generation. Among the mechanisms of seepage, researchers have found is the ability to mirror the emotional states of close others. Psychologist Casey Brown and colleagues have termed this "empathic accuracy." They find that the ability to read the emotions of another in couples or other dyadic relationships is associated with shared depressive symptoms. In children, it has also been shown experimentally that the heart rate of infants increases in response to their mother's induced stress. Developmental psychologist Sara Waters describes this phenomenon as "stress may be caught, not taught," evident even before the capacity for language.

But what enables individual agency in charting a more positive course when exposed to tragedy? And if trauma is carried forward into future generations, what factors can mute the valence of or end a troubled legacy in subsequent generations? In her book, *Ordinary Magic: Resilience in Development*, psychologist Ann Masten has shaped our understanding about such resilience, about those who thrive rather than falter when faced with adversity. Resilience is possible because of the availability of protective factors—within individuals and/or provided by families, schools, communities, and societies.

Among many protective factors, knowledge about one's history and place in the family story can serve as a critical resource. Research suggests that parents' reminiscing style guides the development of an autobiographical memory in children, as early as in preschool. Psychologist Robyn Fivush and colleagues find that parents who share "more elaborated and coherent personal narratives" have children with a more "differentiated and coherent sense of self." Further, adolescents who know more stories about their family history show higher levels of emotional well-being. What is important in the telling of these stories is not only that they convey the challenges of life but that they also offer insights into how such obstacles are overcome. They offer the possibility for growth and change. This sense of agency over desired outcomes is vital for positive development. Negative outcomes from traumatic experiences are not inevitable.

As we explored this familial heritage, we thought not only about the psychological patterns that were passed on but also about a world and a time period, where societal institutions, religious and secular, strangled one's ability to thrive, especially if Jewish, because of antisemitism, or female, because of narrowly prescribed opportunities. Whatever the mechanisms of transmission, Eisig's children were the repository of the past. While the memories receded, the undercurrents persisted, affecting every aspect of their lives, never acknowledged and never put to rest.

* * *

Rhona—

I often stumbled in the writing of this book. Sharing this story sometimes felt like a betrayal of my family—my mother, in particular—exposing a dark side and making public what many would keep private. But if there are universal lessons here, the perpetuation of the family silence would feel like another form of betrayal. I chose to tell this story because I believe that a new understanding of a stigmatized and hidden past can bring unexpected gifts, as it did for me.

This journey has been life-changing. At each step along the way, my mother and her family of origin have been in the room with us, a shadow presence. In Jon Caroll's words, this is the dance of life—the heritage left to us—however mysterious, painful, or uplifting. At last, I can see how I am the sum of all that has come before me. I carry within me, my mother, my grandfather. I am of Montreal, Vienna, and the Belarussian shtetls. And as much as I have fled, I have also clung to the family. My adult home in California holds some of the furniture, paintings, lamps, and books that once filled the apartment of my parents. I still hold close the china plates and candlesticks that accompanied the family's escape from Vienna.

But also, I am different.

What buffered the effects of my mother's sadness and her ultimate disappointment in me? While I absorbed the dark moods, fears, and vigilance of my mother, I was blessed with many protective influences. A gentle father who encouraged my intellectual curiosity, an uncle who taught me to live in my imagination, an aunt who offered unconditional love, and a sister-in-life, my cousin Hannah, who became my closest ally and cheered me on. And I never had to face the early loss of loved ones and of place, abandonment and poverty, and the extremes of antisemitism that my mother and her family did. Of course, my era brought its own challenges.

Not wanting to repeat the patterns in my mother's life, I was driven to make my own way. I managed to avoid the mismatched expectations that plagued the marriages of my grandparents and parents. In Harvey, I found a life partner who shared my intellectual curiosity and helped me separate from my mother for self-preservation. He wholeheartedly supported my career and my choices. As he, too, carried a legacy of darkness— a father whose life was destroyed as an unwitting victim of government-sponsored mind control experimentation. He helped me overcome the burdens I carried, just as I helped him. Together, we focused on self-creation, as individuals and as a couple, utilizing every resource to bring positivity into our lives and to protect our children as best as we could, from threats in the world and from our own limitations.

My chosen field of psychology proved to be an extraordinary helpmate. It offered me a framework to understand human development. Did our family history lead Hannah and me toward mental health careers—she, to become a clinical social worker, and I, a professor of clinical and community psychology? Did this history steer me, perhaps unconsciously, to study the impact of expectations and differential treatment on the lives of children. To elicit their often silenced voices as informants. To design interventions that would enable all children to thrive. This need to liberate others emerges also in the type of sculpture I create, cutting away the stone to free the figure or form that lies within each block. Perhaps, this was a metaphor for releasing others (and myself) to live more positive lives. In this way, I moved beyond the all-black paintings of my early childhood.

Like my grandfather, I am immersed in creative work, judged on the worth of my contributions and a judge of the work of others. I carry his and my mother's critical voices in my head. I also hold exceptionally high expectations for whatever I and others do, but the toughest criticism is saved for myself. "Rewrite Rhona" was the nickname given to me by my graduate students, hopefully with affection, as I held them to the highest standards. But I worked hard to be constructive in my feedback, to identify strengths, offer encouragement, and build a caring community.

Family secrets led me to become a discloser, to speak openly and transparently. In contrast, Hannah, like her mother Hedy, held her thoughts close, preferring not to share intimate feelings. To some in our family, we were viewed as our mothers had been viewed—Hannah, the good and sweet one, and Rhona, the outspoken one. And yet, we had the deepest of bonds, an unvoiced debt between us that mirrored what Hedy and Lotte had forged but without the ambivalence that had characterized their relationship. I carried the burden of living in a conflict-ridden home, while she was freer to enjoy her childhood. In return, she graciously shared her sweet mother with me, without jealousy or constraint.

What about this next generation, the lives of our twin sons, now nearing middle age? My grandfather loved the written word and a well-crafted argument, as did my mother. Both our sons are writers—one, a professor of political science and dean who served in the federal government, and the other, a documentary filmmaker and screenwriter. As were their ancestors, both are sensitive to populations who are marginalized, committed to politics, social movements, and justice. They actively care for others, family and friends, as did their grandmother Lotte. Each of our sons carries high expectations and a critical voice—its severity muted and kinder in this fourth generation. One has a magical voice as did his great-grandfather and at one time, pursued a career in the theatre. In our parenting, we gave them the freedom to follow their passions. They describe us as a family that talked a great deal while gathered around the dinner table. A family in which we came to know each other well, not only as parent and child but also as unique individuals, with strengths and foibles. And in this talk, both serious and teasing, we tried, not always successfully, to help each other grow in our pursuit of purposeful and loving lives.

In recent years, our small Lubetzky family has been greatly diminished. Hannah passed away in 2011, far too early at the age of sixty-three, just six years after her mother's death, and her husband Rabbi Michael followed her three years later. These losses were devastating to me. With Hannah's death went our shared history, her sweetness, and her advocacy for me and our family quest. I hold her deep in my heart. And Dan, my newly claimed Israeli cousin, died in 2019. I remain grateful to have connected with him and his daughter Sharon.

I think back to a pivotal moment during the 1988 b'nai mitzvah of our twin sons at thirteen years of age. We are standing at the temple ark in front of the entire congregation. The rabbi hands the Torah scroll to the last surviving elders, Rhona's mother and Harvey's father. In turn, together they give the Torah to us and finally, we present it to our sons. The ritual represents the passing down of the sacred texts, the word of God, to the next generation. In this act, we also pass on our traditional values and the links to family—our history and stories—and we offer these as a gift to those who follow us. L'Dor V'dor, the Hebrew words for the phrase "from generation to generation." Then, we did not know the important stories and now, we do.

As the last of the elders, we have continued to pass on the Torah, now to our two grandsons and the five grandchildren of Hannah and Michael, on the occasion of their b'nai mitzvah. We bequeath the stories to them as well. Stories that had their beginnings in the mid-19th century, stories that took two Lubetzky brothers from the Belarussian shtetls of Turets and Gorodeja to Vienna, and their descendants to Montreal, the San Francisco Bay Area, and Jerusalem. This family history contains much sadness, a suicide and the loss of many in the Holocaust. It also reveals a thirst for learning, a rich Viennese cultural and intellectual heritage, and a committed Jewish way of life. It is a tale of courage, resourcefulness, and immigrant survival across generations, with devotion to family at its core. These are among the gifts bequeathed to us from our ancestors.

Now that I have learned the history, can I reconcile with a past that I cannot change?

It was at that critical moment in the archives of the City of

Vienna, when I saw my mother no longer listed as living with her family, that I viscerally felt her ejection from home. For the very first time, waves of empathy overcame me. And it was a healing moment. I could clearly see the burdens she carried, the abandonment, losses, and her own thwarted ambitions. I could understand the source of her worries about not having enough—food, material things, and love—and why she held on to me so tightly, born after she suffered multiple miscarriages. I could understand the roots of so many warnings—to avoid loving as loss looms everywhere, to trust no one as harm abounds. I also realized that the criticism she wielded mirrored the criticism she received in her childhood. My need to flee Montreal for marriage and a career was a blow that she could not accept. The choice I made, unusual for Jewish daughters at that time, led to an estrangement between us that could never be bridged. Just as she had done for her own mother, she expected her only child to remain at her side. Her rage, fueled by her mother's rejection and by what she had sacrificed with that choice, became directed toward me.

Perhaps we are not meant to know this much about the inner and outer worlds of our parents and grandparents. While I cannot judge her for the secrets she kept, I know that the silence about the past harmed her and left a void in my understanding of the family and ultimately of myself. If only my mother had been able to share her life with me. And if I had understood, might she have shed that bony hardness, just a little?

With new-found understanding, I again visit her grave in Montreal. Once there, I find myself approaching reconciliation, no longer possible with her but attainable with her memory. I see myself as the descendant of a complex multigenerational family. The players in this dance of life are no longer ghostly figures, they are more fully human. I have come to know them with some degree of intimacy—from Eisig's writings and the last letters of Gabriel, from Musa's entreaties to her brother Reuben, from interviews with Hedy, from the records, and from our experience of the places in which they had lived and died. Now, I have a grandfather, not in living form but with a clear representation in my mind. Despite the churn of his life, I find qualities to appreciate and I see traces of him in his progeny. When I think of my grandmother, I recognize what she had lost, whereas before, I had seen only her helpless and irrational behavior. When I think of Max, Lotte, and Hedy, I recognize the roots of their inequitable pact over the care of their mother. And when I think of my mother, I can acknowledge the many positive qualities that have also become part of me—her intellectual curiosity, her love of books, and her limitless capacity to care for others.

Following Jewish tradition, I place a pebble on my mother's headstone and I do so with new feeling. I know that she did the best she could, as did I, and I also understand that what happened between us was not my fault. It was predetermined by events in the past over which I had no control, part of the legacy of Eisig Lubetzky. Even though she could not forgive me, I am finally able to make peace with her. I can freely say the words that we, of the Jewish faith, say in the face of a death, "May her memory be a blessing." And may the memory of our ancestors, this small Lubetzky family, born in Belarus, remain in our hearts, a blessing to the next generations.

Photographs

Eisig Lubetzky,Vienna (undated), *Atelier Brigitta, Wien*

Musa Brainin Lubetzky, Vienna (undated), *Atelier Rosa, Wien*

Eisig, Musa, Max, Lotte, and Hedy, Vienna (early 1921),
Photography Studio unknown

Eisig's original 1921 gravestone, Zentralfriedhof, Vienna (2010),
Photo by H. Weinstein

Rhona in front of Messerschmidtgasse, Vienna (1969),
Photo by H. Weinstein

Old synagogue, Gorodeja (2010), *Photo by H. Weinstein*

Young Reuben Brainin (undated), *Verlag Jehudia, Warsaw*

A draft page of Eisig's unpublished manuscript (1907),
*Photo courtesy of Yitzhak Isaac Lubetzky Collection,
Reuben Brainin Fonds, Jewish Public Library Archives,
Box 52 File 1, Montreal.*

Eisig, Musa, Max, and Lotte, Vienna (undated),
Ferd. Grega Fotograf, Wien

Eisig and Musa, Vienna (undated),
Photography Studio unknown

Lotte at a dressing table, Montreal (1925),
Lubetzky family photo

Alec Strasberg, Montreal (about 1922),
Strasberg family photo

Hedy with Max and Musa, Vienna, (early 1930s), *Ludwig u. Karl Pretscher Photographie, Wien*

Wedding picture of Max and Olga, Vienna (1936), *Atelier Glantz, Wien*

Gabriel Lubetzky, Vienna (1936),
Picker family photo

Gabriel and kleine Hedy's last visit to
Gorodeja family (1934), *Picker family photo*

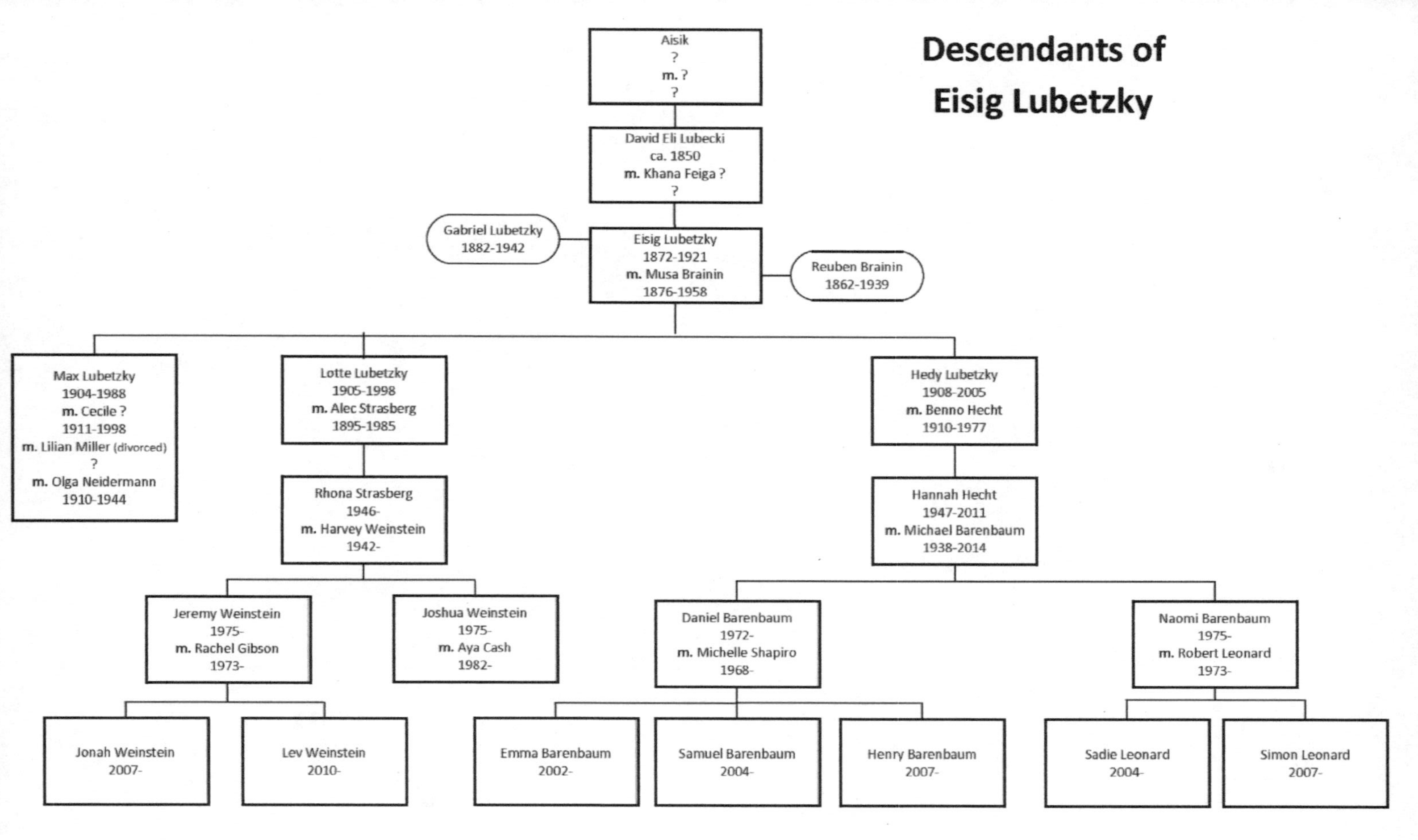
Descendants of
Eisig Lubetzky
Aisik
?
m. ?
?
David Eli Lubecki
ca. 1850
m. Khana Feiga ?
?
Gabriel Lubetzky
1882-1942
Eisig Lubetzky
1872-1921
m. Musa Brainin
1876-1958
Reuben Brainin
1862-1939
Max Lubetzky
1904-1988
m. Cecile ?
1911-1998
m. Lilian Miller (divorced)
?
m. Olga Neidermann
1910-1944
Lotte Lubetzky
1905-1998
m. Alec Strasberg
1895-1985
Hedy Lubetzky
1908-2005
m. Benno Hecht
1910-1977
Rhona Strasberg
1946-
m. Harvey Weinstein
1942-
Hannah Hecht
1947-2011
m. Michael Barenbaum
1938-2014
Jeremy Weinstein
1975-
m. Rachel Gibson
1973-
Joshua Weinstein
1975-
m. Aya Cash
1982-
Daniel Barenbaum
1972-
m. Michelle Shapiro
1968-
Naomi Barenbaum
1975-
m. Robert Leonard
1973-
Jonah Weinstein
2007-
Lev Weinstein
2010-
Emma Barenbaum
2002-
Samuel Barenbaum
2004-
Henry Barenbaum
2007-
Sadie Leonard
2004-
Simon Leonard
2007-

Authors' Note

This book presented a number of challenges in uncovering and documenting the history of Eisig Lubetzky and his family. As we were unfamiliar with the languages, our first challenge was to find and translate Hebrew, Yiddish, and German materials into English. In the case of unpublished and handwritten material, translation was especially difficult. Also, in quoting from these materials, the page numbers of the English translations did not match the page numbering of the original text. Where available, we used page numbers for the original sources.

A second challenge lay in the varied name and/or spelling of individuals, places, and titles of books and journals. These varied by language, historical time period, person, translator, and type of document, even those filed by the same individual at different times. For clarity in our own writing, we tried to make consistent name/spelling choices, but when referencing the work of others, we relied on the name/spelling choices made by these other authors and translators.

Among many examples, we chose the name/spelling "Eisig Lubetzky," as it was used in many of the biographical documents, but it also has been spelled in the following ways: Aisig or Aisik Lubetzky, I. A. Lubetzky, Yitzhak Eisig Lubetzky or as Loubetsky, Loubetzky, Lubetsky, Lubetzki, Lubecki, and Lubecka. Musa Brainin Lubetzky's first name was sometimes spelled as Mussa but she was more formally known as Marie. Similarly, all the Lubetzky family members, siblings, and children had several names of varied spelling and we have chosen one name for our writing.

Upon arrival in Canada and the United States, Eisig Lubetzky's children (Max, Lotte, and Hedy) most often used the spelling Loubetsky. The name of the writer, Nissan Touroff, has also been spelled Nissim Touroff and Nissan Turov. We chose to use the place name of Turets (Russian); also called Turzec (Polish), Turetz (Yiddish), Turec (Belarussian), Tooretz, Turez and Turzets on the Jewish Geneology website. We selected the place name Gorodeja (Russian); also called Horodeya, Haradzieja (Belarussian), Horodziej (Polish), Horodia (Yiddish), Horodzieja, Haradzeja, Gorodzey, Gorodev, and Gorodej. There were other instances, such as Maly Trostinets, where the names of people or places have been spelled differently by authors, depending upon their language. Similarly, the names of journals varied in their spelling.

Third, depending on the source, we found variation in listed dates of birth. We adopted Eisig Lubetzky's birthdate as 1872, as it was on his original gravestone and noted by his biographers, yet in registration forms and on the death certificate, the birthdate is listed as 1874. We chose 1882 for Gabriel Lubetzky's birthdate, as it was listed on the asset forms he filed with the Austrian Government, whereas the filings at Yad Vashem noted his birthdate as 1892.

Fourth, we made a number of stylistic choices. When others spoke or wrote about Lubetzky, we used his last name. When we wrote about him in the context of his personal history and family life or drew inferences about him, we referred to him in familial terms as Eisig. The family tree we included in this book focused on the direct descendants of Eisig Lubetzky, except for two exceptions. We added Gabriel Lubetzky, one of Eisig's four siblings, and Reuben Brainin, one of Musa Brainin Lubetzky's eight siblings, as they are featured in this story. As the journey of discovery and the writing of this book was in every way a collaborative effort, we used the pronoun "we" or the third person perspective, except for sections in four chapters. In these cases, where only one of us is speaking, the text is set off by a bolded heading and italicized.

Finally, as this is a work of non-fiction, we have been careful to describe the events as accurately as possible, often using multiple sources. However, on several occasions, we have taken the liberty of slightly modifying an event or time sequence to make the story line clearer. These small changes do not affect the veracity of the final story. Given the complexities of language, materials from a century ago, destruction of records, and conflicting information, we have tried to tell a story that accurately tracks the history of a family.

Endnotes

Chapter Two: The Montreal Family—1946-1968

gently into the night. Dylan Thomas, Do not go gentle into that good night, *The Poems of Dylan Thomas,* published by New Directions. Copyright © 1952, 1953 Dylan Thomas. Copyright © 1937, 1945, 1955, 1962, 1966, 1967 the Trustees for the Copyrights of Dylan Thomas. Copyright © 1938, 1939, 1943, 1946, 1971 New Directions Publishing Corp.

bubbe. A Yiddish word for grandmother.

Chapter Three: Leave and Return—1968-1998

John Marks titled. *The Search for the Manchurian Candidate: The CIA and Mind Control (*Times Books, 1979).

Chapter Four: A Serendipitous Discovery—1998

Writer, cantor, and dirigent. "Isaak, Eisik Lubetzki (1872-1921)" in *German Encyclopedia Judaica* (Nahum Goldmann's Eshkol Publishing Society, 1934).

Jewish Public Library. https://jewishpubliclibrary.org, accessed May 12, 2025.

I've read two chapters. *Book of Remembrance, Tooretz-Yeremitz* (Tooretz-Yeremitz Societies, 1977).

written by Moshe Ungerfeld. Yitzhak Isaac Lubetsky, *Book of Remembrance*, 61.

which he titled. Nisssan Turov, "The Man Who Escaped Himself: On Isaac Lubetzky," *Mozenim*, 35, no. 1 (1972): 76-79.

How did Ungerfeld. Accessed May, 20, 2020, http://www.encyclopedia.com.

book by Nissan Turov. *The Problem of Suicide: A Socio-Psychological Study* (Devir Publishing, 1953).

two of Lubetzky's writings. "Zionism and its Opponents: An Open Letter to Max Nordeau," *Ha-shiloah* 4:22 (1898): 377-381. "The Sin," *Ha-shiloah* 22 (1910): 127-132, 11-23, 108-117, 439-450, 307-318, 207-222, 497-511.

Hashiloach. Also spelled Ha-shiloach depending on the translation.

Nissan Turov. Nissan Touroff, accessed May 20, 2020, http://www.encyclopedia.com.

I saw him once. Nissan Turov, "Essays on the Suicides of Famous Personas (Isaac Lubetzky)," *Ha-doar*, 37, (1945): 219-241.

in his book. William Cutter, *Midrash and Medicine: Healing Body and Soul in the Jewish Interpretive Tradition* (Jewish Lights Publishing, 2011).

The Dybbuk. Written by S. Ansky sometime between 1913 and 1916 originally in Russian but later translated into Yiddish and Hebrew. Accessed January 13, 2018, http://www.yivoencyclopedia.org/article.aspx//.

As of today. Moshe Ungerfeld, 1972.

an amazing story. Eisig Lubetzky, "A Lonely Stalk of Grain," *Ha-Eshkol* 4, (1902): 94-111.

Although the Jewish population. V. Charny, "Jewish Population of Towns in Minsk Gubernica," accessed January 3, 2018, http://www.jewishgen.org.

No shtetl stood alone. Samuel Kassow, "Shtetl," *YIVO Encyclopedia of Jews in Eastern Europe,* accessed on January 21, 2018, http://www.yivoencyclopedia.org/article.aspx/Shtetl.

The Jewish community. Yerahamiel Markowitz, *Book of Remembrance,* 11.

Gorodey, the hometown. Eisig Lubetzky, "A Lonely Stalk of Grain."

Volozhin Yeshiva. Shaul Stampfer, "Volozhin, Yeshiva of," *The YIVO Encyclopedia of Jews in Eastern Europe,* accessed September 22, 2025, https://encyclopedia.yivo.org/article/1531.

autobiographical fiction. See Alan Mintz, *"Banished from Their Father's Table: Loss of Faith and Hebrew Autobiography,"* (Indiana University Press, 1989).

1903 Kishniev massacre. See Wolf Moskovich, "Kishinev," *The YIVO Encyclopedia of Jews in Eastern Europe,* accessed September 22, 2055, encyclopedia.yivo.org/article/366.

The Haskalah movement. A maskil was a follower of Haskalah. Shira Schoenberg, "Modern Jewish History: The Haskalah." Jewish Virtual Library, accessed September 22, 2025, https://www.jewishvirtuallibrary.org/the-haskalah#:~:text=by%20Shira%20Schoenberg&text=The%20Haskalah%2C%20or%20Jewish%20Enlightenment,the%20Reform%20and%20Zionist%20movements.

Chapter Five: A Child Prodigy Escapes the Shtetl

veiled autobiography. Book One. Yitzhak Isaac Lubetzky Collection, Reuben Brainin Fonds, Jewish Public Library Archives, Montreal.

literary tradition of autobiographical writing. Mintz, 1989.

Second unpublished manuscript. Veiled autobiography, Book Two. Yitzhak Isaac Lubetzky Collection.

Chapter Six: Let My Words Speak For Me

It is time that this is done. Ungerfeld, 1977.

Lubetzki penetrated the page. Turov, 1945.

the main synagogue. Akiwa Zimmerman, "Chordirigenten (Choir Directors)," *Wien-eine Stadt und ihre Kantoren (Vienna-a city and its cantors), undated.*

Jews were the people. Steven Beller, *Vienna and the Jews:1867-1938, A Cultural History* (Cambridge University Press, 1989).

in his memoir. Stefan Zweig, *The World of Yesterday* (Viking Press, 1943; University of Nebraska Press, 1964).

of other authors. Beller, 1989. Marsha L. Rozenblitt, *The Jews of Vienna, 1867-1914: Assimilation and Identity* (State University of New York Press, 1983).

Hebrew literary criticism. Holtzman, Avner. "Hebrew Criticism and Scholarship," *YIVO Encyclopedia of Jews in Eastern Europe*. Accessed September 22, 2025, https://encyclopedia.yivo.org/article/113.

Lubetzky's name. Holtzman, Avner. "Hebrew Literature (Appendix: Hebrew Writers)," *YIVO Encyclopedia of Jews in Eastern Europe*. Accessed September 22, 2025, https://encyclopedia.yivo.org/article/57.

a master's thesis. Shoshanah Sperber, *"Isaac Lubetzky: Writer and Critic"* (Master's thesis, Tel Aviv University, 2008). Supervisor: Professor Avner Holtzman, Department of Hebrew Literature. Available online from the university.

Assuming that a true depiction. Avner Holzman, "Seeds and Sighs: the Life and Work of Ya'akov Shalom Katznelbogen," in *In the Streets of London: Notes and Stories* (Ameda-Beitan, 2002), 153.

a fascinating correspondence. Ahad Ha'am, *Letters, Vol. 1*(1896-1898) (Yavneh Moriah, 5683-5688 [1923-1928]), 259, 306; Ahad Ha'am, *Letters, Vol.2* (1899-1901) (Yavneh Moriah, 5684 [1924], 30-31, 13-14, 193-194. Ahad Ha'am Archive, National Library of Israel.

Ahad Ha'am. Accessed May 27, 2020, http://www.wikipedia.com, http://www.yivoencyclopedia.com.

Samuel the Pious. See bibliography of Lubetzky's Hebrew writings in Shoshana Sperber, 2008.

Fast After a Dream. Eisig Lubetzky, "Fast After a Dream," *Ha-shiloah,* 4:19 (5658-5659 [July-December 1898]), Tammuz-Kislev, 47-57.

Fast After a Dream. Eisig Lubetzky, "Fast After a Dream," *Ha-shiloah,* 4:20 (5658-5659 [July-December 1898]), Tammuz-Kislev, 143-152.

Lonely Stalk of Grain. Eisig Lubetzky, "Lonely Stalk of Grain," *Ha-eshkol* 4, (5662 [1902]), Krakow, 95-111.

The Sin. Eisig Lubetzky, Eisig, "The Sin," *Ha-shiloah,* 22:127-132, Shvat-Tammuz, (5760, January-June 1910), 11-23; 108-117; 439-450; 207-222; 497-511.

best-known commentary. Eisig Lubetzky, "Zionism and its Opponents: An Open Letter to Max Nordeau," *Ha-shiloah* 4:22, Tammuz-Kislev (5658-5659 [July-December 1898]), 377-381.

Lubetzky quoted Nordeau. Max Nordeau, "Zionism and Its Opposers," in *The Question of the Jews and Its Solution* (Jewish Agency for Israel, 1960), 59.

Bershadsky is not a genius. Eisig Lubetzky, "Bershadsky," *Ha-tsofeh*, 84, (27 Nissan 5663 [April 24, 1903]), 367. Quoted in Sperber, 83.

And about Yosef Brenner. Moshe Ungerfeld, 1972.

We should note. Y. L Peretz, "In the World of Wisening Letters," *Ha-tsofeh*, 515, (October 4, 1904), 932. Quoted in Sperber, 97.

contemporary mentions. Avner Holtzman, *Aesthetics and National Revival: Hebrew Literature Against the Visual Arts* (Zamora Beitan, 1999), 53, 285. See also Einat Baram-Eshel, *The Flourishing of the Hebrew Novella in the Beginning of the 20th Century* (Magnes, 2001), 82-86.

unafraid to express views. Gershom Bader, "I. A. Lubetzky," *Hadoar* (November 7,1921).

The end result. Nissan Turov, 1945.

Yiddish story by Lubetzky. Eisig Lubetsky, "Und ich sage uch . . . (And I tell you)." In *Nackte Lieder: Jiddische Literatur aus Wien, 1915-1938*, Thomas Soxberger, ed., (Mandelbaum Verlag, 2008).

Chapter Seven: The Darkness Within

In the boxes labeled Lubetzky. Yitzhak Isaac Lubetzky Collection, Reuben Brainin Fonds, Jewish Public Library Archives, Montreal.

Undated and unsigned. Yitzhak Isaac Lubetzky Collection.

From this archived correspondence. Ahad Ha'am letters, 1898-1901.

alternating periods of depression. Yossi Goldstein, "Ahad Ha'am in Historical Perspective." in Peter Y. Medding, ed., *A New Jewry: America Since the Second World War, Studies in Contemporary Jewry, An Annual VIII*, (Oxford University Press, 1992), 173. See also Steven J. Zipperstein, *Elusive Prophet: Ahad Ha'am and the Origins of Zionism* (University of California Press, 1993), 162.

from Musa to her brother. December, 1910. In Yitzhak Isaac Lubetzky Collection in Reuben Brainin Fonds, Jewish Public Library Archives, Montreal.

Kanader Adler. Based in Montreal, it was the foremost Yiddish newspaper in Canada from 1907-1977, accessed May 27, 2020, www.wikipedia.com.

14 largely undated letters. Reuben Brainin Fonds, Jewish Public Library Archives, 1010_3_027A.

Lubetzky sarcastically accused. Eisig Lubetzky, "From the Book Market," *Hashiloach* 19 (Tevet-Av 5668-5669 [July-December 1908]): 109-114, 273.

Brainin "was praised." Stanley Nash, "Re'uven Brainin," accessed September 19, 2025, https://encyclopedia.yivo.org/article/666.

a book by. Carole B. Balin and Wendy I. Zierler, eds., *To Tread on New Ground: Selected Hebrew Writings of Hava Shapiro* (Wayne State University Press, 2014).

support for the controversial plan. Naomi Caruso, *Reuven Brainin: The Fall of an Icon* (Canadian Jewish Archives New Series 49, 2007).

"more suicides than most." Frederic Morton, *A Nervous Splendor, Vienna 1888-1889* (Penguin Books, 1979), 67.

Chapter Eight: By His Own Hand

The rhythms of the everyday. See Robert Solomon Wistrich, "Ghosts From Vienna's Past," *Shalom: The European Jewish Times*, Fall, 2008, accessed January 28, 2025, Http://www.shalom magazine.com/Article.php? id= 490306. Also see Claudia Reichl-Ham, "From the Brilliant Metropolis of a Great Power to the 'Swelled Head' of a Rump State: Vienna in the First World War," Cairn.info, accessed January 28, 2025, https://shs.cairn.info/publications-de-claudia-reichl-ham—139336?lang=en, and Hannes Leidinger, "Revolutions (Austria-Hungary)," *International Encyclopedia of the First World War*, October 8, 2014, accessed January 28, 2025, https://encyclopedia.1914-1918-online.net.

an article appeared. Y. Krepel, "Even Schoolchildren are Trading Currencies—The Hebrew-Yiddish writer Yitshok Eyzik Lubetski Poisons Himself." *Yidishes Tageblat (The Jewish Daily News)*, September 28, 1921.

the fall of the Austrian kroner. Emanuel H. Vogel, "The Currency Problem of Austria," *The Annals of the American Academy of Political and Social Science, 98. Supplement: Present Day Social and industrial Conditions in Austria*. November, 1921, 28-34. Also see Walter M. Iber, "Post-war Economies (Austria-Hungary)," in *International Encyclopedia of the First World War*, 2020, accessed September 19, 2025, https://encyclopedia.1914-1918-online.net/article/post-war-economies-austria-hungary/ and Christian Beer, Ernest Gnan, and Maria Teresa Valderrama, "A (not so brief) history of inflation in Austria," accessed January 25, 2025, https://ideas.repec.org/a/onb/oenbmp/y2016i3b1.html.

He was cruel. Shalom Streit, "In Front of the Screen and Behind it." *Ha-poel Ha-tzair*, 14: 43-44, (September 26, 1921).

day in print. Gershom Bader, "I. A. Lubetzky," *Hadoar*, (November 7, 1921).

As Reizen noted. *Freiheit*, August 25, 1927, Yitzhak Isaac Lubetzky Collection, Reuben Brainin Fonds, Jewish Public Library Archives, Montreal.

as described by. Reizen, 1927.

German newspapers. Krepel, 1921.

of our literature. Streit, 1921.

rich narrative voice. Bader, 1921.

in literary journals. Moshe Ungerfeld, 1972.

like Moses at Sinai. Lubetzky's letters to Ahad Ha'am. Ahad Ha'am Archive, National Library of Israel.

bitter at his lot. Reizen, 1921.

in his final moments. Streit,1921.

as unusual or lethal. Nissan Turov, 1945.

In the words of. Einat Baram-Eshel, 2001, 83.

Chapter Nine: Aftermath

funeral of Reuben Brainin. "Thousands Pay Last tribute to Reuben Brainin at Montreal Rites," Archive of the Jewish Telegraphic Agency, accessed May 28, 2020, www.jta.org.

husband's every need. Reizen, 1927.

the family news. Yitzhak Isaac Lubetzky Collection.

Chapter Ten: Lotte—Vienna to Montreal

Canadian Council for Refugees. accessed on March 12, 2025, https://ccrweb.ca/en/hundred-years-immigration-canada-1900-1999.

Eisig Lubetzky's nemesis. "Brainin, Re'uven." *The YIVO Encyclopedia of Jews in Eastern Europe,* accessed May 29, 2020, http://www.yivoencyclopedia.org.

None is Too Many. Irving Abella and Harold Troper, *None Is Too Many: Canada and the Jews of Europe, 1933-1948.* (University of Toronto Press, 1983, 2000, 2012).

impacted the prospects. "BRIA 10 2 a United States Immigration Policy and Hitler's Holocaust," accessed September 21, 2025, https://teachdemocracy.org/bill-of-rights-in-action/bria-10-2-a-united-states-immigration-policy-and-hitler-s-holocaust.

Chapter Eleven: In the Shadow of the Holocaust

It has been well-demonstrated. Daniel A. Gross, "The U.S. Government Turned Away Thousands of Jewish Refugees, Fearing That They Were Nazi Spies," November 18, 2015, accessed January 29, 2025, https://www.smithsonianmag.com/history/us-government-turned-away-thousands-jewish-refugees-fearing-they-were-nazi-spies-180957324/.

By May of 1939. "Expulsion, Deportation and Murder–History of the Jews in Vienna. City of Vienna," accessed January 29, 2025, https://www.wien.gov.at/english/jewishvienna/history/nationalsocialism,html.

stolpersteine. Gunther Demnig, accessed September 21, 2025, https://www.stolpersteine.eu/en/.

Forgotten Transports. Lukáš Přibyl. *Forgotten Transports: To Estonia.* Documentary, Czech Republic, Menemsha Films, 2008.

800,000 were Jews. Kathleen Fields, "Remembering the German 'Holocaust by Bullets in Belarus." Interview with historian Anika Walke, Center for the Humanities, Washington University, accessed May 5, 2020, http://www.humanities,wustl.edu. Also see "The Holocaust in Belarus," Facing History and Ourselves, accessed May 29, 2020, http://www. facinghistory.org.

Maly Trostenets. *Jewish Virtual Library,* accessed May 29, 2020, http://www.jewishvirtuallibrary.org.

essays by their descendents. Pia Schölnberger, *Das Massiv der Namen: Ein Denkmal für die österreichischen Opfer der Shoa in Maly Trostinec* (Czernin, 2019).

Chapter Twelve: From Generation to Generation L'Dor V'Dor

Historian Jeremy D. Popkin. "Family Memoir and Self-Discovery," *Life Writing,* 12, no. 2 (2015): 127-132.

Psychologists Ross Parke and Glen Elder. *Children in Changing Worlds: Sociocultural and Temporal Perspectives* (Cambridge University Press, 2019).

The writer James Wood. "The Other Side of Silence: Rereading W.G. Sebald," *The New Yorker*, June 5 & 12, 2017.

Psychologist Carole K. Holahan. "Achievement Across the Life Span: Perspectives From the Terman Study of the Gifted," *Gifted Child Quarterly* 65, no. 2 (2021): 185-195.

Recent statistics. "Any Mood Disorder," *Transforming the Understanding and Treatment of Mental Ilnesses*, NIMH Information Resource Center, accessed September 20, 2025, https://www.nimh.nih.gov/health/statistics/any-mood-disorder. See also "Suicide," *Transforming the Understanding and Treatment of Mental Ilnesses*, NIMH Information Resource Center, updated August, 2025, accessed September 20, 2025, https://www.nimh.nih.gov/health/statistics/suicide#part_2557.

In his book. Natan Meir, *Stepchildren of the Shtetl: The Destitute, Disabled, and Mad of Jewish Eastern Europe, 1800-1939*, Stanford Studies in Jewish History and Culture (Stanford University Press, 2020).

Psychologists Stephen P. Hinshaw and Dante Cicchetti. "Stigma and Mental disorder: Conceptions of Illness, Public Attitudes, Personal Disclosure, and Social Policy," *Development and Psychopathology*, 12 (2000): 555-598.

such books as Kay Redfield Jamison. *An Unquiet Mind: A Memoir of Moods and Madness* (Vintage, 1996). See also William Styron, *Depression* (Vintage Minis, 2017).

of what physician. V. J. Felitti, R. F. Anda, D. F. Williamson, et al., "Relationship of Childhood Abuse and Household Dysfunction to Many of the Leading Causes of Death. The Adverse Childhood Experiences (ACE) Study." *Am J Prev Med,* 14, no. 4 (1998): 245-58.

what has been called by Maurice Eisenbruch. "From Post-Traumatic Stress Disorder to Cultural Bereavement: Diagnosis of Southeast Asian refugees." *Soc Sci Med* 33, no.6 (1991): 673-680. See also Pauline Boss, "The Context and Process of Theory Development: The Story of Ambiguous Loss," *Journal of Family Therapy and Review* 8, no. 3 (2016): 269-286.

epigenetics of trauma transmission. Rachel Yehuda, "Trauma and the Family Tree," *Scientific American Magazine,* 327, 1, (2022): 50. See also Rachel Yehuda and Amy Lehrner, "Intergenerational Transmission of Trauma Effects: Putative Role of Epigenetic Mechanisms," *World Psychiatry* 17, no. 3 (2018): 243-257.

emotional states of close others. Casey L. Brown, Kevin J. Grimm, Jenna L. Wells, et al., "Empathic Accuracy and Shared Depressive Symptoms in Close Relationships," *Clin Psychol Sci* 11, no. 3 (2023): 509-525.

induced stress. Sara F. Waters, Tessa V. West, and Wendy Berry Mendes, "Stress Contagion: Physiological Covariation Between Mothers and Infants," *Psychol Sci* 25, no. 4 (2014): 943-942.

subsequent generations. Child development psychologist Ann S. Masten, *Ordinary Magic: Resilience in Development* (The Guilford Press, 2015).

in preschool. Robyn Fivush, Tilmann Hebermas, Theodore E. A. Waters., et al., "The Making of Autobiographical Memory: Intersections of Culture, Narratives and Identity," *International Journal of Psychology* 46, no. 5 (2011): 321-345.

Sources

Archives

Israelitishcke Kultusgemeinde (Vienna Israelite Community), Vienna

Jewish Public Library, Montreal

National Library of Israel, Jerusalem

Osterreichische Nationalbibliothek (The Austrian National Library), Vienna

Osterreichisches Staatsarchiv (National Archives of Austria), Vienna

Yad Vashem, Jerusalem

Translated and Transcribed Materials

Ahad Ha'am (Marina Zilbergerts, trans.). *Letters, Vol. 1*, 1896-1898, 4-5, 8-17, 25-28. Yavneh Moriah, 1923. Ahad Ha'am 1856-1927 (Creator of the Archive), Ahad Ha'am Archive, 1892-1933, ARC.4* 791/521, National Library of Israel, Jerusalem.

Ahad Ha'am (Marina Zilbergerts, trans.). *Letters, Vol. 2*, 1899-1901, 1-3, 6, 18-24, 29-34, 36-38. Yavneh Moriah 1924. Ahad Ha'am 1856-1927 (Creator of the Archive), Ahad Ha'am Archive, 1892-1933, ARC.4* 791/521, National Library of Israel, Jerusalem.

Asset Lists (Josef Brainin, trans.). Gabriel Lubetzky, Olga Lubetsky, 1938. Obtained from Osterreichisches Staatsarchiv, Wien.

Bader, Gershom (Marina Zilbergerts, trans.). "I. A. Lubetzky." *Hadoar* (November 7,1921): 303-316.

Brainin, Reuben (Ma'ayan Sela, trans.). *Diary Entry for September 29, 1921.* Reuven Brainin 1862-1939 (Creator of the Archive), Brainin, Ruben, 1897-1938, P8, Brainin, Ruben—Private Collection, National Library of Israel, Jerusalem.

Brainin, Reuben (Ma'ayan Sela, trans.). *Letters to and from Lubetzky.* Reuben Brainin Fonds, Jewish Public Library Archives, 1010_3_027A, Montreal.

Hecht, Hedy. Life history interviews conducted by Rhona Weinstein, 1997-2001.

Krepel, Yoyne (Mandy Cohen, trans.). "Even Schoolchildren are Trading Currencies—the Hebrew-Yiddish Writer Yitshok Eyzik Lubetski Poisons Himself." *Yidishes Tageblat* (September 28, 1921).

Lubetzky, Eisig. (Ken Blady, Danny Luzon, Ma'ayan Sela, and Mandy Cohen, trans.) A collection of unpublished manuscripts, articles, and letters. Yitzhak Isaac Lubetzky Collection, Reuben Brainin Fonds, Jewish Public Library Archives, Montreal.

Lubetzky, Eisig (Ma'ayan Sela, trans.). "Fast After a Dream." *Ha-shiloah* 4:19 (1898): 47-57; 4:20 (1898): 143-152.

Lubetzky, Eisig (Abrasha Bogen, trans.). "Zionism and its Opponents: An Open Letter to Max Nordeau." *Ha-shiloah* 4:22 (1898): 377-381.

Lubetzky, Eisig (Ma'ayan Sela, trans.). "Lonely Stalk of Grain." *Ha-Eshkol* 4 (1902): 95-111.

Lubetzky, Eisig (Ma'ayan Sela, trans.). "From the Book Market." *Ha-shiloah* 19 (1908): 273.

Lubetzky, Eisig (Yochi Cohen-Charash and Donny Inbar, trans.). "The Sin." *Ha-shiloah* 22 (Shvat-Tammuz, 5760, [January-June 1910]): 127-132, 11-23; 108-117; 439-450; 207-222; 497-511.

Lubetzky, Eisig. "Und ich sage uch . . . (And I tell you)." In *Nackte Lieder: Jiddische Literatur aus Wien* 1915-1938 *(Naked Songs: Jewish Literature from Vienna)*, edited by Thomas Soxberger. Mandelbaum Verlag, 2008.

Lubetzki, Isaak, Eisik (1872-1921) (Abrasha Bogen, trans.). *German Encyclopedia Judaica*, Nahum Goldmann's Eshkol Publishing Socieity, 1934.

Lubetzky, Gabriel (Simone Stirner, trans.). Letters from Vienna to Hedy and Musa in Montreal, personal papers, 1936-1939.

Lubetzky, Gabriel (Ma'ayan Sela, trans.). Letters from Vienna to Hedi in Israel, personal papers, 1936-1939.

Registration Forms (Meldezettel) for Eisig Lubetzky and family. Obtained from Osterreichisches Staatsarchiv (National Archives of Austria), Vienna.

Reizen. Avrom (Ken Blady and Mandy Cohen, trans.). "Episodes from my Life." *Freiheit* 5, August 25, 1927.

Sperber, Shoshana (Ma'ayan Sela [thesis] and Marina Zilbergerts [bibliography], trans.). "*Isaac Lubetzky: Writer and Critic*." Master's thesis, Department of Hebrew Literature, Faculty of Humanities, Tel Aviv University, 2008.

Streit, Shalom (Ma'ayan Sela, trans.). "In Front of the Screen and Behind It." *Ha-poel Ha-tzair* 14 (1921): 43-44.

Touroff, Nissan (Ma'ayan Sela, trans.). "Essays on the Suicides of Famous Personas (Isaac Lubetzky)." *Hadoar* 37 (1945): 219-241.

Touroff, Nissan (Yochi Cohen-Charesh, trans.). "Igra Rama (From the Top): Itzhak Eisik Lubetski." In *The Problem of Suicide: A Socio-Psychological Study*. Devir Publishing, 1953.

Ungerfeld, Moshe (Ma'ayan Sela, trans.). "The Man Who Escaped Himself: On Isaac Lubetzky." *Mozneim* 35, no.1 (1972): 76-79.

Ungerfeld, Moshe (Abrasha Bogen, trans.). "Yitzhak Aisik Lubetzki." In *Book of Remembrance: Tooretz-Yeremitz*, edited by Michael Walzer-Fass and Moshe Kaplan. Tooretz-Yeremitz Societies, 1977.

Ungerfeld, Moshe. "Yitzhak Isaac Lubetzky (English)." In *Book of Remembrance: Tooretz-Yeremitz*, edited by Michael Walzer-Fass and Moshe Kaplan. Tooretz-Yeremitz Societies, 1977, 61-62.

Bibliography

Abella, Irving M., and Harold M. Troper. *None is too Many: Canada and the Jews of Europe 1933-1948*. Lester & Orpen Dennys, 1983; University of Toronto Press, 2012.

Abramsky, Chimen, Maciej Jachimcyzk, and Antony Polonsky, eds. *The Jews in Poland*. Basil Blackwell, 1986.

Abramsky, Sasha. *The House of Twenty Thousand Books*. The New York Review of Books, 2014.

Aleichem, Sholem. (Aliza Shevrin, trans.). *Tevye the Dairyman and Motl the Cantor's Son*. Penguin Classics, 2009.

Archive of the Jewish Telegraphic Agency. "Thousands Pay Last tribute to Reuben Brainin at Montreal Rites." Accessed May 28, 2020. www. jta.org.

Balin, Carole B., and Wendy I. Zierler, eds. *To Tread on New Ground: Selected Hebrew Writings of Hava Shapiro*. Wayne State University Press, 2014.

Baram-Eshel, Einat. *The Flourishing of the Hebrew Novella in the Beginning of the 20th Century*. Magnes, 2001.

Beller, Steven. *Vienna and the Jews: 1867-1938, A Cultural History*. Cambridge University Press, 1989.

Beer, Christian, Ernest Gnan, and Maria Teresa Valderrama. "*A (not so brief) history of inflation in Austria,*" Austrian Central Bank, accessed January 25, 2025, https://ideas.repec.org/a/onb/oenbmp/y2016i3b1.html.

Biale, David. *Eros And the Jews: From Biblical Israel to Contemporary America*. University of California Press, 1997.

Bonyhady, Tim. *Good Living Street: The Fortunes of My Viennese Family*. Allen & Unwin, 2011.

Boss, Pauline. "The Context and Process of Theory Development: The Story of Ambiguous Loss." *Journal of Family Theory & Review* 8, no. 3 (2016): 269-86.

Brown, Casey L., Kevin J. Grimm, Jenna L. Wells, et al. "Empathic Empathy and Shared Depressive Symptoms in Close Relationships." *Clin Psychol Sci*. 11, no. 3 (2023): 509-25.

Buloff, Joseph (Joseph Singer, trans.). *A Memoir of Laughter, Survival, and Coming of Age in Eastern Europe*. Harvard University Press, 1991.

Canadian Council for Refugees. Accessed on March 12, 2025, https://ccrweb.ca/en/hundred-years-immigration-canada-1900-1999.

Caruso, Naomi. *Reuven Brainin: The Fall of An Icon*. Canadian Jewish Archives, 2007.

Cassedy, Ellen. *We Are Here: Memories of the Lithuanian Holocaust*. University of Nebraska Press, 2012.

Charny, V. "Jewish Population of Towns in Minsk Gubernica." Accessed March 3, 2018, http://www.jewishgen.org.

City of Vienna. "Expulsion, Deportation and Murder–History of the Jews in Vienna," accessed January 29, 2025. https://www.wien.gov.at/english/jewishvienna/history/nationalsocialism,html.

Clare, George. *Last Waltz in Vienna: The Destruction of a Family 1842-1942*. Pan Books, 1982.

Cohen, Roger. *The Girl from Human Street: Ghosts of Memory in a Jewish Family*. Counterpoint Press, 2016.

Cutter, William. *Midrash and Medicine: Healing Body and Soul in the Jewish Interpretative Tradition*. Jewish Lights Publishing, 2011.

Davidowicz, Lucy S. *The Golden Tradition: Jewish Life and Thought in Eastern Europe*. Syracuse University Press, 1996.

Demnig, Gunther. Stolpersteine. Accessed September 21, 2025., https://www.stolpersteine.eu/en/.

De Waal, Edmund. *The Hare with Amber Eyes: A Hidden Inheritance*. Ecco, an imprint of Harper Perennial, 2010.

Eisenbruch, M. "From Post-Traumatic Stress Disorder to Cultural Bereavement: Diagnosis of Southeast Asian Refugees." *Soc Sci Med* 33, no. 6 (1991): 673-80.

Elon, Amos. *Herzl*. Holt, Rinehart and Winston, 1975.

Elon, Amos. *The Pity of It All: A Portrait of the German-Jewish Epoch 1743-1933*. Picador, 2002.

Epstein, Barbara. *The Minsk Ghetto, 1941-1943: Jewish Resistance and Soviet Internationalism*. University of California Press, 2008.

Epstein, Helen. *Where She Came From: A Daughter's Search for Her Mother's History*. Little Brown, 1997.

Facing History and Ourselves. "The Holocaust in Belarus." Accessed May 29, 2020, http://www.facinghistory.org.

Fass, Paula S. *Inheriting the Holocaust: A Second Generation Memoir*. Rutgers University Press, 2009.

Felitti, Vincent J., Robert F. Anda, Dale Nordenberg, et al. "Relationship of Childhood Abuse and Household Dysfunction to Many of the Leading Causes of Death in Adults: The Adverse Childhood Experiences (ACE) Study." *A J Prev Med* 14, no. 4 (1998): 245-58.

Fields, Kathleen. "Remembering the German 'Holocaust by Bullets' in Belarus." Interview with historian Anika Walke, Center for the Humanities, Washington University, accessed September 21, 2025, https://humanities.wustl.edu/search?search=Fields%2C+Kathleen.+"Remembering+the+German+'Holocaust+by+Bullets'+in+Belarus."+Interview+with+historian+Anika+Walke&sort_by=created.

Fivush, Robyn, Tilmann Habermas, Theodore E. A. Waters, et al. "Intersections of Culture, Narratives, and Identity." *International Journal of Psychology* 46, no. 5 (2011): 321-45.

Foer Safran, Jonathan. *Everything Is Illuminated*. Houghton Mifflin, 2002.

Grinker, Roy Richard. *Nobody's Normal: How Culture Created the Stigma of Mental Illness*. W. W. Norton & Company, 2022.

Gross, Daniel A. "The U. S. Government Turned Away Thousands of Jewish Refugees, Fearing That They Were Nazi Spies." November 18, 2015. *Smithsonian Magazine*, accessed January 29, 2025, https://www.smithsonianmag.com/history/us-government-turned-away-thousands-jewish-refugees-fearing-they-were-nazi-spies-180957324/

Harding, Thomas. *One House, Five Families, and a Hundred Years of German History*. Picador, 2016.

Haumann, Heiko. *A History of East European Jews*. CEU Press, 2002.

Healy, Maureen. *Vienna and the Fall of the Hapsburg Empire: Total War and Everyday Life in Word War I*. Cambridge University Press, 2004.

Hinshaw, Stephen P. *Another Kind of Madness: A Journey Through the Stigma and Hope of Mental Illness*. St. Martin's Press, 2017.

Hinshaw, Stephen P., and Dante Cicchetti. "Conceptions of Illness, Public Attitudes, Personal Disclosure, and Social Policy." *Development and Psychopathology* 12 (2000): 555-98.

Hirsch, Marianne, and Leo Spitzer. *Ghosts of Home: The Afterlife of Czernowitz in Jewish Memory*. University of California Press, 2010.

Hochschild, Adam. *Half the Way Home: A Memoir of Father and Son*. Viking, 1986.

Holahan, Carole. "Achievement across the Life Span: Perspectives from the Terman Study of the Gifted." *Gifted Child Quarterly* 65, no. 2 (2021): 185-95.

Holtzman, Avner. *Aesthetics and National Revival: Hebrew Literature Against the Visual Arts*. Zmora Beitan, 1999.

Holtzman, Avner. "Seeds and Sighs: The Life and Work of Ya'akov Shalom Katznelbogen." In *The Streets of London: Notes and Stories*. Ameda-Beitan, 2002.

Holtzman, Avner. "Hebrew Literature (Appendix: Hebrew Writers)." *YIVO Encyclopedia of Jews in Eastern Europe*, accessed September 22, 2025, https://encyclopedia.yivo.org/article/57.

Holtzman, Avner. "Hebrew Criticism and Scholarship." *YIVO Encyclopedia of Jews in Eastern Europe*, accessed September 22, 2025, https://encyclopedia.yivo.org/article/113.

Iber, Walter M. "Post-war Economies (Austria-Hungary)." *International Encyclopedia of the First World War*, accessed September 19, 2025, https://encyclopedia.1914-1918-online.net/article/post-war-economies-austria-hungary/.

Ignatieff, Michael. *Russian Album: A Memoir*. Penguin Canada, 1987.

Jablonka, Ivan (Jane Kurtz, trans.). *A History of the Grandparents I Never Had*. Stanford University Press, 2016.

Jamison, Kay Redfield. *An Unquiet Mind: A Memoir of Moods and Madness*. Vintage, First Edition, 1997.

Leidinger, Hannes. "Revolutions (Austria-Hungary)," In *International Encyclopedia of the First World War*, October 8, 2014, accessed January 28, 2025, https://encyclopedia.1914-1918-online.net.

Lieblich, Amia (Naomi Seidman, trans.). *Conversations With Dvora: An Experimental Biography of the First Modern Hebrew Woman*. University of California Press, 1997.

Marks, John. *The Search for the Manchurian Candidate: The CIA and Mind Control.* Times Books, 1979.

Marsden Gillis, Christina. *Where Edges Don't hold: A Small Island Miscellany*. CreateSpace Independent Publishing Platform, 2017.

Mastens, Ann S. *Ordinary Magic: Resilience in Development.* Guilford Press, 2015.

Mazower, Mark. *Hitler's Empire: How the Nazis Ruled Europe*. Penguin Books, 2008.

Medding, Peter Y., ed. *Studies in Contemporary Jewry Volume VIll: A New Jewry, America Since the Second World War.* Oxford University Press, 1992.

Mendelsohn, Daniel. *The Lost: A Search for Six of Six Million.* HarperCollins, 2006.

Meir, Natan M. *The Destitute, Disabled, and Mad of Jewish Eastern Europe, 1800-1939*. Stanford University Press, 2020.

Mintz, Alan. *Banished from Their Father's Table: Loss of Faith and Hebrew Autobiography*. Indiana University Press, 1989.

Morton, Frederic. *A Nervous Splendor: Vienna 1888-1889.* Little, Brown, 1979.

Morton, Frederic. *The Forever Street.* Simon & Schuster, 1984.

Morton, Frederic. *Thunder At Twilight: Vienna 1913/1914.* Charles Scribner's Sons, 1989.

Nash, Stanley, personal communication, October 3, 2013.

Nash, Stanley. "Re'uven Brainin." *YIVO Encyclopedia of Jews in Eastern Europe,* accessed September 22, 2025, https://encyclopedia.yivo.org/article/666.

NIMH Information Resource Center. "Any Mood Disorder." *Transforming the Understanding and Treatment of Mental llnesses,* accessed September 20, 2025, https://www.nimh.nih.gov/health/statistics/any-mood-disorder.

NIMH Information Resource Center. "Suicide," *Transforming the Understanding and Treatment of Mental Illnesses,* updated August, 2025, accessed September 20, 2025, https://www.nimh.nih.gov/health/statistics/suicide#part_2557.

Nordeau, Max. "Zionism and Its Opposers." In *The Question of the Jews and Its Solution.* Jewish Agency for Israel (1960): 59.

Parke, Ross D., and Glen H. Elder, Jr. (eds.). *Children in Changing Worlds: Sociocultural and Temporal Perspectives.* Cambridge University Press, 2019.

Popkin, Jeremy D. " Family Memoir and Self-Discovery," *Life Writing* 12, no. 2 (2015): 127-38.

Příbyl, Lukáš. *Forgotten Transports: To Estonia.* Documentary, Czech Republic, Menemsha Films, 2008.

Reichl-Ham, Claudia. "From the Brilliant Metropolis of a Great Power to the Swelled Head: Vienna in the First World War." *Cairn.Info.* Accessed September 22, 2025, https://shs.cairn.info/publications-de-claudia-reichl-ham—139336?lang=en.

Rome, David. *The Canadian Story of Reuben Brainin: Part 1 and Part 2.* National Archives Canadian Jewish Congress, 1993, 1996.

Rome, David (ed., trans.). *Through the Eyes of The Eagle: The Early Montreal Yiddish Press (1907-1916).* Vehicule Press, 2001.

Rosner, Elizabeth. *Survivor Café: The Legacy of Trauma and the Labyrinth of Memory*. Counterpoint Press, 2017.

Roth, Joseph (Michael Hofmann, trans.). *The Hotel Years*. New Directions Publishing Corporation, 2015.

Roth, Joseph (Michael Hofmann, trans.). *The Wandering Jews: The Classic Portrait of a Vanished People*. W. W. Norton & Company, 2001.

Rozenblitt, Marsha L. *The Jews of Vienna, 1867-1914: Assimilation and Identity*. State University of New York Press, 1983.

Ruderman, David B. *Early Modern Jewry: A New Cultural History*. Princeton University Press, 2010.

Schölnberger, Pia. *Das Massiv der Namen: Ein Denkmal für die österreichischen Opfer der Shoa in Maly Trostinec*. Czernin, 2019.

Shoenberg, Shira. "Modern Jewish History: The Haskalah." Jewish Virtual Library, accessed September 22, 2025, https://www.jewishvirtuallibrary.org/the-haskalah#:~:text=by%20Shira%20Schoenberg&text=The%20Haskalah%2C%20or%20Jewish%20Enlightenment,the%20Reform%20and%20Zionist%20movements.

Schorske, Carl E. *Fin-de-Siècle Vienna: Politics and Culture*. Vintage Books, 1981.

Sebald, W. G. (Anthea Bell, trans.). *Austerlitz*. The Modern Library, 2001.

Soxberger Thomas. *Nackte Lieder: Jiddische Literatur aus Wien 1915-1938*. Mandelbaum verlag, 2008.

Soxberger, Thomas. *Revolution Am Donaukanal: Jiddische Kultur und Politik in Wien 1904 bis 1938*. Mandelbaum kritik & utopie, 2013.

Stampfer. Shaul. "Volozhin, Yeshiva of," *The YIVO Encyclopedia of Jews in Eastern Europe*, accessed September 22, 2025, https://encyclopedia.yivo.org/article/1531.

Styron, William. *Depression*. Vintage, 2017.

Suleiman, Susan Rubin (1993). *Budapest Diary: In Search of the Motherbook*. Plunkett Lake Press, 2011.

Teach Democracy. "BRIA 10 2 a United States Immigration Policy and Hitler's Holocaust." Accessed September 21, 2025. https://teachdemocracy.org/bill-of-rights-in-action/bria-10-2-a-united-states-immigration-policy-and-hitler-s-holocaust.

Tec, Nechema. *Defiance*. Oxford University Press, 1993.

Thomas, Dylan. "Do not go gentle into that good night," published by New Directions. Copyright © 1952, 1953 Dylan Thomas. Copyright © 1937, 1945, 1955, 1962, 1966, 1967 the Trustees for the Copyrights of Dylan Thomas. Copyright © 1938, 1939, 1943, 1946, 1971 New Directions Publishing Corp.

Turov, Nissan. *The Problem of Suicide: A Socio-Psychological Study*, Devir Publishing, 1953.

Vogel, David (Dalya Bilu, trans.). *Married Life*. The Toby Press, 2007.

Vogel, Emmanuel H. "The Currency Problem of Austria, Supplement: Present Day Social and Industrial Conditions in Austria." *The Annals of the American Academy of Political and Social Science* 98. (1921): 28-34.

Walzer-Fass, Michael and Moshe Kaplan, eds. *Book of Remembrance: Tooretz-Yeremitz*. Tooretz-Yeremitz Societies, 1977.

Waters, Sara F., Tessa V. West, and Wendy Berry Mendes. "Physiological Covariation between Mothers and Infants." *Psychological Science* 25, no. 4 (2014): 934-42.

Wengeroff, Pauline (Shulamit. S. Magnus, trans.). *Memoirs of a Grandmother: Scenes from the Cultural History of the Jews of Russia in the Nineteenth Century* (Volume One). Stanford University Press, 2010.

Weinstein, Harvey M. *Psychiatry and the CIA: Victims of Mind Control*. American Psychiatric Press, 1990.

Weinstein, Joshua Ari, "Table Talk: My Grandmother Died." *The Threepenny Review*, Fall 1999.

Weinstein, Rhona S. *Reaching Higher: The Power of Expectations in Schooling*. Harvard University Press, 2002, 2004.

Wickersham, Joan. *The Suicide Index: Putting My Father's Death In Order*. Harcourt, 2008.

Wiesel, Elie (Marian Wiesel, trans.). *Open Heart*. Alfred A. Knopf, 2012.

Wood, James. "The Other Side of Silence: Rereading W. G. Sebald." *The New Yorker*, June 5 and 12, 2017.

Yehuda, Rachel and Amy Lehrner. "Intergenerational Transmission of Trauma Effects: Putative Role of Epigenetic Mechanisms." *World Psychiatry* 17, no. 3 (2018): 243-57.

Yehuda, Rachel. "Trauma and the Family Tree." *Scientific American Magazine* 327, no. 1 (July 2022): 50.

Zborowski, Mark and Elizabeth Herzog. *Life Is With People: The Culture of the Shtetl*. Schocken Books, 1952.

Zipperstein, Steven J. *Elusive Prophet: Ahad Ha'am and the Origins of Zionism*. University of California Press, 1993.

Zweig, Stefan. *The World of Yesterday*. Viking Press, 1943; University of Nebraska Press, 1964.

Acknowledgments

This book is the culmination of some twenty-five years of research and writing, exploring what had been a lifelong curiosity for Rhona—a photograph of a grandfather she had not known and the absence of a story. There are so many to thank—funders, fixers, research assistants, translators, reviewers, and family members. In retrospect, we are amazed at how many people assisted us in this journey and we are grateful that their help was so enthusiastically offered. We learned mightily from our village of collaborators.

We begin with gratitude to The Tauber Foundation, especially to Ingrid Tauber who offered generous financial support, and to The Institute for Jewish and Community Research, which acted as the fiscal agent. We also appreciate the research funding we received from faculty enabling grants at the University of California, Berkeley and the accompanying support from the Psychology Department for this project. These funds allowed us to engage Berkeley graduate students and others as researchers and translators.

This has been a fascinating treasure hunt and we are grateful for all our key informants. It was Abrasha Bogen and cousin Judy King in Montreal, both deceased, who offered the first clue about Eisig Lubetzky, and Marianne Urbah in Paris, also deceased, whose own genealogical research introduced us to the village of Turets and the history of Eisig Lubetzky. Rabbi William Cutter of Hebrew Union College in Los Angeles was instrumental in providing the first writings of Eisig that we had seen. It was Rabbi Cutter who brought our family book to Israel that ultimately led to Shoshana Sperber's master's thesis on Lubetzky. Sperber's extensive analysis of his writings was an important contribution to the literature and exceptionally helpful as we pieced his story together.

Archivists are critical to the development of a historical perspective through their careful preservation of documents and artifacts. Too often underappreciated, their vital work provides the foundation for an evidence-based understanding of people and events in the past. We acknowledge the invaluable assistance of the late Paul Hamburg and of Ruth Haber, librarians for Jewish Studies at UC Berkeley; Shannon Hodge and Sam Pappas, archivists at the Jewish Public Library in Montreal; Rachel Misrati, archivist at the National Library of Israel; and the now retired Mag. Wolf-Erich Eckstein, archivist at The Israelitische Kultusgeminde Wein. And we offer our appreciation to scholar Aaron Krishtalka who translated the Yiddish for us at the Jewish Public Library and who identified documents for further exploration.

Trying to uncover a 150-year-old story and making our way in Lithuania and Belarus would have been impossible without the expert and caring assistance of Franklin Swartz, International Director of Voluntas, and his wife Galina Swartz. They, along with driver and translator Alex, assisted us with research in government records, tracing locales, interpreting, and educating us in the history of the Jews in that part of the world. Our time in Belarus and our understanding of Eisig were undoubtedly enriched by their help.

In Vienna, the historians Evelyn Adunka and Thomas Soxberger filled in much of the history of the Jewish community at the turn of the 20th century. Walter Juraschek was an amazing guide to Vienna and the impact of the Anschluss on the Jews. The Brainin family was not only welcoming to us but also reinforced our sense of belonging to a larger network of loving relatives. They not only made us feel at home but also contributed to our appreciation of the life of the contemporary Jewish community. Our cousin Josef Brainin helped us erect a new marker over the grave of Eisig Lubetzky to assure that Eisig's presence would be remembered.

In Israel, our cousins, the late Dan Picker and his daughter Sharon, filled in the gaps of Gabriel Lubetzky's story and the book that Sharon created about her great-grandfather was invaluable as we learned of Gabriel's last days.

There were so many documents to translate—Yiddish to English, German to English, Hebrew to English—that made the work of uncovering the history a great challenge. It was especially important for the literary works that our translators were knowledgable about the artistic conventions of the time. The excellent work of these translators afforded us some confidence in having captured both the imagery and the ideas expressed by the authors. We thank all of our dedicated translators who worked so diligently on these materials: Yochi Cohen-Charash, Ma'ayan Sela, Mandy Cohen, Marina Zilbergerts, Simone Stirner, Danny Inbar, and Danny Luzon (then graduate students at UC Berkeley); and also Ken Blady (a fixture of the Bay Area Jewish community as a teacher and translator of Yiddish), Heribert Adam, Abrasha Bogen (deceased), Fritz Seil (deceased), and Josef Brainin. We are grateful as well to Marcy McGaugh who transcribed the interviews and our nephew Gary Sternklar who prepared the family tree.

We greatly benefited from the editorial feedback and encouragement of Tom Jenks and numerous colleagues, friends, and family. These include: Heribert Adam, Kogila Adam-Moodley, David Hollinger, Jo-Ellen Brainin-Rodriguez, Rudy Mendoza-Denton, Ozlem Ayduk, Daniel Barenbaum, Naomi

Leonard, Ronald Blumer, Muffie Meyer, Carolyn and Philip Cowan, Irving and Ellen Zucker, Sarah Freedman, Laurel Fletcher, Paula Fass, Dan Slobin, Ross Parke, Bonnie Leadbeater, Diane Wolf, Corinne Houpt, Therese Williams, Laura Sky, Debby and Mayer Perelmuter, Dorothy Kaufmann, Jeremy Weinstein, and Josh Weinstein. We alone are responsible for any errors contained within this book.

We feel very fortunate to have worked with Eric, Peggy, and Alex Johnson of Alive Book Publishing around the final preparation of the book. Their respect for authors and love of books made our working relationship a pleasure.

We also would like to acknowledge each other. While we did a pretty good job of sharing the responsibility for raising our twin sons, this was the first time that we collaborated on a research and writing project! With different styles of writing, it proved challenging to meld our words together. But each sentence was written in collaboration despite minor and even major disagreements. A marriage of more than fifty years offers a strong foundation to support two strong-willed members of a couple in a struggle to find one voice. And despite the warning from one son not to let this destroy our marriage, we forged ahead and completed it, the process enriching our lives.

Lastly, we thank our sons and daughters-in-law who have given us so much joy and our two grandsons who continue to fill our lives with amazement. Neither Aunt Hedy nor Rhona's sister-in-life Hannah lived long enough to read this manuscript, but their curiosity, their belief in the project and in the two of us were significant in carrying us through the long years of research and writing. The book is a gift to them and to the family of Hannah and Michael who also carry the legacy of Eisig Lubetzky.

About the Authors

Rhona S. Weinstein, a Professor of Psychology Emerita at the University of California, Berkeley, is the author of the award-winning book *Reaching Higher: The Power of Expectations in Schooling* (Harvard University Press), and co-editor of *Achieving College Dreams: How a University-Charter District Partnership Created an Early College High School* (Oxford University Press). Her research has traced the covert influence of expectations—how they shape classrooms, constrain possibilities, and, when thoughtfully transformed, open doors for children too often left behind. In collaboration with teachers and principals, she has redesigned schools and classroom practices to promote equal opportunity to learn.

Harvey M. Weinstein is a psychiatrist and human rights scholar, a Senior Research Fellow at the Human Rights Center and a retired Clinical Professor in the School of Public Health, University of California, Berkeley. His multidisciplinary research has taken him into the moral consequences of ethnic cleansing and genocide, exploring how individuals, communities, and nations seek justice, reckon with loss, and find pathways toward reconciliation. He is the author of *Psychiatry and The CIA: Victims of Mind Control* (American Psychiatric Press), first published in Canada as *A Father, A Son and the CIA* (James Lorimer) and translated into Japanese (Wave), and co-editor of *My Neighbor, My Enemy: Justice and Community in the Aftermath of Mass Atrocity* (Cambridge University Press).

Born in Montreal, the Canadian-American co-authors have lived in the San Francisco Bay area for their entire careers, have traveled the world, and currently reside in Walnut Creek, California. Married for almost sixty years, they take pleasure in their twin sons and spouses, two grandsons, and two granddogs. For more than two decades, they have spent their summers on Pender Island, off the coast of British Columbia, a sanctuary that inspired their writing, woodwork, and sculpture. *The Empty Envelope* is their first joint writing project.

ABOOKS

ALIVE Book Publishing and ALIVE Publishing Group
are imprints of Advanced Publishing LLC,
3200 A Danville Blvd., Suite 204, Alamo, California 94507

Telephone: 925.837.7303
alivebookpublishing.com

www.ingramcontent.com/pod-product-compliance
Lightning Source LLC
LaVergne TN
LVHW091112080826
845145LV00008B/1888